I0800250

IMAGES
of America

ISLE OF PALMS

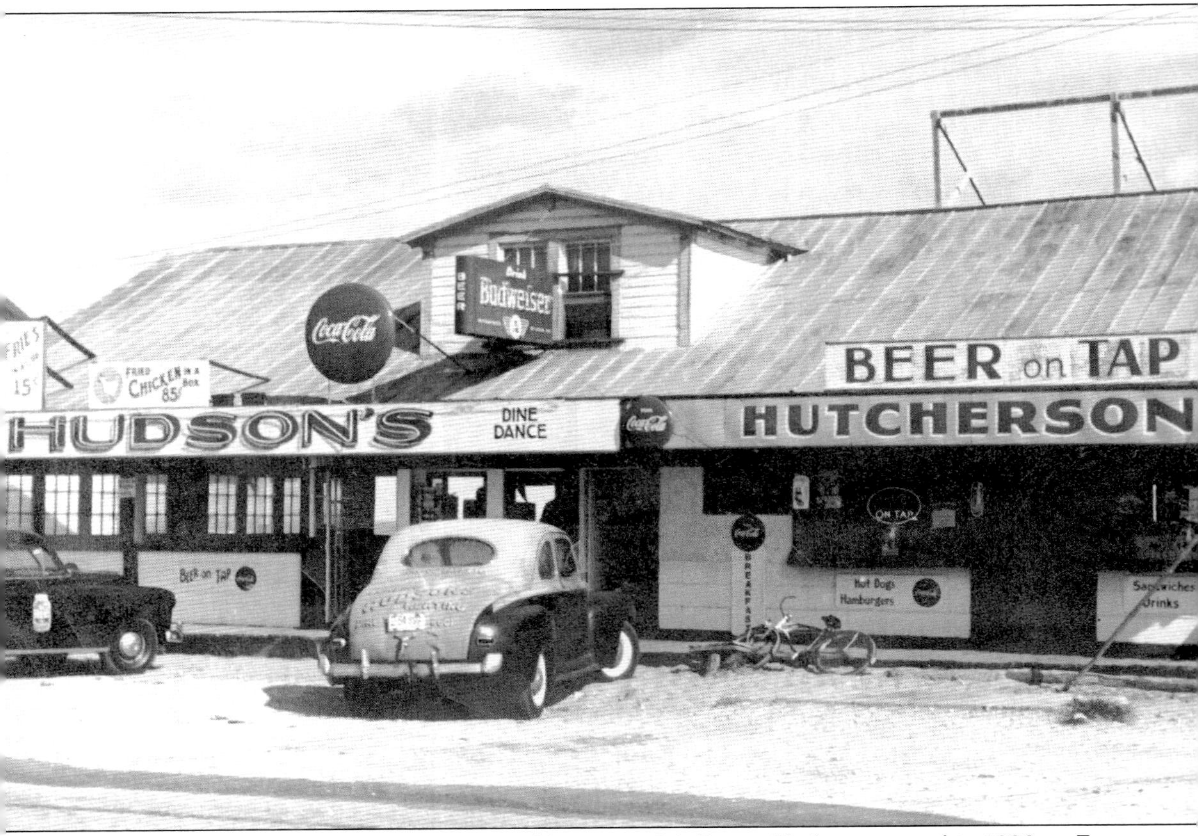

Hudson's Pavilion, owned and operated by Forrest McQueen Hudson, opened in 1928 on Front Beach. The Hudson family lived in an apartment on top of the dancing pavilion, which also housed the very first U.S. Post Office on Isle of Palms. When Mr. Hudson died at the age of 39, his wife took over the successful business before turning it over to her son and daughter. Forrest M. Hudson Jr. eventually acquired the entire building and added a bar, restaurant, surf shop, bathhouse, snack bar, and game room. Mr. Hudson also managed a float and umbrella rental shack on the beach. Mark Hudson, son of Forrest, opened the first fireworks stand there after receiving permission from the chief of police. He made $88 on the Fourth of July when he was 10 years old! Hudson's catered to the massess who flocked to the beach every summer until the pavilion's doors closed in 1988.

IMAGES
of America

ISLE OF PALMS

Wendy Nilsen Pollitzer

ARCADIA
PUBLISHING

ISBN 978-0-7385-1802-2

Published by Arcadia Publishing
Charleston, South Carolina

Printed in the United States of America

Library of Congress Catalog Card Number: 2005924397

For all general information contact Arcadia Publishing at:
Telephone 843-853-2070
Fax 843-853-0044
E-mail sales@arcadiapublishing.com
For customer service and orders:
Toll-Free 1-888-313-2665

Visit us on the Internet at www.arcadiapublishing.com

For Lillian Nilsen, my guiding light and spiritual companion during the entirety of this project.

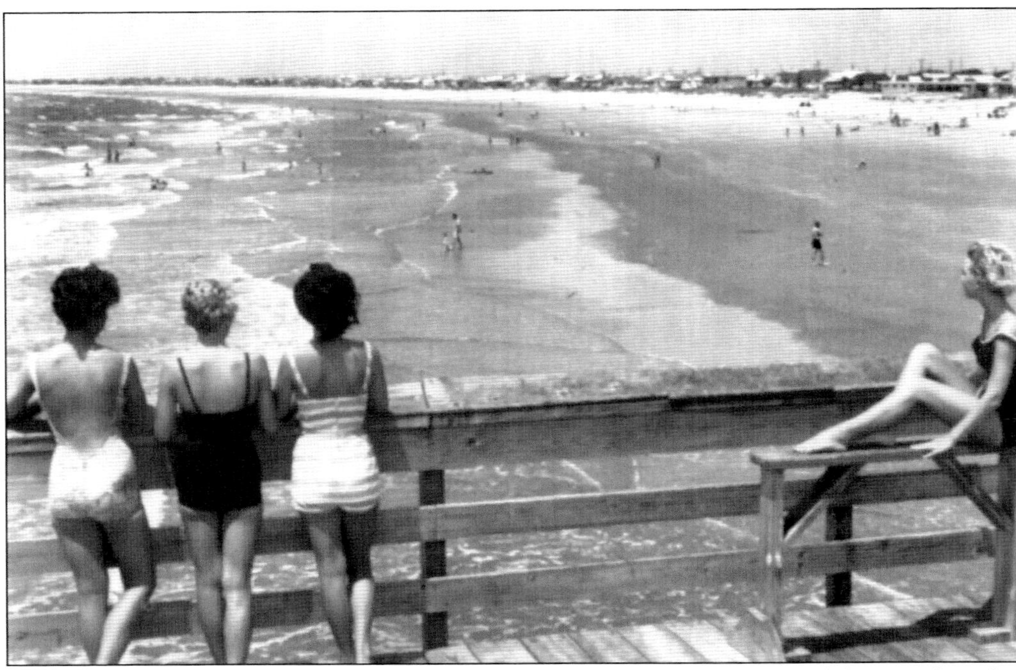

The Isle of Palms fishing pier was built in 1953. Obviously, people enjoyed the pier for other things besides fishing. These ladies gaze at the many beachgoers on Front Beach, a favorite spot for locals and tourists alike.

Contents

Acknowledgments

It is not possible to compile a book of this nature without the help of the many people who shared their stories, pictures, and time with me. I credit the integrity of the book to all of the former and current residents who so willingly contributed.

W.W. Wannamaker's *Long Island South* and Philip G. Clarke Jr.'s *Isle of Palms* were extremely informative, as were articles by Amy Adams Leamon, Sully Witte, and Thomas Waring found on *iloveiop.com*. The City of Isle of Palms produced a 50th Anniversary tape in 2003 that was also very useful.

I want to thank Henry and Anne Shaffer for a substantial donation of reference material. Mr. Shaffer at one point was in the process of writing a book to be titled *My Island Love Affair*, but unfortunately lost everything in a computer crash. He graciously gave me all his notes and memorabilia.

Sandy Stone also gave me an impressive collection of postcards dating back to the early 1900s. Thank you, Sandy, for trusting me with your precious artifacts.

The Darby and Way families were very generous with their memories. I cannot express my gratitude enough to The Beach Company for their contribution of many priceless photos. In particular, Jason Ward, the company's marketing support specialist, gave much of his time to this worthwhile project.

The majority of this book comes from the pictorial donations and oral history from familiar island names. In no order, I would like to sincerely thank Phyllis Shaffer, Marge Sexton, Dr. Jimmy Sexton, Jerry Ciandella, Mayor Mike Sottile, Tom and DeeDee Harper, Gene White, Shay Gregorie, Janet Mauldin, Timi Kennedy, Cathy Kennedy, Henry and Francis Finch, Hammond Bamberg, Norma Kulseth, Vincent Sottile, the entire Nilsen family, Stanley Pearson, Theron and Dale Hegler, Bobby Ross, Ray and Mary Clarkin Taylor, Tim McKevlin, Mark Hudson, Megan Stevens, Chris Casias, Marilyn Thomas Roland, John Stanley, Douglas Kerr, Wendi Potter Lynn, Jane Yates, Bill and Juanita Casey, Chip Campsen, Terrye Campsen Seckinger, Mayor Carmen Bunch, Kathy Carroll, the Windjammer, South Carolina Department of Natural Resources, Isle of Palms Marina, Isle of Palms Exchange Club, East Cooper Regional Medical Center, The Citadel Archives and Museum, and Poe Library on Sullivan's Island.

Writing this book and compiling its pictures was no easy task with two small daughters. Though I brought my daughter, Julia, with me on most visits, I relied heavily on my parents and husband to watch my oldest, Abbie. My greatest thanks are extended to Shirley, Stewart, and Richard for being so patient with my frequent absence and to Anne and Ricky for their help, as well.

My grandmother dreamed of being a writer. Work and raising four children postponed her writing. She died before she could fulfill her dream, so, with Elsie Blume, I share this mutual dream-come-true.

Last, but certainly not least, I want to thank Adam Latham, my editor, for being so patient with me during this process. His guidance gave me faith to accomplish this goal.

INTRODUCTION

Isle of Palms is a very popular tourist destination. The small barrier island is home to only 4,500 permanent residents but accommodates as many as 25,000 visitors during peak months each year. The pristine beaches and proximity to Charleston make it an ideal refuge for the active and inquisitive traveler.

The Seewee Indians first lived on the land, originally called Hunting Island. They led a simple life of hunting, fishing, and growing vegetables. Wild game was very abundant on the island, providing plenty of food for the entire tribe. Furs and skins were used to barter with the Spanish, French, and English.

More and more settlers were coming from England, creating a larger demand for fur and skins from the wild game. The Seewee thought they were being cheated in the trade, so they decided to take their concerns directly to the King of England. For a year, they built dugout canoes and thatched sails out of palm fronds. The men loaded the canoes with the furs and provisions and headed for England. They got off to a good start, until they encountered a tropical storm. All the cargo and most of the Indians perished in the storm. The Seewee Indians were the first Carolina tribe to disappear completely.

Hunting Island was entirely abandoned except for the occasional hunter or fisherman. In 1696, Sir Thomas Holton from Barbados was granted title to the island. He renamed it Long Island because of its elongated and narrow shape.

In 1898, Nicholas Sottile built the first house on Long Island. A year later, a gentleman from Beaufort discovered the barrier island and became interested in its development. Dr. Joseph S. Lawrence pitched his idea to investors, and together they formed a company that would construct ferry slips in Charleston and Mt. Pleasant, almost eight miles of railroad, two bridges across Cove Inlet and Breach Inlet, and a large dancing pavilion at the end of the terminal on Long Island. He changed the name to Isle of Palms to attract more tourists.

Lawrence became president of the Charleston and Seashore Railroad Company. In just three years, Isle of Palms was home to the Hotel Seashore, a grand pavilion, a seaside restaurant, and accommodating bathhouses.

The conglomerate merged with all the gas, electric, and railroad companies in the Charleston area and was incorporated under the common ownership of Consolidated Railway Gas and Electric Company. The seaside resort was now complete with a gentlemen's clubhouse, a large Ferris wheel, and a steeple chase imported from Coney Island. It was a recreational haven!

In 1913, Consolidated separated from its East of the Cooper operations, forming a new company, Charleston–Isle of Palms Traction Company. Its president was James Sottile, the youngest brother of Nicholas. The company advertised the resort extensively. Sottile had a thriving business until rising costs and the demand for a free ferry initiated the dissolution of his enterprise. In 1924, the Charleston County Sheriff's Office seized the company's ferry boats. Isle of Palms was once again isolated from the mainland.

Charleston County took over the Cove Inlet Bridge and modified it for automobile traffic. The same year, trolleys were discontinued, and the trestle crossing Breach Inlet was rebuilt for automobile traffic. In 1929, the Grace Memorial Bridge replaced the Charleston ferry service. Isle of Palms was now fully accessible.

Hardaway Contracting Company took over Isle of Palms Incorporated in 1934 and slowly developed the island for 10 years. In 1944, J.C. Long, a Charleston attorney, purchased 1,300 acres from Hardaway Contracting Company and formed The Beach Company primarily to develop Isle of Palms. The company built an office in the middle of the island, paved roads, and constructed new homes. They also brought trash collection, public water, and streetlights to the remote barrier island. The Beach Company envisioned a community for the working class and built affordable housing with World War II veterans in mind.

The island was unofficially governed through the Exchange Club, chartered in 1948. Some residents voiced their concerns about the lack of adequate fire and police protection, so they petitioned to vote on incorporation. A total of 121 people voted in favor of incorporating while 68 opposed it. In 1953, Isle of Palms elected its first mayor, Walter I. (Buck) Chapman, and borrowed $5,000 to get organized. Its small population worked together to form the Playground Auxiliary, create a volunteer fire department, and establish the first church on the island. Everyone chipped in, and together they built a solid foundation for future growth.

In 1972, Finch Properties purchased 1,600 acres at the northeastern tip of the island from J.C. Long. With the help of developers from the Sea Pines Company, they started the Isle of Palms Beach and Racquet Club, a gated community with single and multi-family dwellings. The name changed in 1984 to Wild Dunes Beach and Racquet Club, and later simply to Wild Dunes.

In 1989, Isle of Palms suffered the biggest blow in its history. Hurricane Hugo violently slammed into the South Carolina coast, its eye passing directly over Isle of Palms. The island suffered over $100 million in damages and lost over 95 percent of its buildings. Its impact was devastating, but the community worked together like never before to rebuild their island and their lives.

In 1993, the Clyde Moultrie Dangerfield Bridge was dedicated to the man who fought for it through 20 years of debate. Also known as the Isle of Palms Connector, the bridge became the first fixed span to link Isle of Palms with the mainland.

Many controversies have split the island, but it has maintained integrity as a vocal community. Those who disagree with each other at least have one thing in common: they love their island!

Though its growth has far surpassed the expectations of many, Isle of Palms remains one of the most charming beach communities on the entire East Coast.

One

Charleston's Seaside Resort

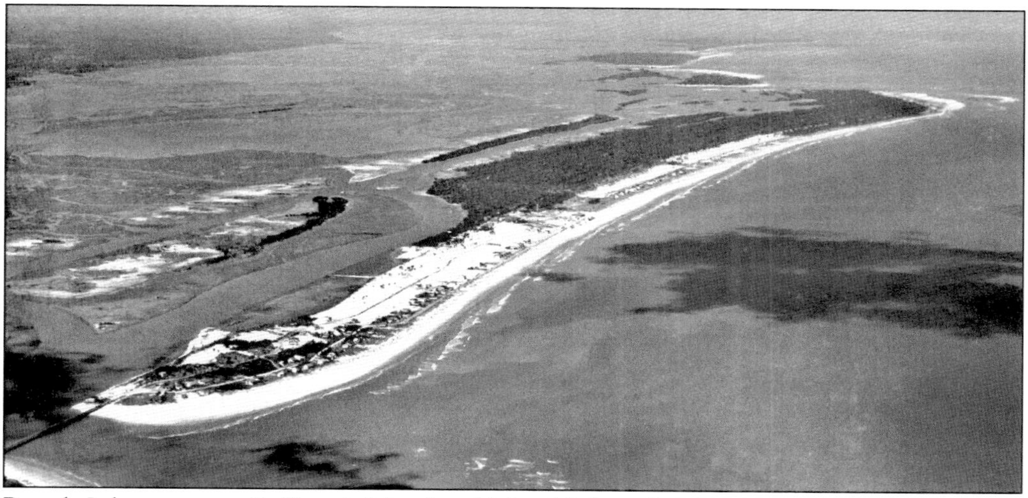

Breach Inlet separates Sullivan's Island and Isle of Palms. On the morning of June 10, 1776, more than 2,500 British troops attempted to cross Breach Inlet at low tide to sneak an attack on Fort Sullivan. They were surprised by the treacherous currents and defeated by 600 American troops, led by Col. William Thomson, and a company of Catawba Indians. Gen. William Moultrie later defeated the entire British fleet, a decisive victory in the American Revolution. The bridge built across the inlet in 1956 is named for Colonel Thomson. Breach Inlet has more historic significance—on the night of February 17, 1864, the Confederate submarine *H.L. Hunley* embarked from Breach Inlet on its way to sink the Union blockade vessel *Housatonic*. The sneak attack was successful, making the *H.L. Hunley* the first submarine to sink an enemy ship, but the submarine and her crew perished in the process. The bridge that replaced the Thomson Memorial Bridge in 2002 is named after the *H.L. Hunley*, ensuring Breach Inlet's second role in history.

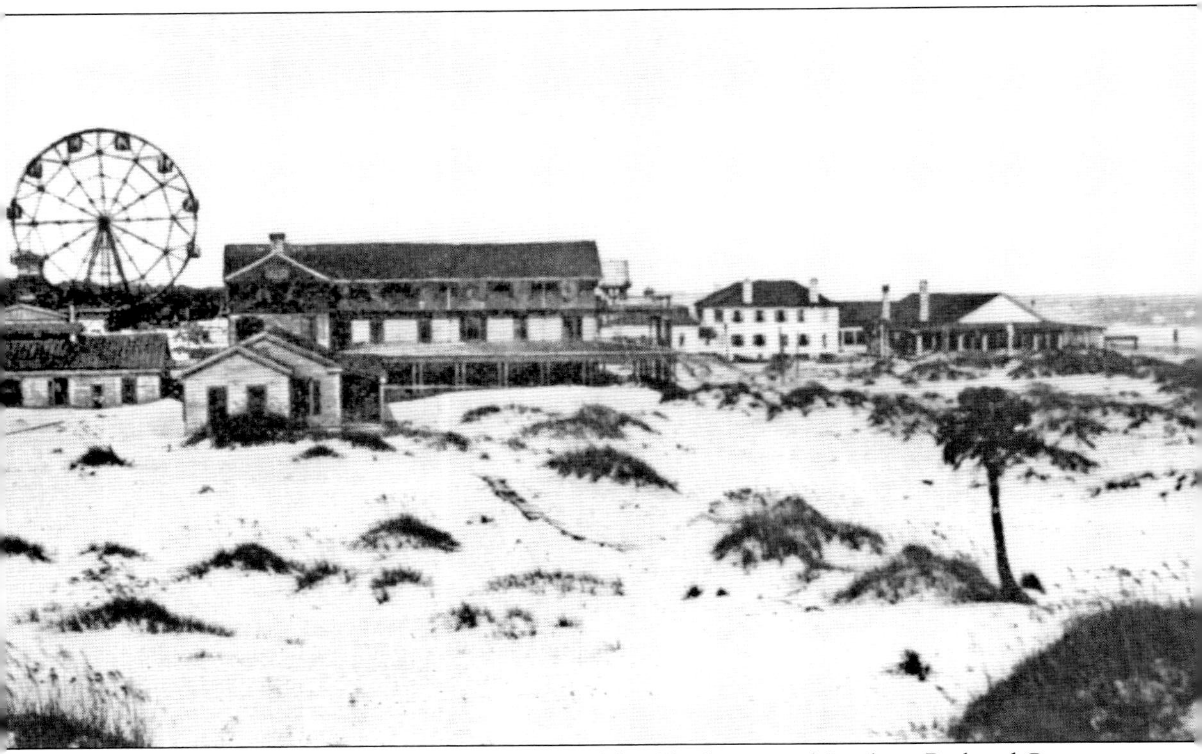

In 1898, Dr. Joseph S. Lawrence, president of the Charleston and Seashore Railroad Company, began plans to develop the relatively unknown Long Island. After promoting the idea to investors, Dr. Lawrence drew contracts for the construction of two ferry slips on Cumberland Street in Charleston and across the harbor in Mt. Pleasant. He also built seven miles of railroad, complete with two trolley trestles, across Cove Inlet to Sullivan's Island and across Breach Inlet to Long Island. He changed the name from Long Island to the more euphonious Isle of Palms, patterned after Isle of Pines in Cuba. Following several mergers and name changes, the Charleston–Isle of Palms Traction Company began a large-scale promotional campaign advertising Isle of Palms as Charleston's seaside resort in the early 1900s. The company operated the Hotel Seashore, the amusement park, and the pavilion seen here. Isle of Palms was on its way to being the "Coney Island of the South," as anticipated by Dr. Lawrence. The island prospered for two decades as a successful resort but encountered financial difficulties after World War I.

Sabal palms or cabbage palms, for which Isle of Palms is named, tolerate more salt water than other coastal trees. They persist long after oaks, cedars, and pines have died from tidal flooding. The leaf bases on young sabals are called boots. Older trees usually are bootless because either fire or storm has taken the boots off. The Seewee Indians used palm fronds as roofs for their dwellings. Their trunks were often used to build fortification walls and dock pilings.

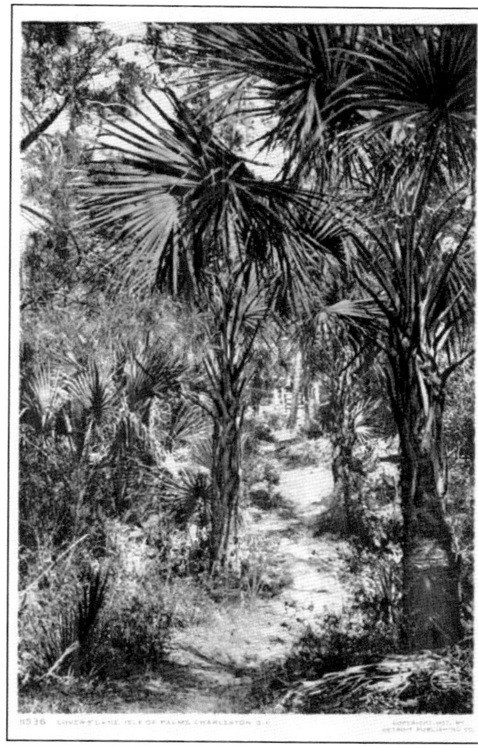

Nicholas Sottile built the first house on Isle of Palms in 1898. He hired a ferry boat captain to transport his cargo from Charleston to a small wharf on Hamlin Creek. A Charleston businessman and mayor pro tem under John P. Grace, Nicholas sought refuge on Isle of Palms until his death in 1928. In this picture, Nicholas stands proudly in front of his island getaway while his family poses on the porch. The house, then on the front row, still stands at 807 Ocean Boulevard.

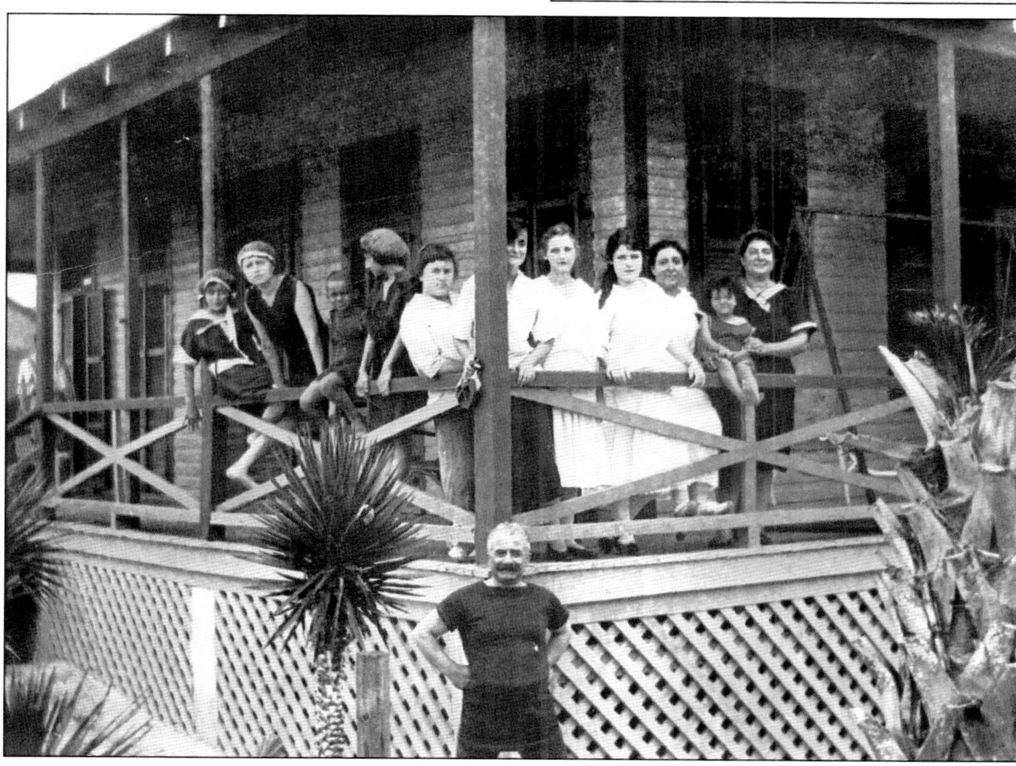

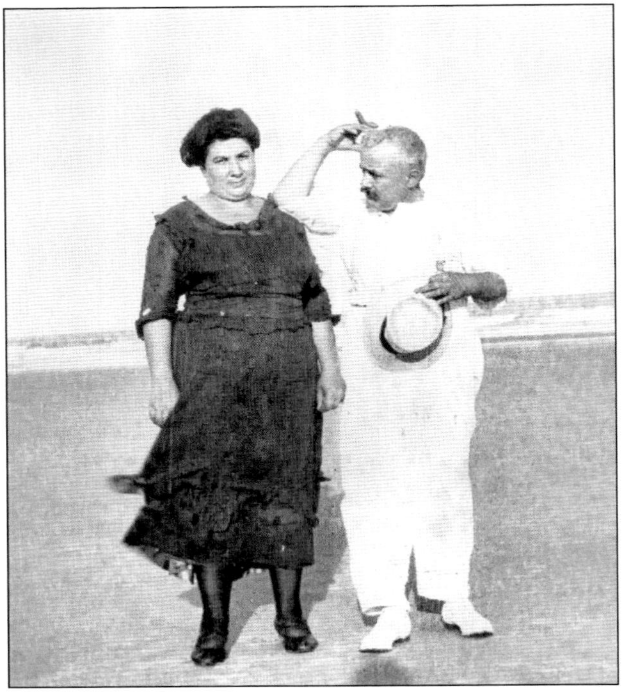

Nicholas and his second wife, Josephina Randazzo, stroll on the beach. The couple had five children: Nicholas, Francis (Frank), Josephine, Salvador (Sally), and Vincent. Nicholas's first wife, Maria Nunzia, died at a very early age, leaving Nicholas with three young daughters—Rosina Sottile (Kennerty), Lucille Sottile (Conlon), and Marie Sottile (Daley). They all had strong Isle of Palms ties. The current mayor of Isle of Palms, Mike Sottile, is the son of Frank.

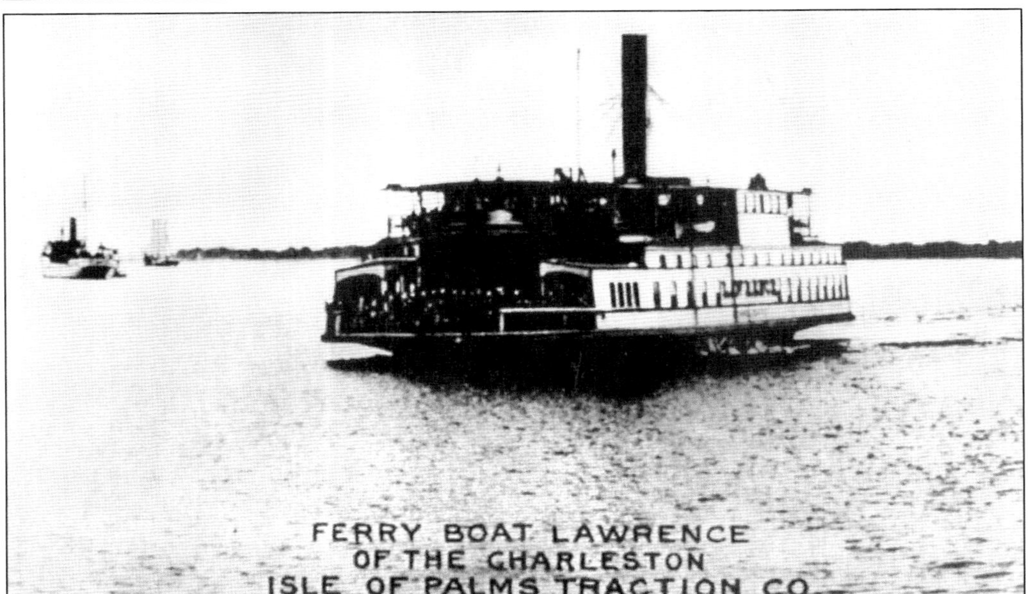

The ferryboat *Lawrence* departed from Cumberland Street in downtown Charleston to take passengers to Mt. Pleasant. There, the commuters embarked on a seven-mile rail journey through Mt. Pleasant and Sullivan's Island. The boat was originally called *Commodore Perry*, but Consolidated Railway Gas and Electric Company changed its name to *Lawrence* after the company's president. Dr. Lawrence bought the valuable waterfront real estate, the *Commodore Perry*, and the *Sappho* for $25,000. Consolidated later formed a new company, the Charleston–Isle of Palms Traction Company, in 1913, listing James Sottile as president.

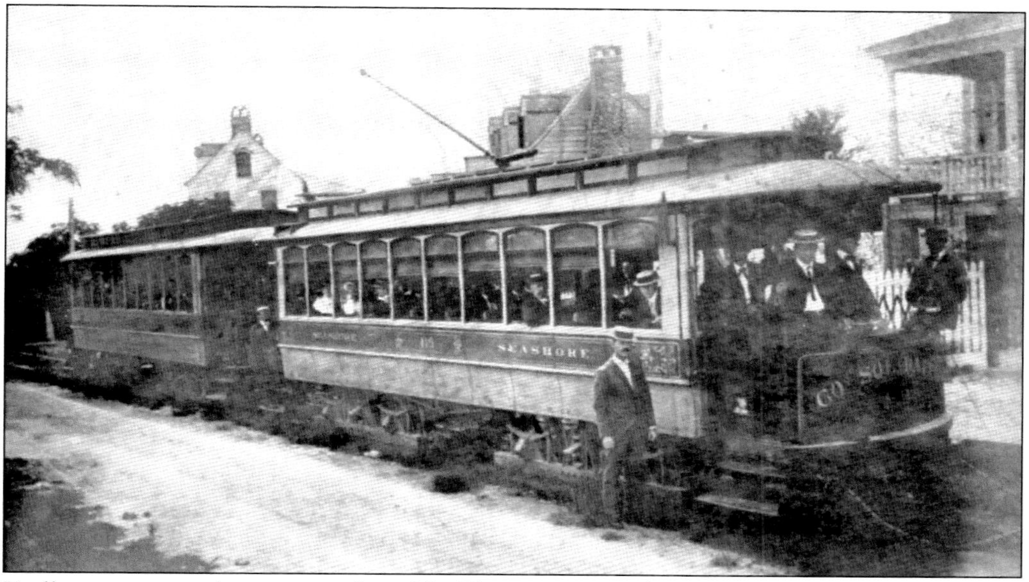

Trolleys transported passengers from Mt. Pleasant eastward on Pitt Street. The trestle across Cove Inlet required a swing bridge for boat navigation. Once on Sullivan's Island, passengers followed the tracks through Middle Street and Railroad Avenue (Jasper Boulevard), across another trestle over Breach Inlet, and through Isle of Palms, stopping at a terminal near the present-day Sea Cabins' pier. The rails followed the curve of what is now Pavilion Drive. The path across Sullivan's Island is still marked by station numbers, which have been converted into street names.

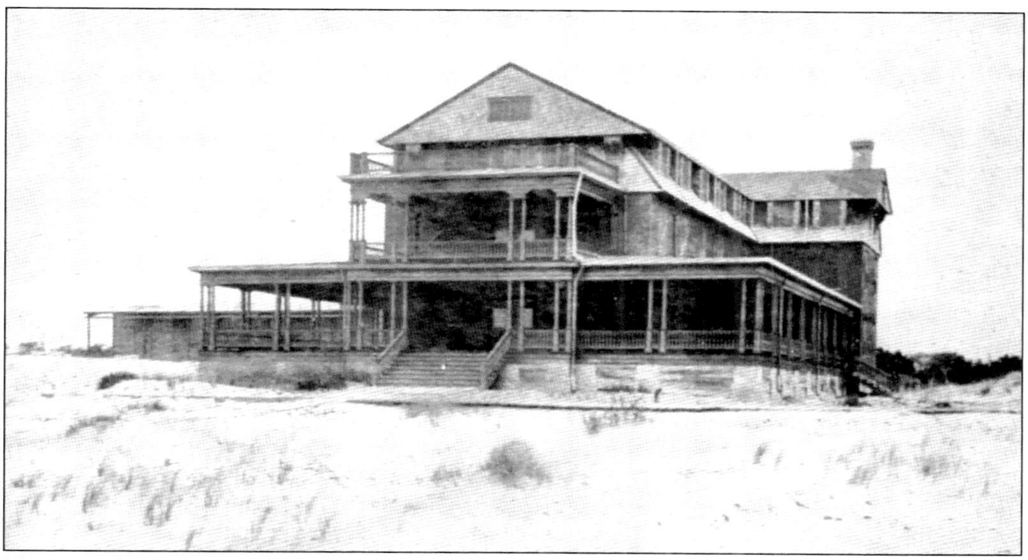

The Hotel Seashore, under progressive management, was one of the largest resorts in the country. Dr. Lawrence opened the hotel in 1902. In 1913, Consolidated sold its ferry, rail, and hotel operations to Charleston–Isle of Palms Traction Company. Passengers left Columbia or Augusta at 8 a.m. and enjoyed a swim before midday dinner. The hotel served dinner from 1 to 4 p.m. for 75¢ a person. After a day at the beach and a night of dancing, guests retired to one of the naturally air conditioned rooms.

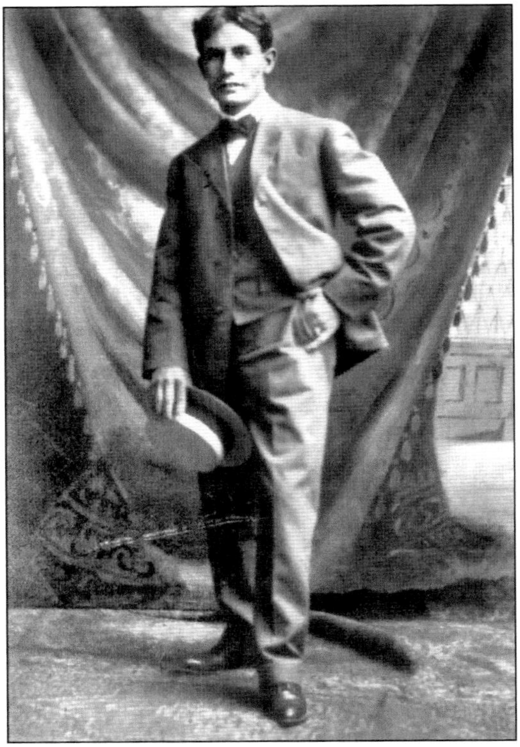

James Sottile, president of the Charleston–Isle of Palms Traction Company, died as one of the 50 wealthiest men in America at 77. After successfully marketing Isle of Palms as Charleston's seaside resort, Sottile moved to Florida and started South Dade Farms, Inc., acquiring nearly 20,000 acres in the Miami area. At his death in 1964, he was worth $100 million. This came long after losing his Charleston fortune in the Depression, when he was down to "his wife's jewels and his children's piggy banks."

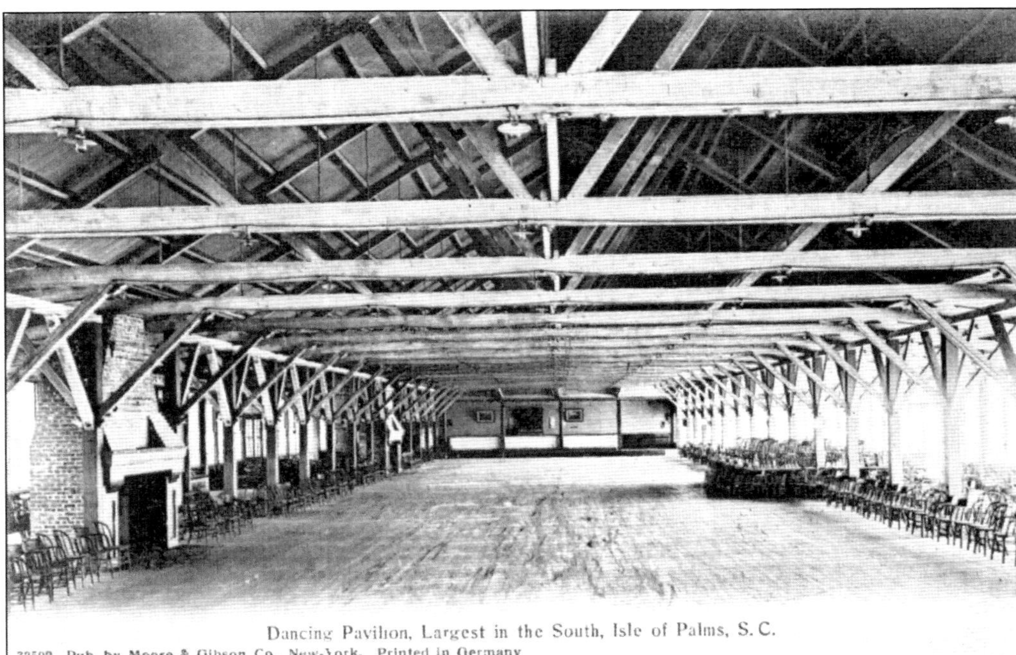

The dancing pavilion was the largest in the entire South, boasting a 400-foot dance floor. The Metz Military Band played regularly, and nationally known orchestras were invited to play on special occasions. This pavilion burned in the early 1900s.

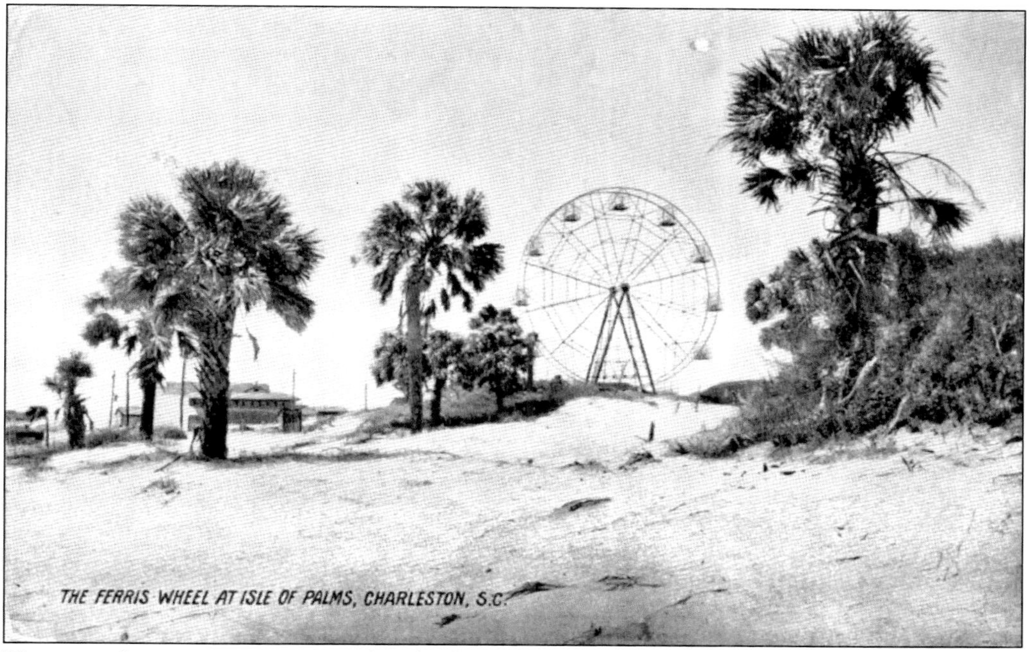

The most famous attraction on Isle of Palms was the monstrous Ferris wheel. Originally built for the Chicago World's Fair in 1892, the Ferris wheel spent time at the Cotton Congress in Atlanta and Coney Island in New York before making its home on the Isle of Palms.

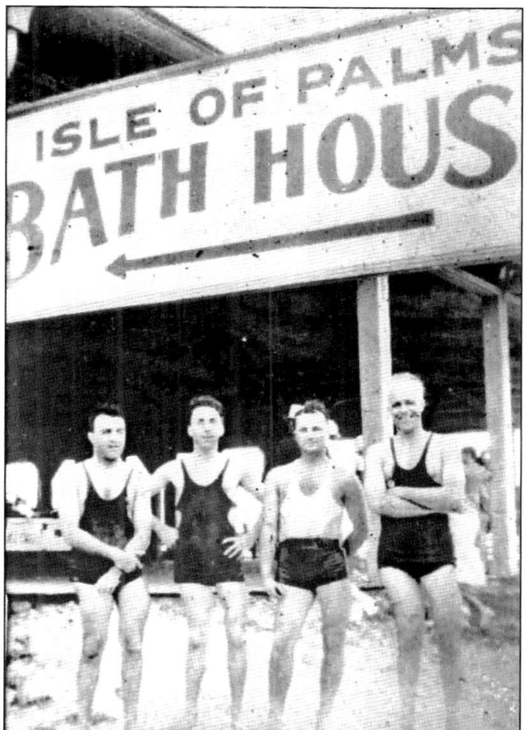

There was a great need for bathhouses, or changing rooms, in the island's early days. Folks just did not wear their bathing suits to the beach like they do today. The ladies and gentlemen were fully clothed when they started the early-morning journey to the beach via ferries and trolleys. They changed into their swimming attire once they arrived and redressed before their departure home. It was common to rent bathing suits from the hotel.

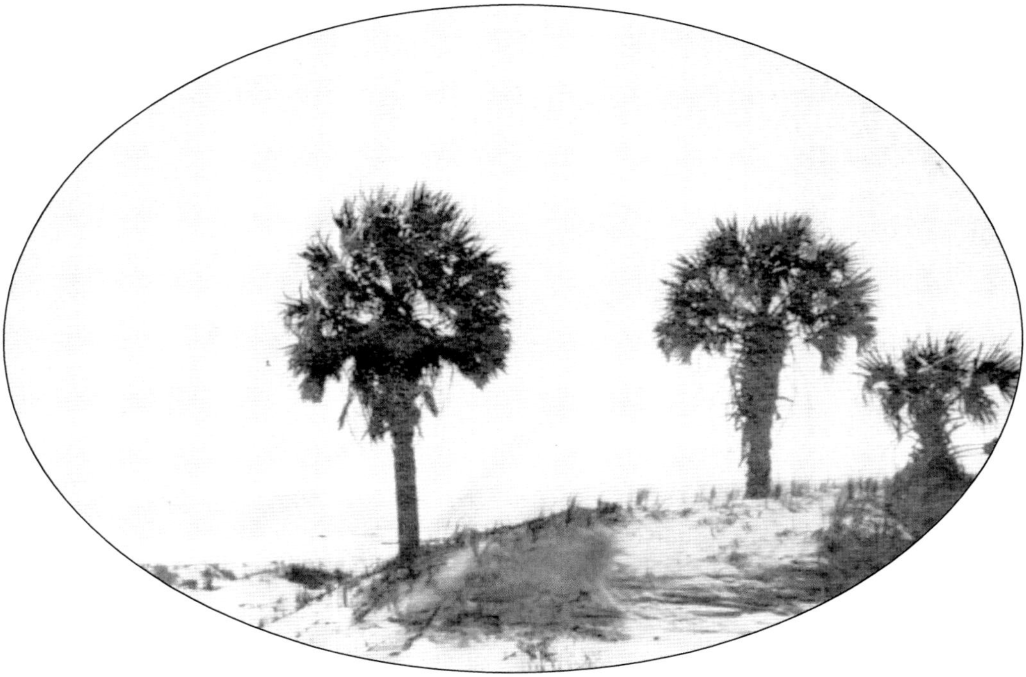

The magnificent dunes, some 30 feet tall, grew over the course of several centuries. Isle of Palms is thought to be between 25,000 and 75,000 years old. Atlantic breezes and annual sand accretion contributed to the formation of these grand dunes.

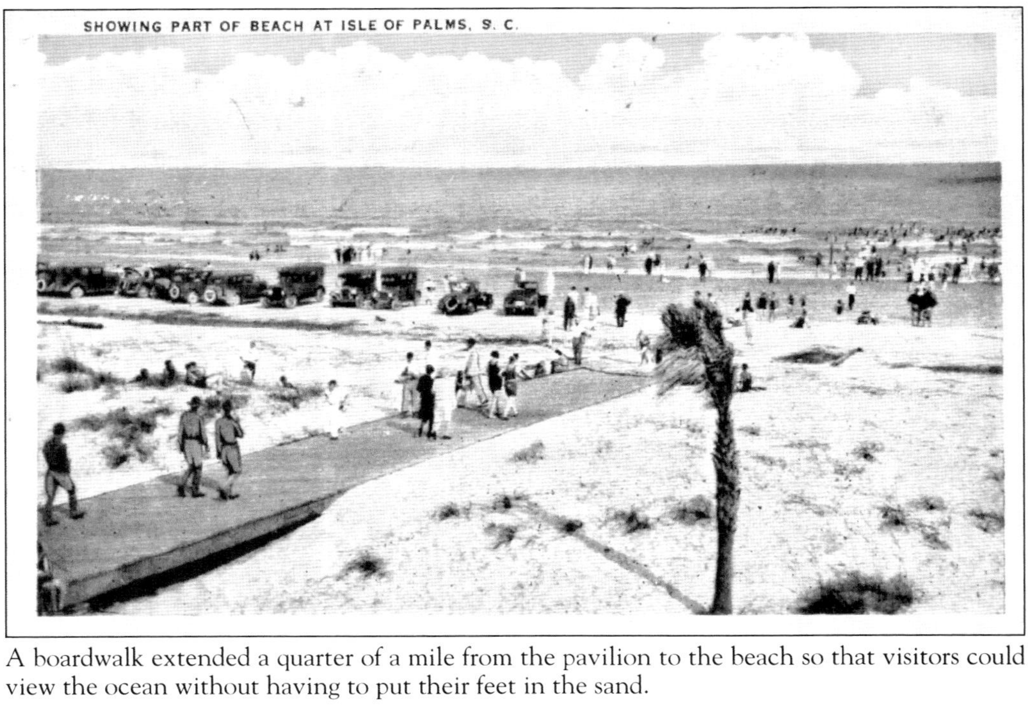

A boardwalk extended a quarter of a mile from the pavilion to the beach so that visitors could view the ocean without having to put their feet in the sand.

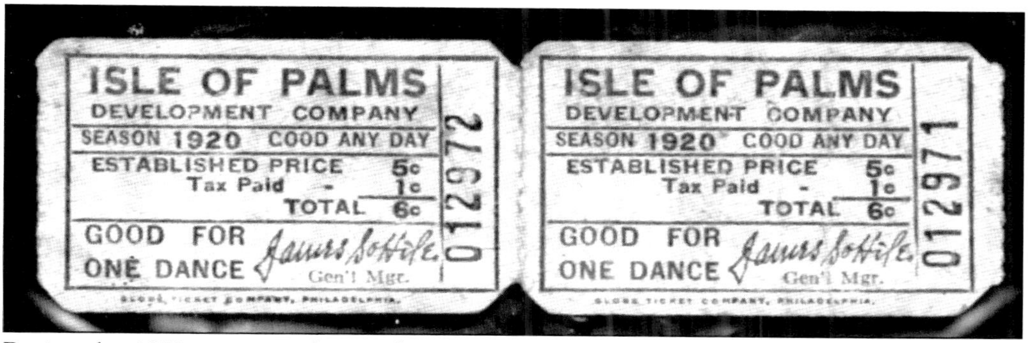

During the 1920 season at the pavilion, a single dance cost 6¢. Gentlemen purchased these tickets for that one memorable dance at the beach with the one they loved. These tickets were also used for lectures, sittings with photographers, and animal shows. Free activities included fireworks, flying-machine exhibits—as they were called then—and boat racing. In addition, a number of athletic events were sponsored by the Charleston–Isle of Palms Traction Company.

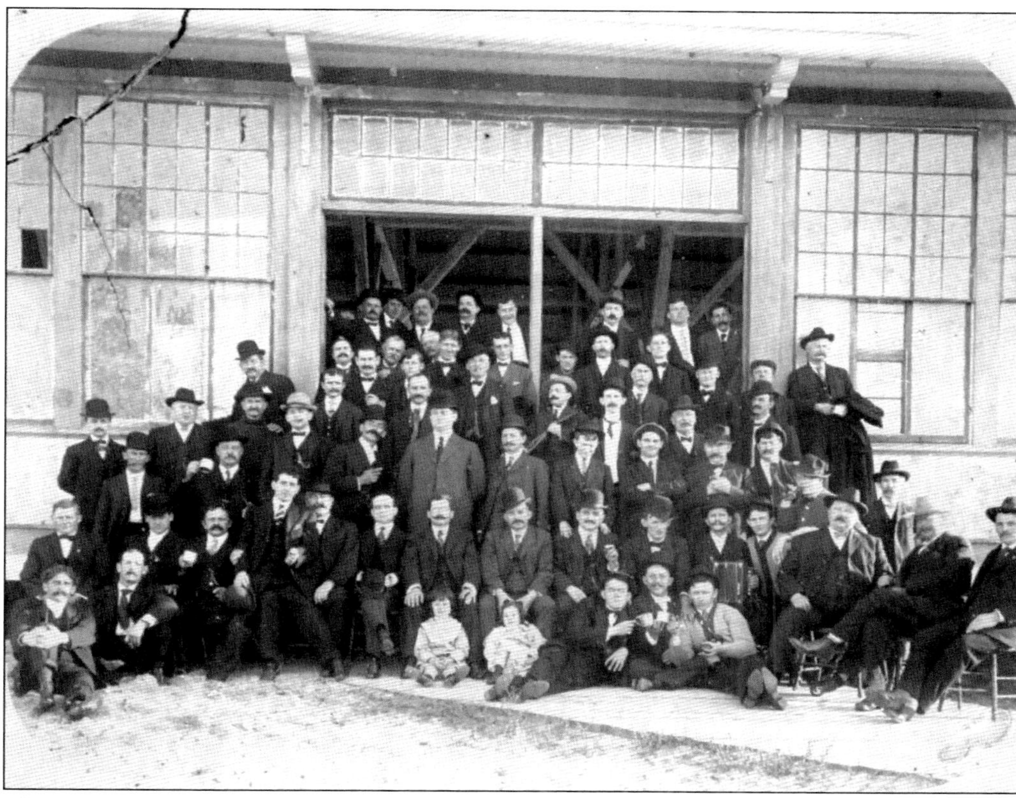

These gentlemen gather in front of the beach side of the pavilion. Statewide and interstate conventions were held at the pavilion and Hotel Seashore. One noted lecturer was Madam Dodge, an anti–women's suffrage leader. Before women were granted the right to vote in 1920, many spoke out against the movement. Madam Dodge thought a woman's emotional instability would make her a dangerous voter. Let's hope these men knew better than to endorse such a movement!

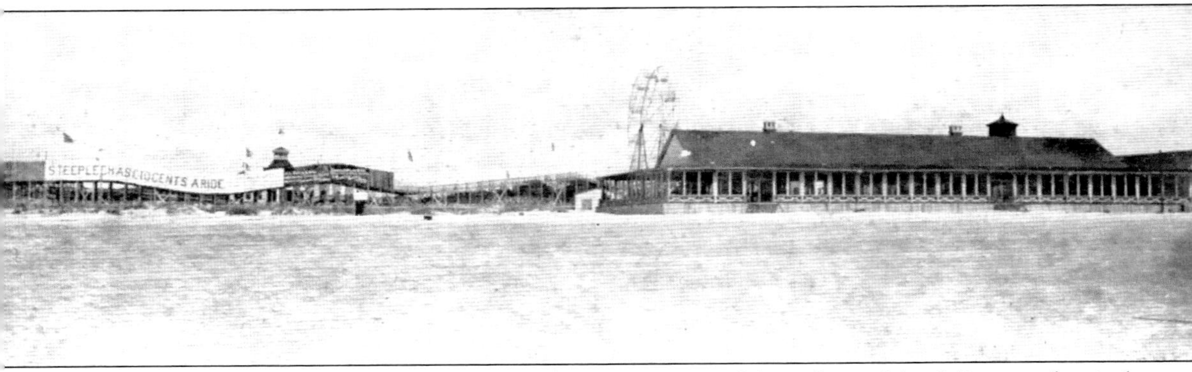

The steeplechase, located next to the pavilion, was imported from Coney Island. Five mechanical horses on rails and rollers raced on a U-shaped course. Riding co-ed added to the fun!

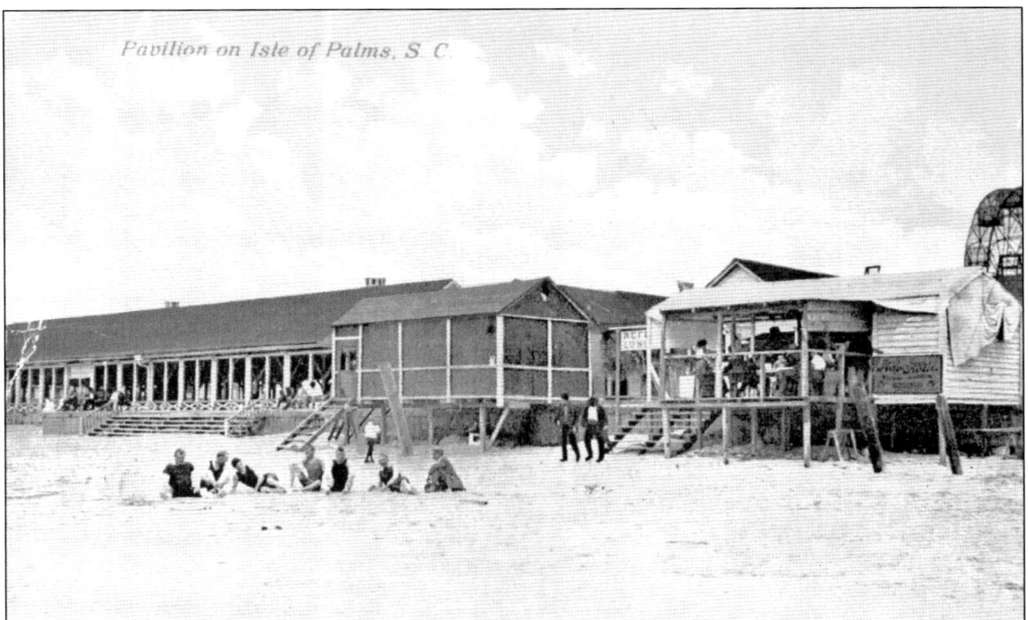

The bathhouses and restaurants were luxurious amenities for people who stayed all day at the beach. The gentlemen in the foreground sit on the sand in their full-body bathing suits, probably rented from the hotel.

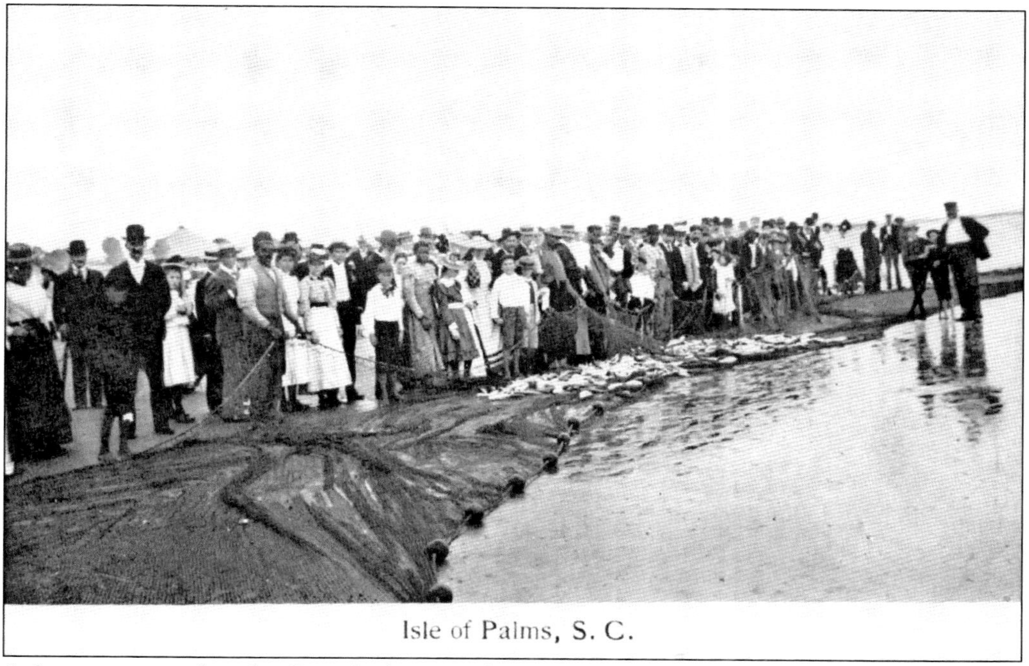

A fun activity in the island's early days was drawing the seine net. Experts pulled the long fish net beyond the breakers and brought its ends to the beach, trapping the encircled fish. Anyone could volunteer to help, and many watched with great interest. The hotel prepared the fish for a delicious seaside meal.

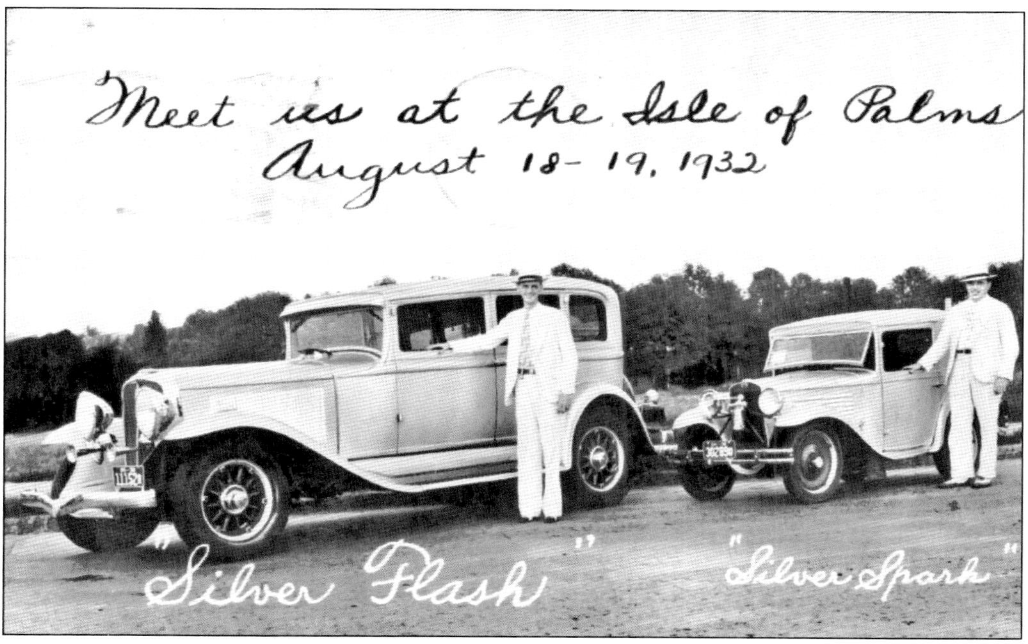

Taken in August 1932, these gentlemen stand in front of their cars, "Silver Flash" and "Silver Spark." Automobile racing was very popular on Isle of Palms. At low tide, cars like these ripped up and down the beach until the activity was banned in 1953.

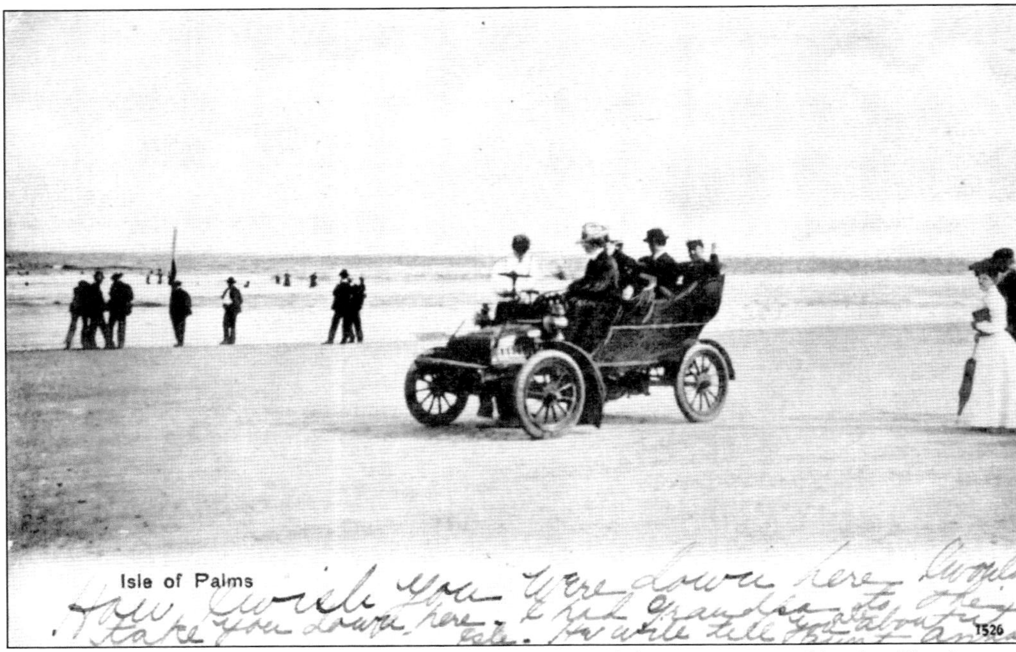

This "horseless carriage" was probably used in an automobile race promoted by the Charleston–Isle of Palms Traction Company. The seven miles of hard beach sand made an ideal drag for the adventurous driver.

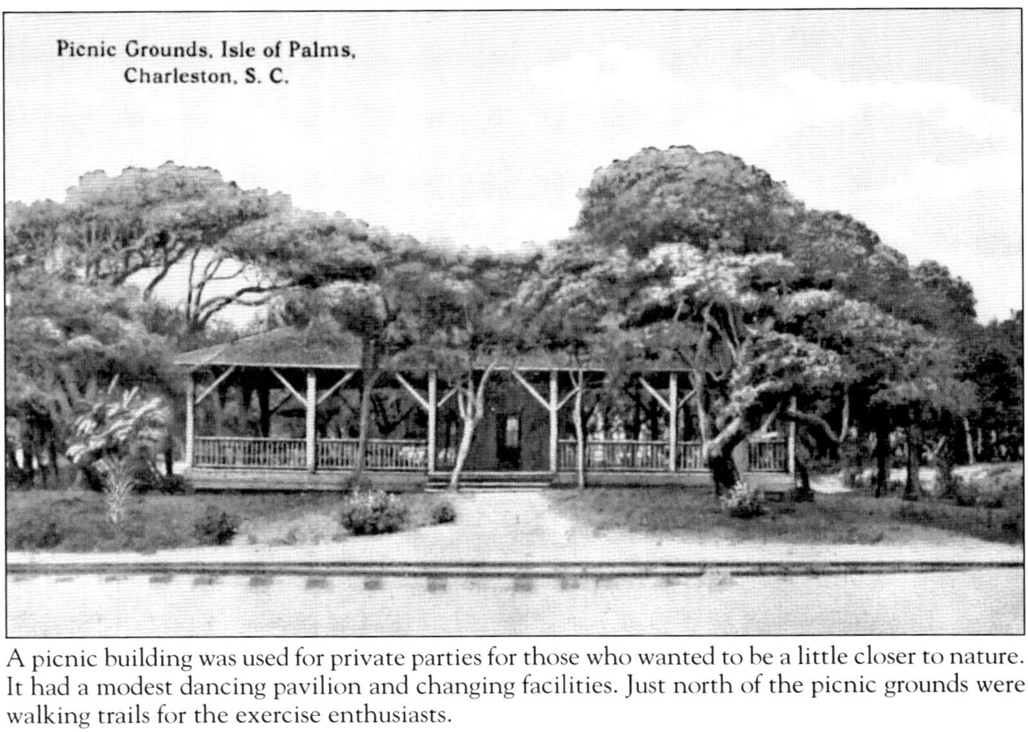

A picnic building was used for private parties for those who wanted to be a little closer to nature. It had a modest dancing pavilion and changing facilities. Just north of the picnic grounds were walking trails for the exercise enthusiasts.

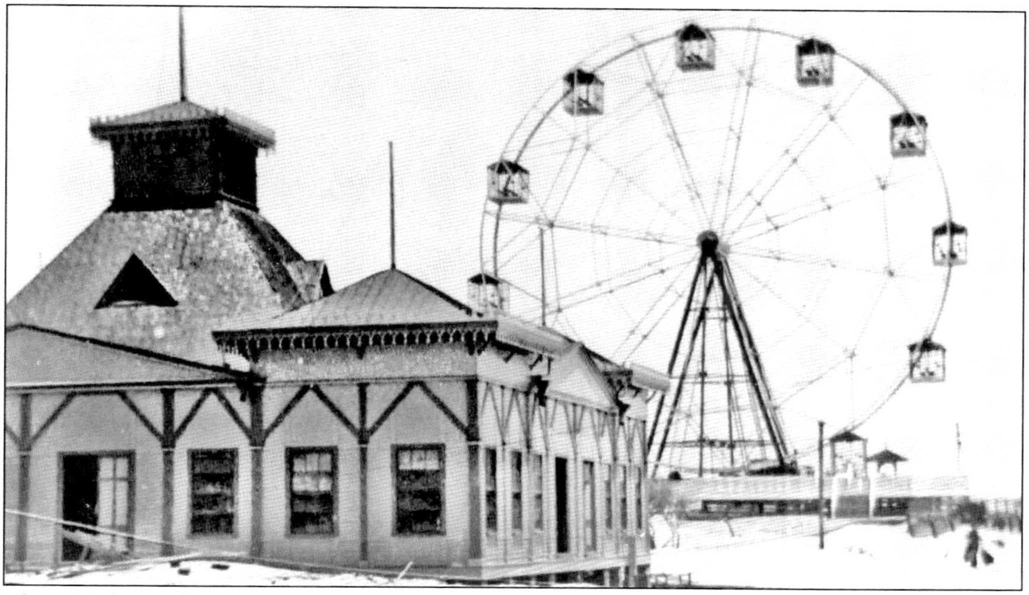

The 186-foot tall Ferris wheel towered over the gentlemen's clubhouse. While women and children patronized the café next door, the men would come here to play cards, conduct business, or simply converse about the politics of the day.

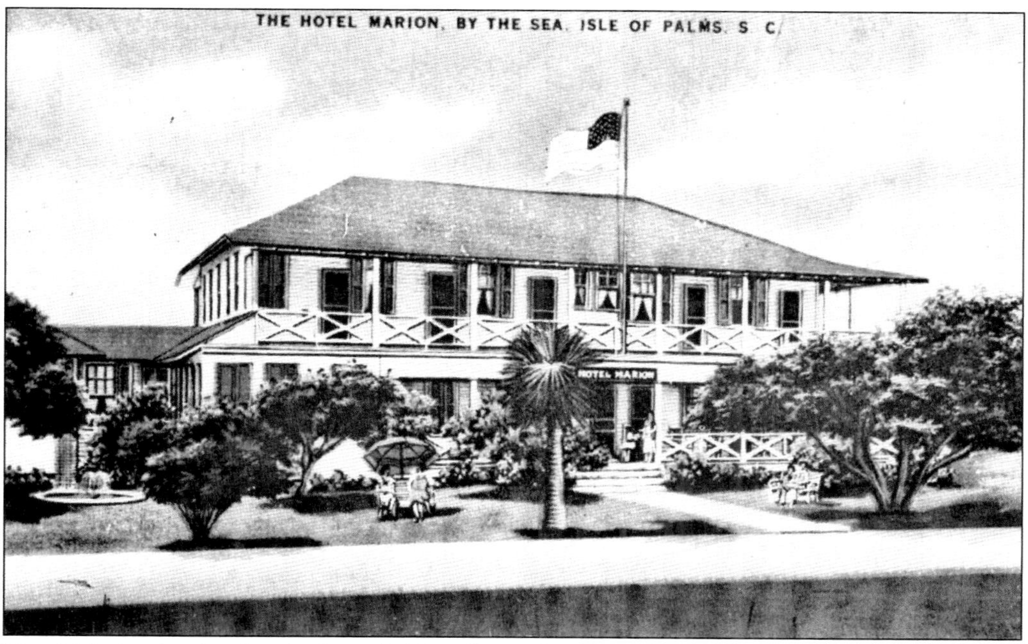

Hotel Marion by the Sea, built in 1912, still stands today at 916 Palm Boulevard as one of the island's oldest structures. Bill Casey and his mother ran the hotel until 1973, when Mr. Casey converted the building into apartments.

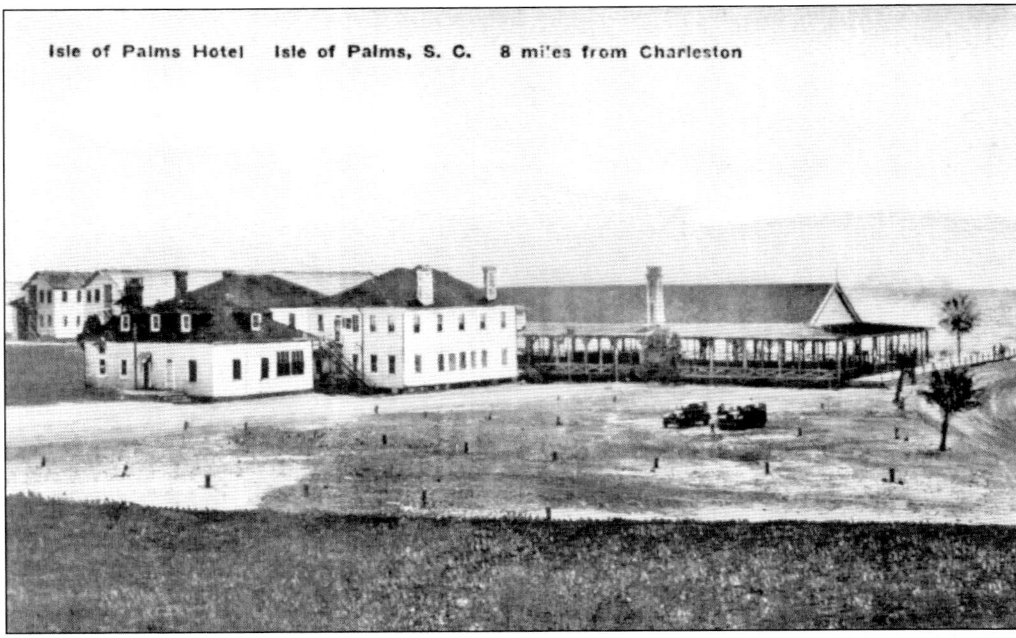

The spacious pavilion had floor-to-ceiling windows on three sides that allowed the cool breezes in from the Atlantic.

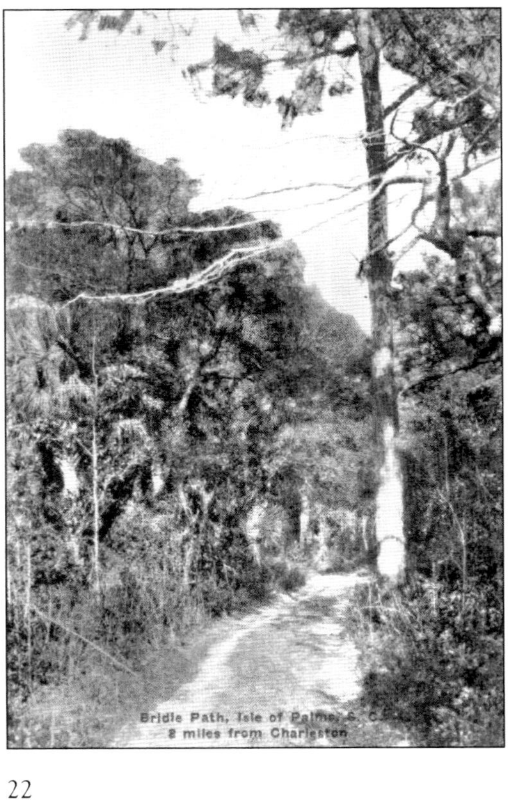

Isle of Palms encountered financial difficulties after World War I. In 1924, the county sheriff, in compliance with a court order, seized the ferryboats. Very few people lived on the island at the time; those who did walked across the railway bridges or took boats from a small wharf on Hamlin Creek to get to the mainland. Isle of Palms was virtually isolated! Until development took off in the late 1940s, bridle paths like this wound their way through tall pines and scattered sabal palms.

The tracks from the wooden trolley trestle that crossed Breach Inlet were removed in 1926, allowing automobile traffic on the bridge. Isle of Palms was now easily accessible. No longer isolated from the mainland, it was ready for further development.

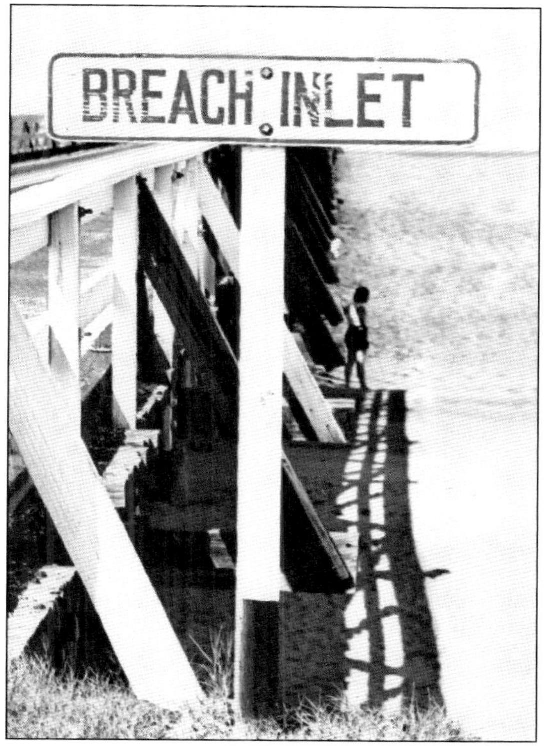

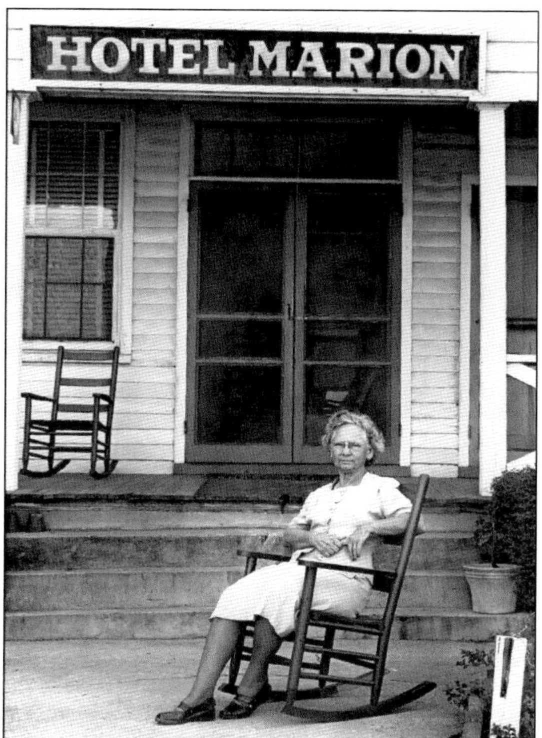

Lela Watkins sits in a rocking chair in front of the Hotel Marion. Originally from Augusta, she saw the need for an additional hotel while vacationing on the island. She built the two-story hotel in 1912 and ran it until her death in the 1950s.

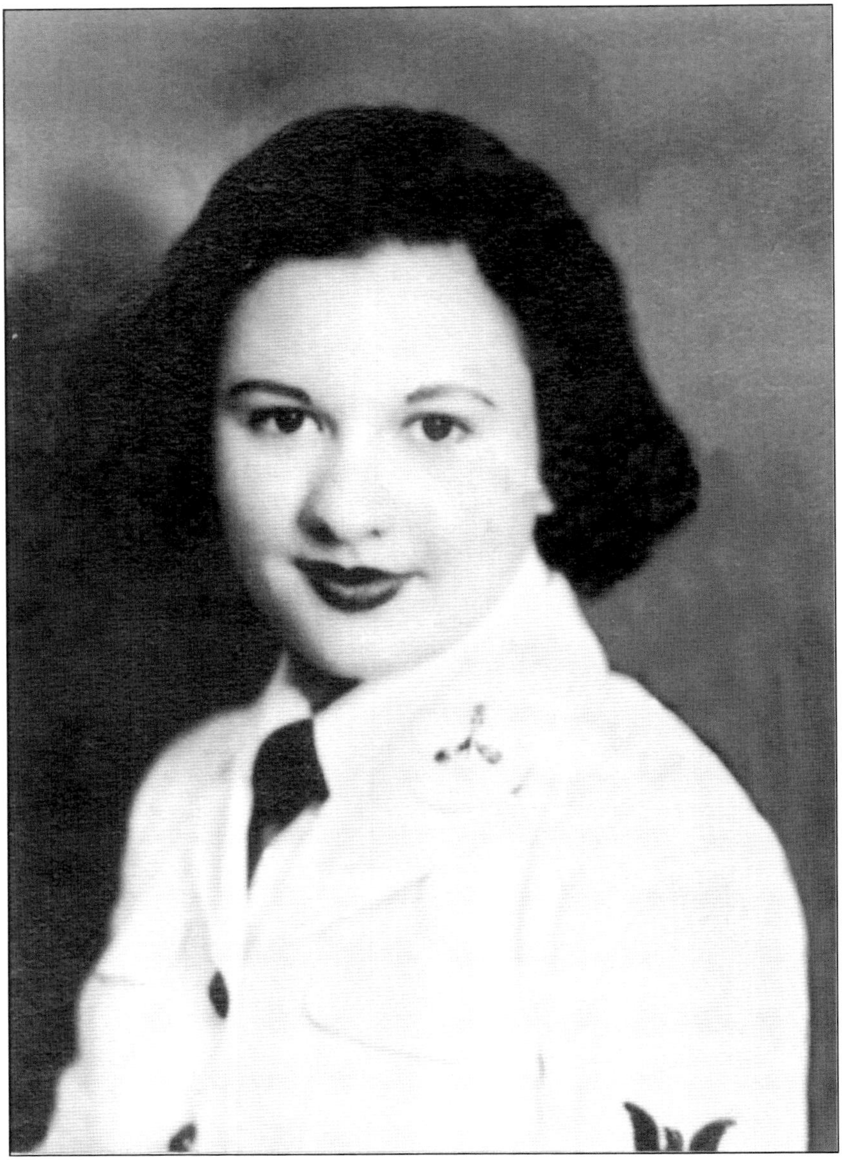

Carmen Bunch came to Isle of Palms in 1945 from New York City. She met her husband, Jack, while in the U.S. Navy. Jack, an island boy, brought his new bride back to his beloved home, and together they ran the Inlet Inn until 1950 and lived upstairs. When she first came to the island, she cried herself to sleep every night. Coming from a city of millions to an island with a population of less than 300 was quite a change! After meeting Marguerite and Louis Stith on Sullivan's Island, Carmen began to feel more at home on the island. They ate at her restaurant every night, and their friendship lasted for decades. When J.C. Long and Frank Sottile offered her the lot of her choice, Carmen chose two on the west side of the island. She thought she would have children who would want to live beside her. Without a penny to her name, she took a loan on the G.I. Bill and bought both the lots. Today, her daughter and granddaughter do, indeed, live next door to her on Seventeenth Avenue. Carmen, once homesick from the big city, is anchored on Isle of Palms.

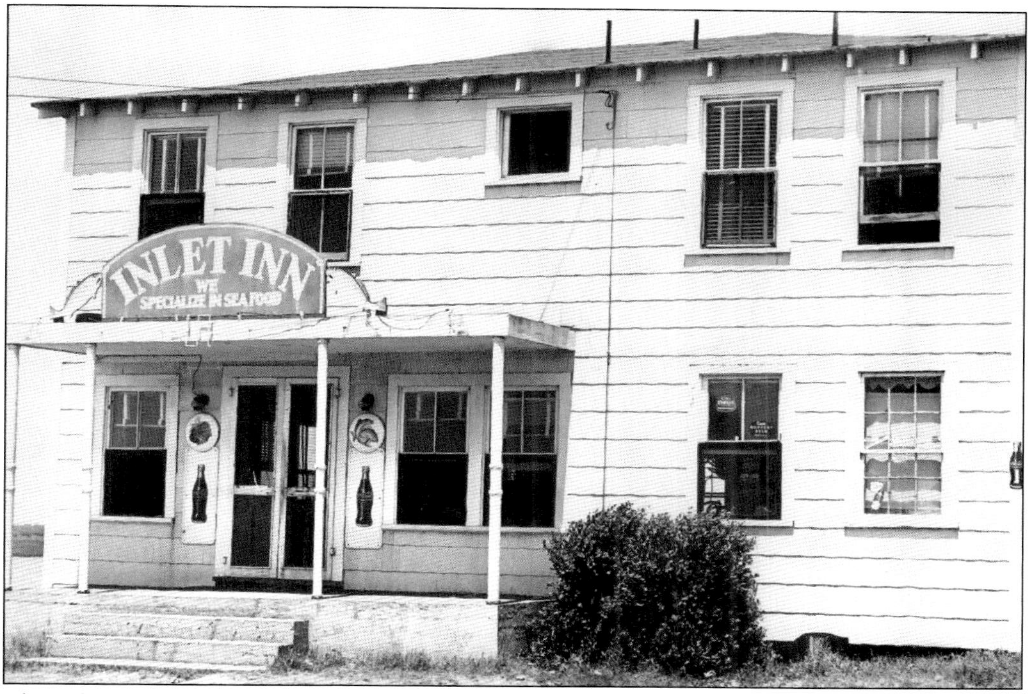

The Inlet Inn restaurant opened in 1938 on Breach Inlet. It was operated by Nell and Griffin Bunch until 1940 and later managed by Jack and Carmen Bunch. The inn, in addition to renting rooms, chartered rowboats from Breach Inlet for $1 a day. The seafood restaurant was one of only two dining establishments on the island.

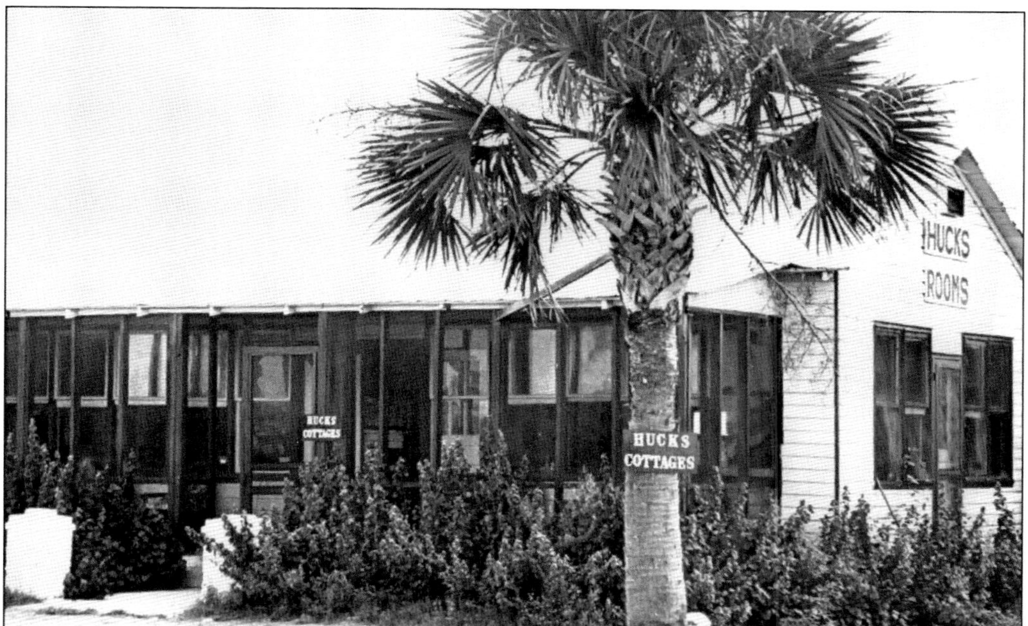

The other restaurant on the island was Hucks Cottages. The bungalow was both an inn and an eatery.

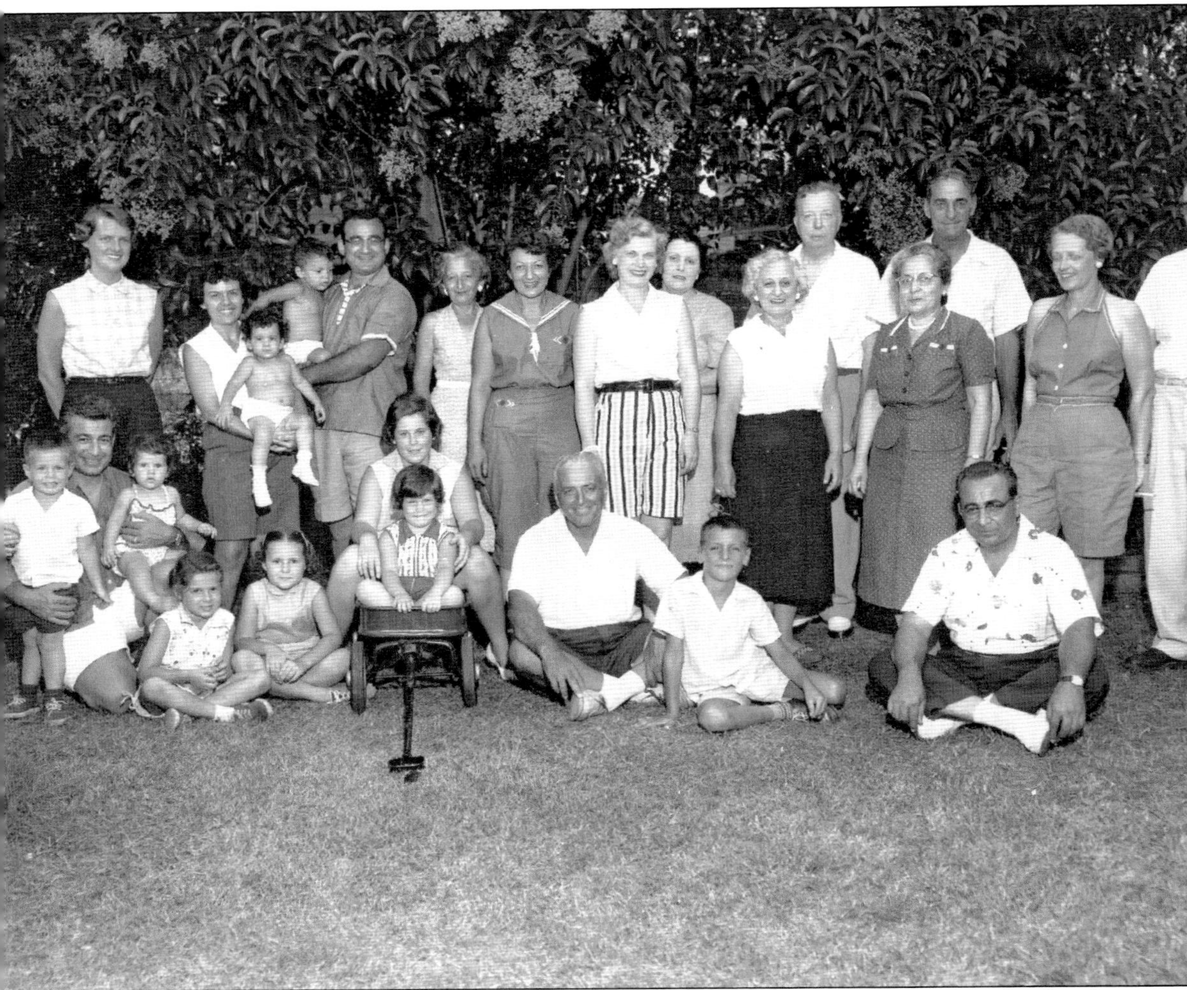

The Sottile family came from Sicily in the late 1800s and settled in Charleston. The five brothers included Giovanni, Nicholas, Santo, Albert, and James. Members of the Nicholas Sottile family include Rosina and William Kennerty and children, William Jr. and Rosemarie; Lucille and J. Julian Conlon; Marie and Caleb Daley; Nicholas and Charlotte Brown and children, Mary Jo and Carol; Frank and Tommie Lee and children, Carol, Michael, and Deborah; Josephine; Sally and Louise Wynne and their children, Elisabeth, Charlotte, Nicholas, Susan, and William; and Vincent Sr. and Pauline and their children, Vincent and Mary.

Two

Incorporation and Development

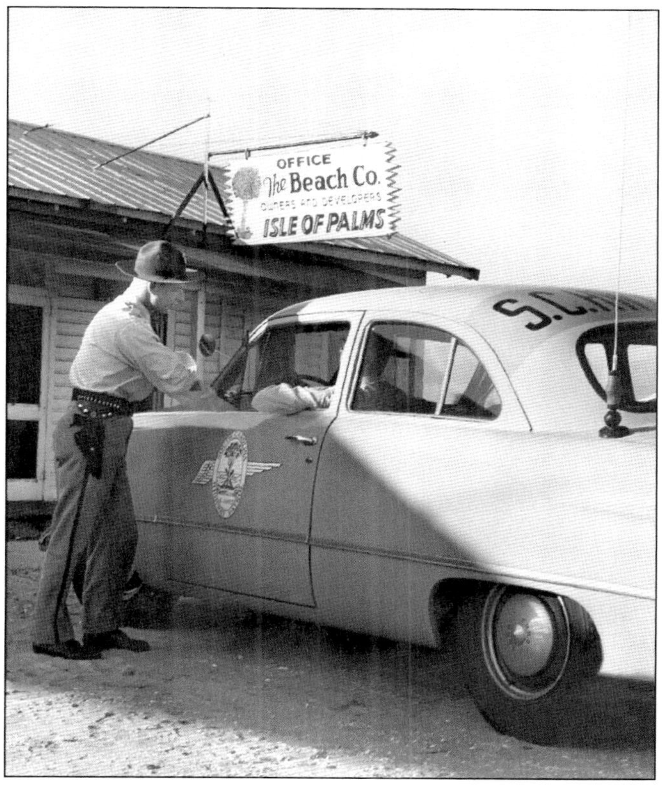

In 1945, J.C. Long founded The Beach Company, one of the state's modern pioneer companies in real-estate development. Its first office on Isle of Palms was a modest, one-story building indicative of the character of the island in the late 1940s. Today, 60 years later, the family-held-and-operated company headquarters itself at Majestic Square on King Street in downtown Charleston. Its conservative and meticulous reputation explains why The Beach Company has grown into one of the most significant real-estate businesses in the Southeast.

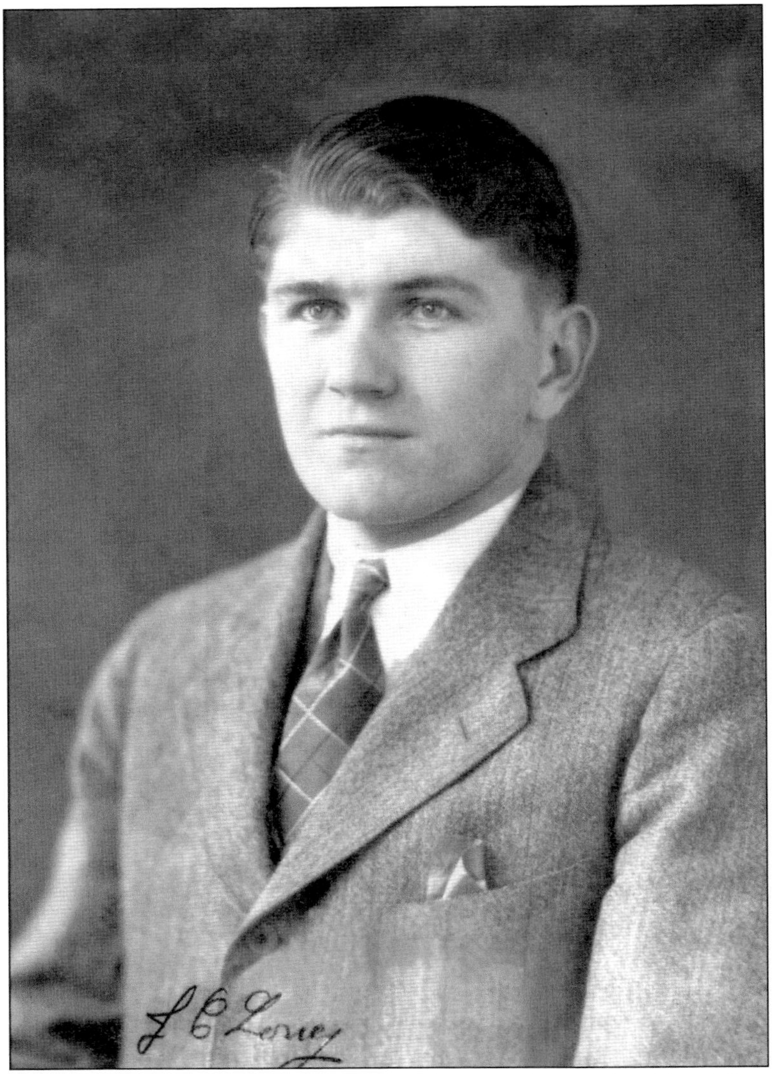

John Charles Long, known to everyone as J.C., was born on September 19, 1903, in Pensacola, Florida. His family moved to Charleston when he was 15. An all-star football player on the Bantam team at the High School of Charleston, J.C. continued his athletics while attending law school at the University of South Carolina, playing on the varsity football, baseball, and basketball teams. In 1931, J.C. started his career as a builder with Ashley Forest, one of the earliest residential developments West of the Ashley. The same year, he was elected to the state senate. After resigning as an alderman at large from Ward 12 in 1951, J.C. became a member of the Educational Finance Commission at the request of Gov. James F. Byrnes. He was also instrumental in widening U.S. 17 in Mount Pleasant. It was in real estate that J.C. made his fortune, becoming the largest single property owner in Charleston County. Practicing law, however, was nearest to J.C.'s heart; he often drew hundreds of spectators to the courtroom to witness his highly emotional arguments. In 1944, he purchased 1,300 acres of land on Isle of Palms, and this small beach community got its second birth. The Beach Company introduced paved roads, new bridges and homes, garbage collection, water, and streetlights. A man of vision, J.C. Long remains one of the most influential residents Isle of Palms has ever known.

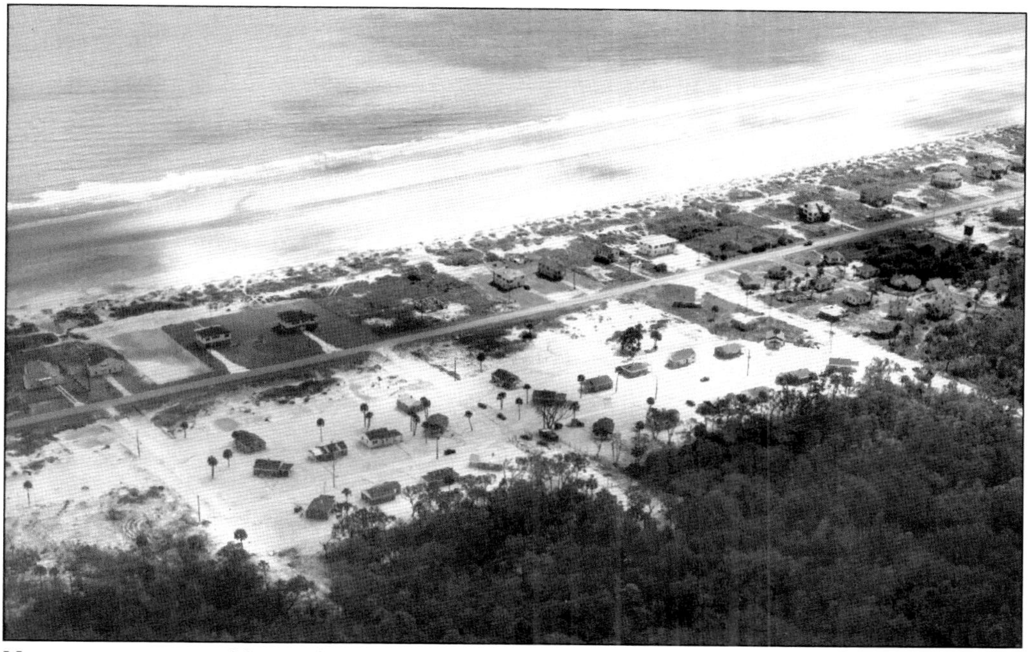

Housing was minimal beyond Palm Boulevard up to Waterway Boulevard. The modest homes were about 1,200 square feet. The dwellings would later be known as "J.C. Long homes."

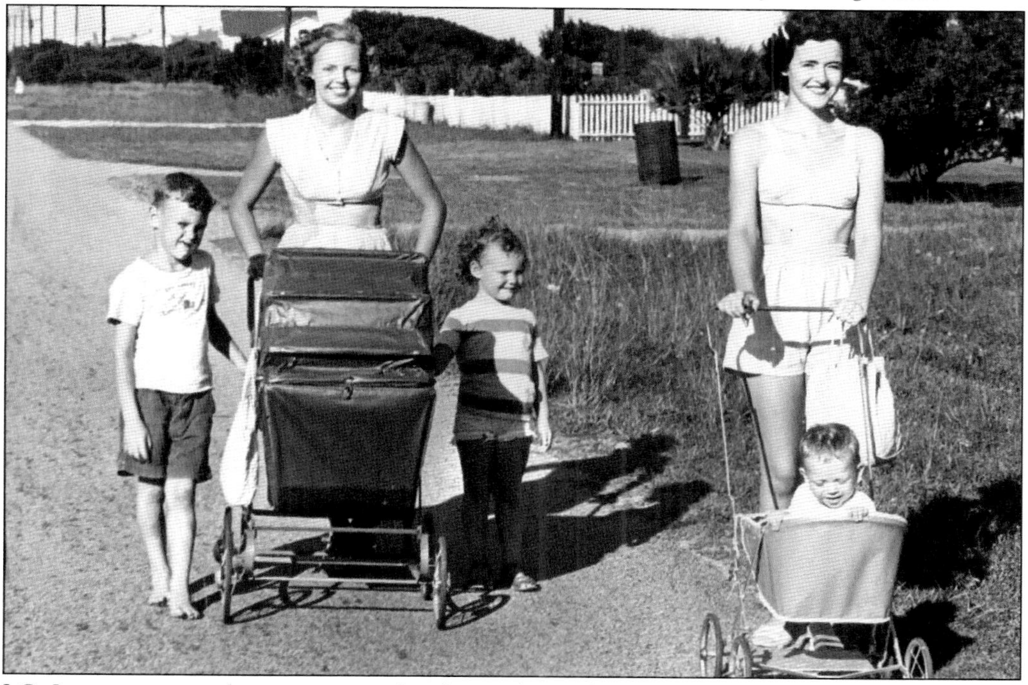

J.C. Long envisioned a community for the working class. He built affordable housing on the island with World War II veterans in mind. Young families were able to live near the beach, a recreational haven for toddlers and children. By 1949, the beach community had 375 homes. These women, along with their precious cargo, enjoy an afternoon stroll.

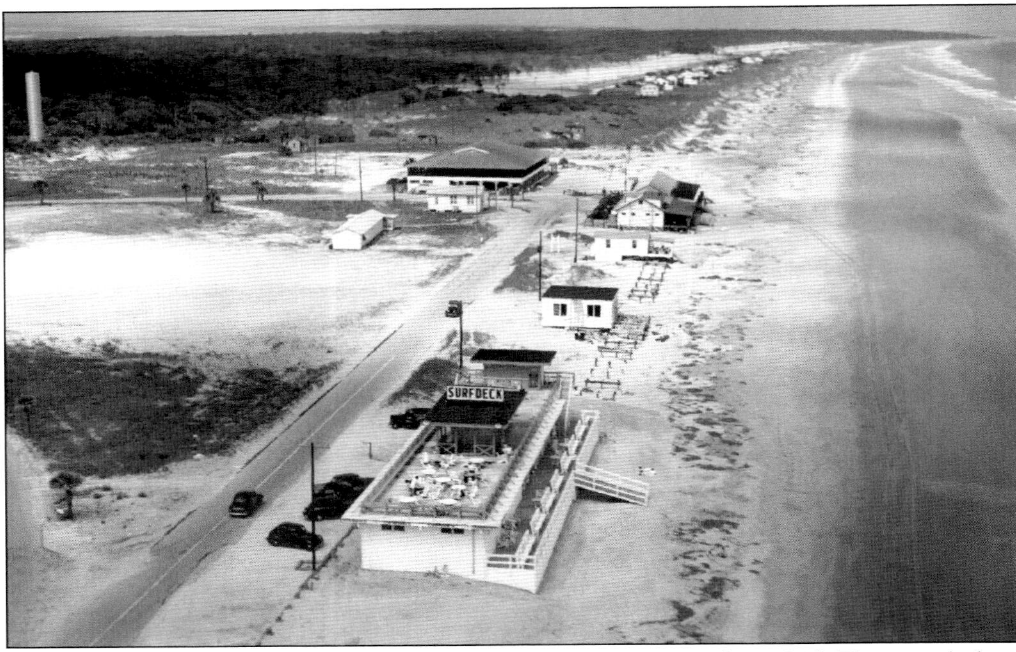

The Surf Deck, a popular hangout for the local teenagers, opened in 1946. This aerial photo shows the large deck that made it so well liked. Sunbathers flocked to the top of the building, and thanks to flood lighting on the beach, night bathing was just as common.

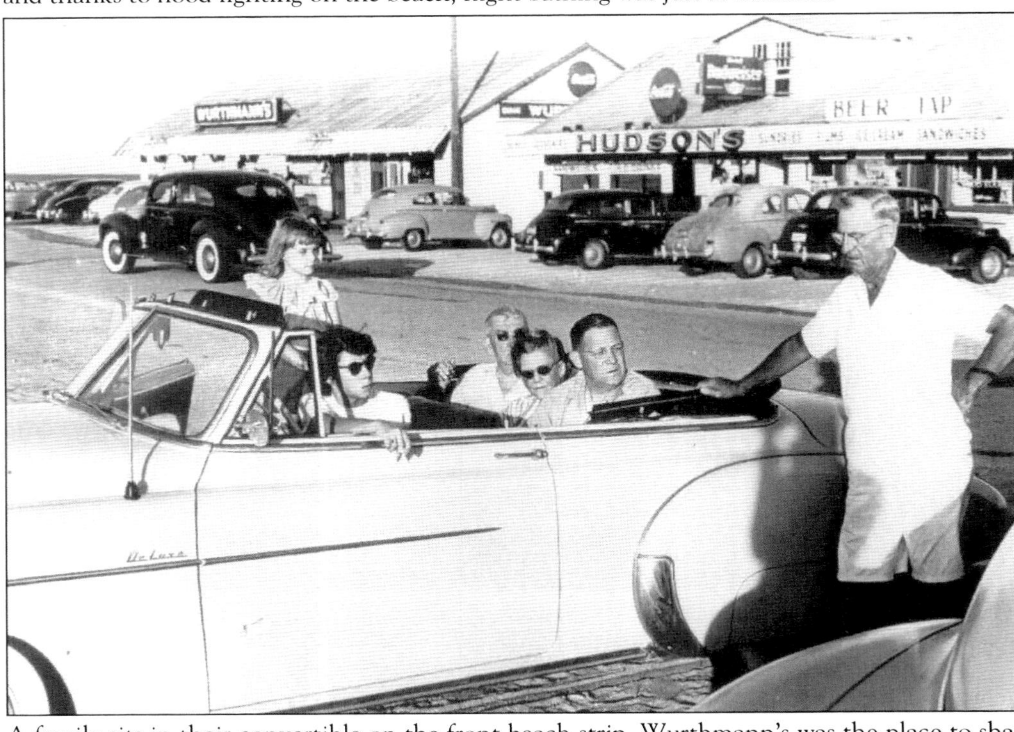

A family sits in their convertible on the front beach strip. Wurthmann's was the place to shag and Hudson's offered cold beer on tap. What a tough decision!

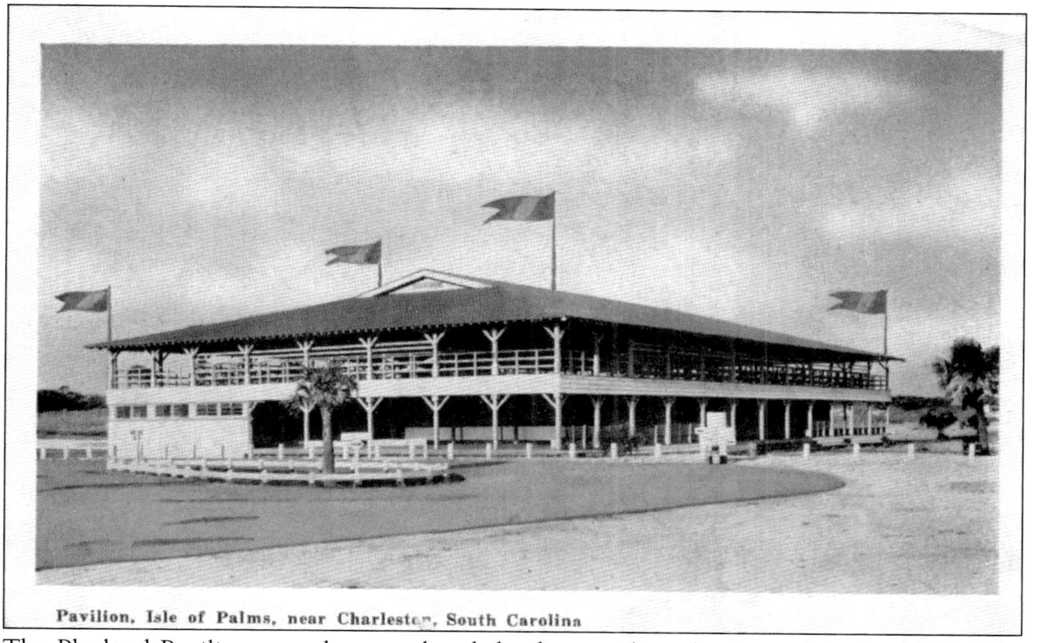

The Playland Pavilion, seen here, replaced the first pavilion that burned in the 1920s. The Hasselmeyer family managed the popular spot, which hosted well-known acts like the Drifters, the Tams, and even James Brown. Many memories were made before fire burned the pavilion to the ground in 1953.

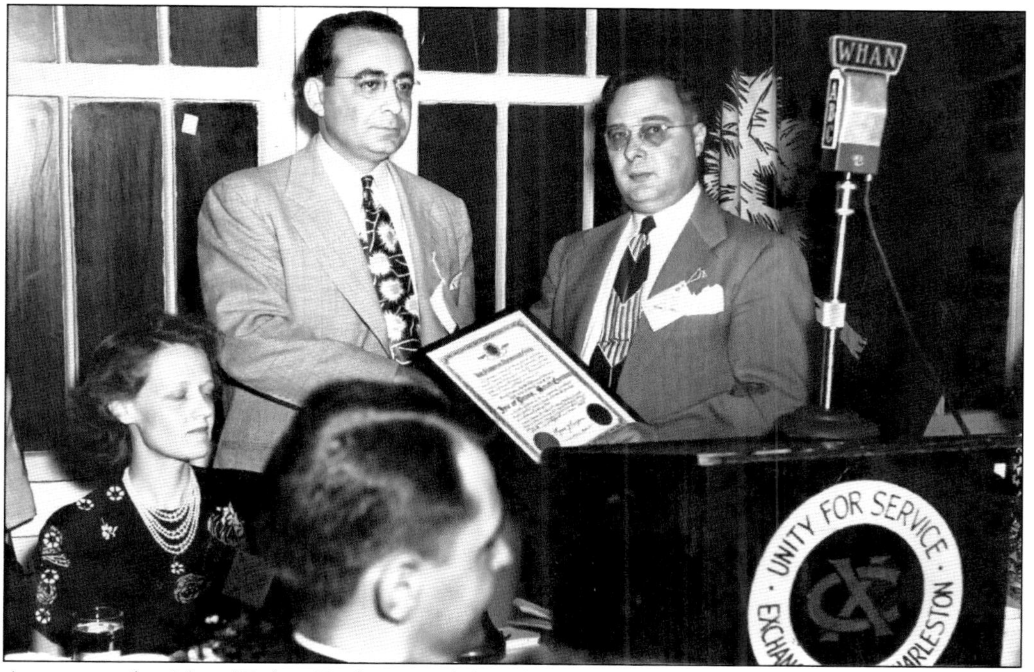

Accepting the Isle of Palms Exchange Club's charter is its president, Frank Sottile. The first meeting was held at the Isle of Palms Pavilion on Saturday, April 24, 1948. The Exchange Club governed the island prior to the city's incorporation in 1953.

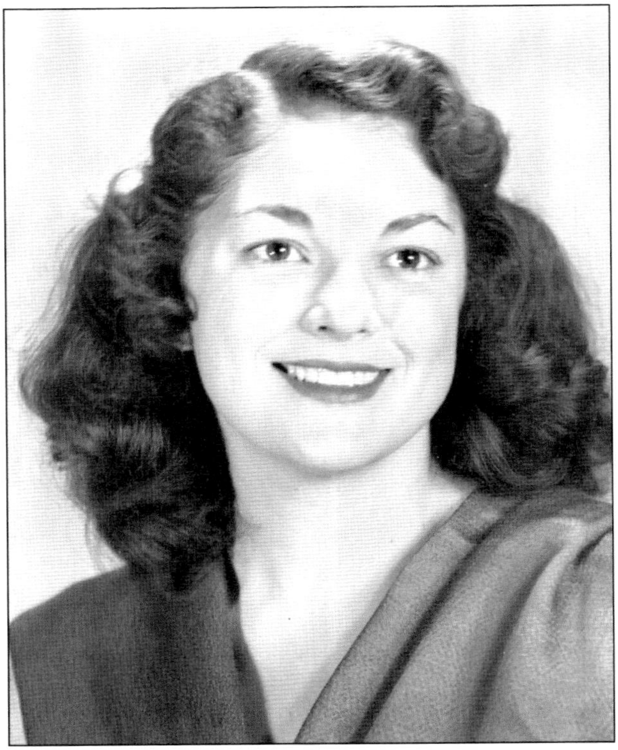

Beauty queen Joan Hartnett, Miss Isle of Palms 1949, is pictured at the Azalea Festival.

The Exchange Club float makes its way through downtown Charleston at the Azalea Festival parade in 1950. The side of the float reads, "Isle of Palms, Charleston's Beach Suburb." The festival hired professional float builders to construct the magnificent displays.

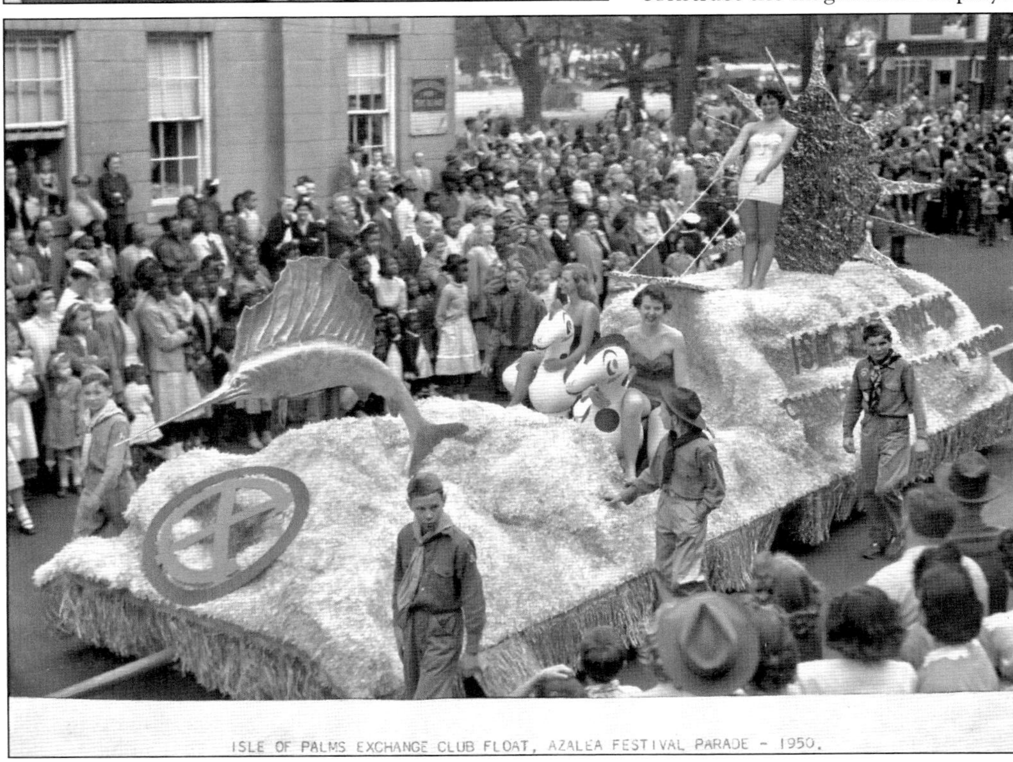

ISLE OF PALMS EXCHANGE CLUB FLOAT, AZALEA FESTIVAL PARADE - 1950.

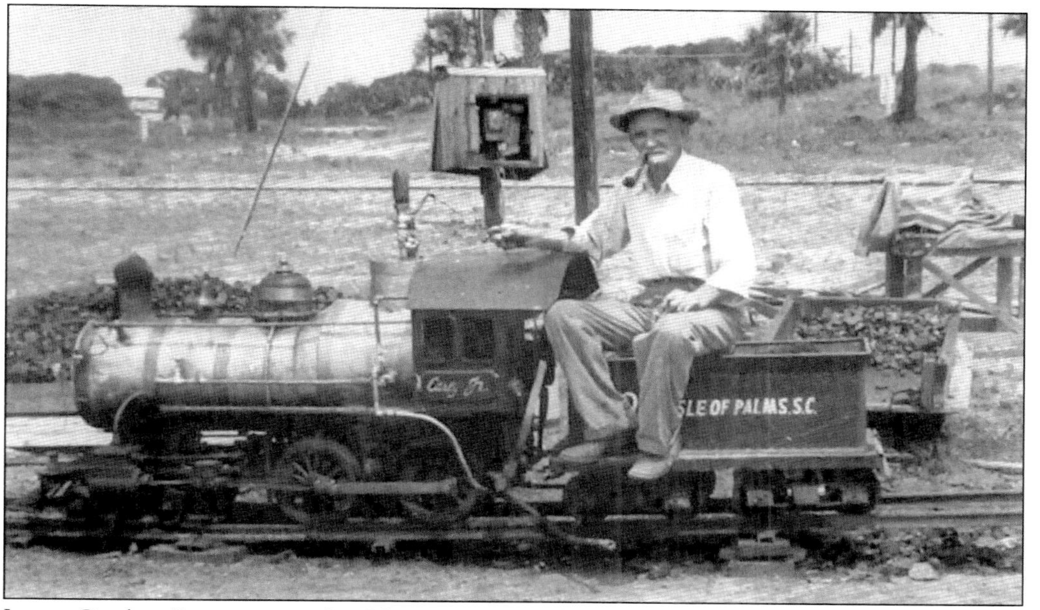

James Gordon Burn sits on the "Casey Jr.," a coal-burning locomotive at the Isle of Palms Amusement Park in the summer of 1949. The park was located near the Oceanside Villas Condos. Mr. Burn was a mechanic for the South Carolina Port Utilities Railroad. Upon retirement, he maintained and operated this train for the park. His grandson is George Bowers, and his great-granddaughters are Kimberly Bowers and Wendy B. Jenkins.

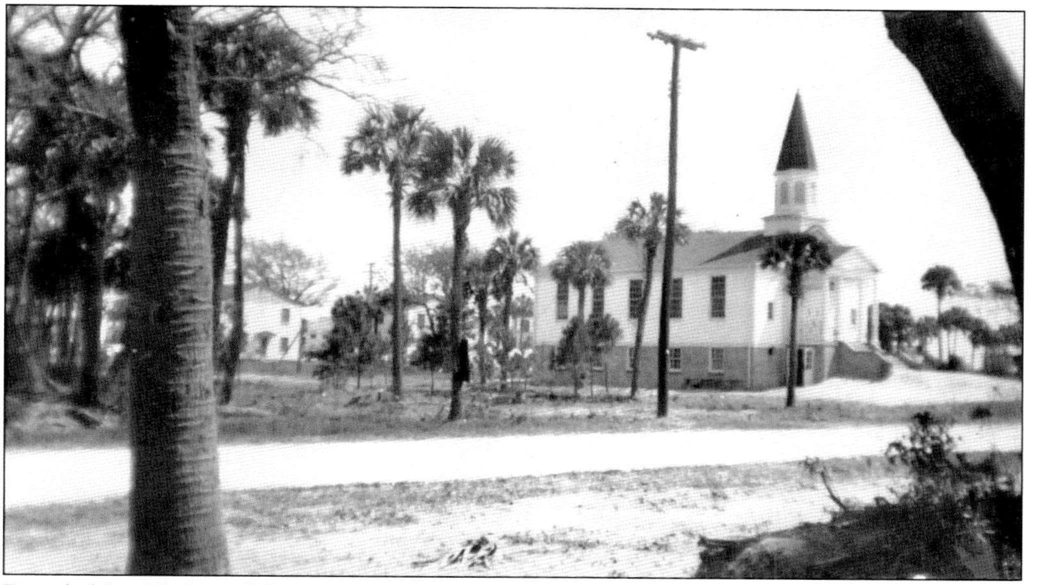

Founded by Clyde and Betty Dangerfield, the Isle of Palms First United Methodist Church sits on a lot donated by J.C. Long. Its charter members include the Dangerfields, Albion and Sara Johnson, Wiley and Viola Horne, J.R. and Penny Deans, Neoni Cameron, Mrs. H.H. Watkins, Ivey Bryan, Wallie Anderson, Cecil and Julie Sears, Lee and Iris Landrum, Elizabeth and Frank Cobb, Mr. and Mrs. J.D. Honsford, Andrew and Frances Jones, James and Sue Gantt, and Norman and Betty Todd. The church's first pastor was Rev. C.J. Lupo.

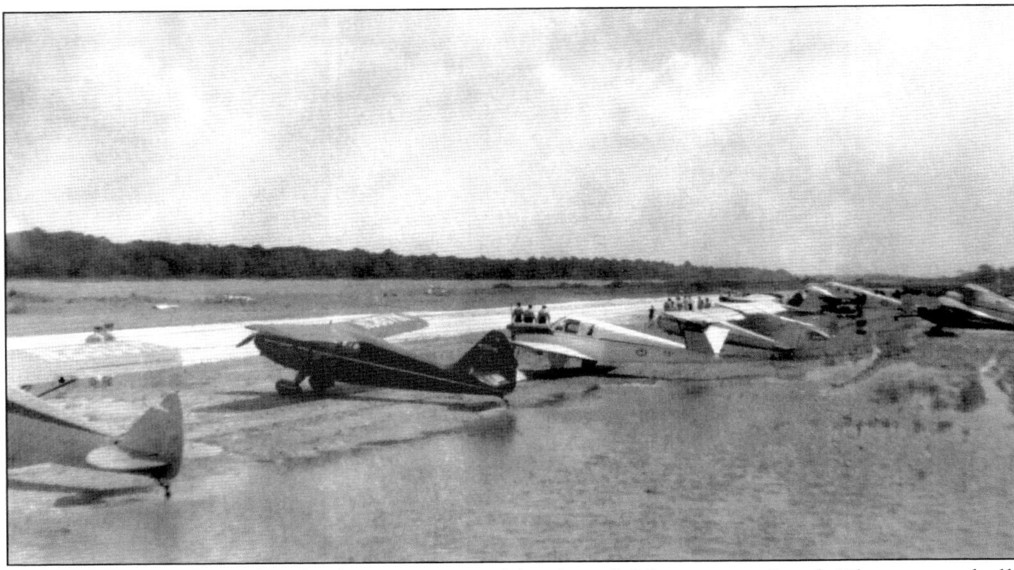

In August 1951, the Isle of Palms airstrip and landing field was completed. The oyster shell–covered runway extended 1,800 feet between Thirtieth and Thirty-ninth Avenues, parallel to the Intracoastal Waterway. The Harold F. Wilson Memorial Airfield closed in 1975.

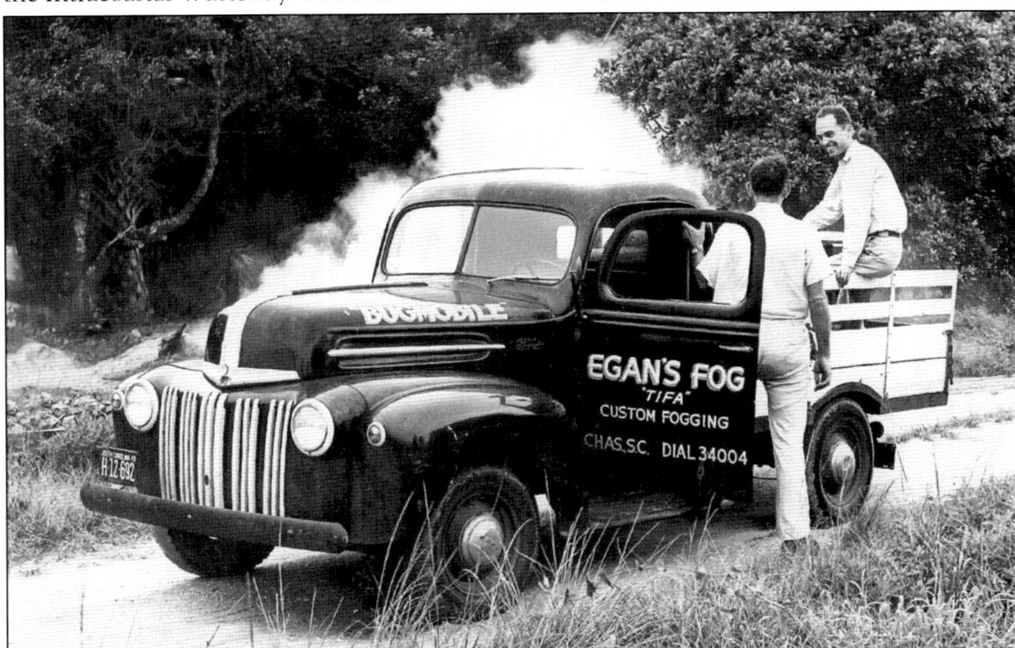

If there is one price to pay to live in the Lowcountry, it is the inconvenience of mosquitoes. In 1952, the Exchange Club started a campaign to wipe out the pests. Volunteers filled burlap bags with sawdust, soaked them with kerosene, and placed them in every ditch, pool, and pond on the island. They also poured burned oil on areas that held stagnant water. Fogging trucks, like this bugmobile, controlled the problem during normal conditions, but after a considerable rain or wind storm, fogging was a waste of time and money.

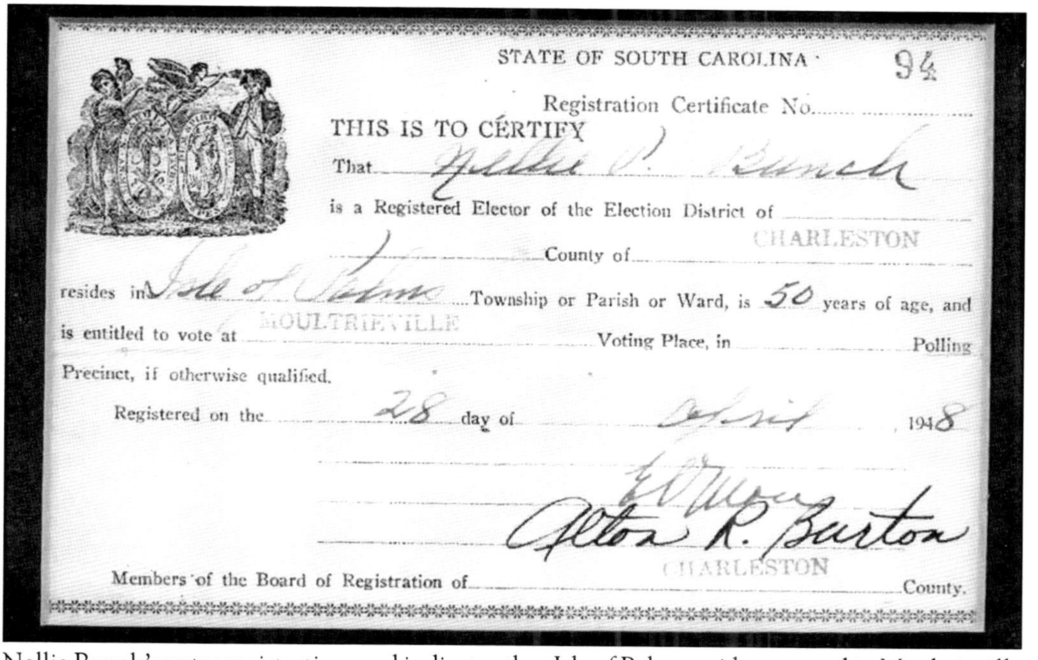

STATE OF SOUTH CAROLINA 94

Registration Certificate No.

THIS IS TO CERTIFY

That Nellie P. Bunch

is a Registered Elector of the Election District of

County of CHARLESTON

resides in Isle of Palms Township or Parish or Ward, is 50 years of age, and is entitled to vote at MOULTRIEVILLE Voting Place, in Polling Precinct, if otherwise qualified.

Registered on the 28 day of April, 1948

Alton R. Burton

Members of the Board of Registration of CHARLESTON County.

Nellie Bunch's voter registration card indicates that Isle of Palms residents voted in Moultrieville (Sullivan's Island) before the city's incorporation in 1953. The election brought 189 voters to the Exchange Club, the island's only polling place. The island was split right down the middle on this controversial referendum. Half of the residents wanted to incorporate, while the other half thought incorporation would ruin the island's character. It would be the first in a series of heated debates between island residents.

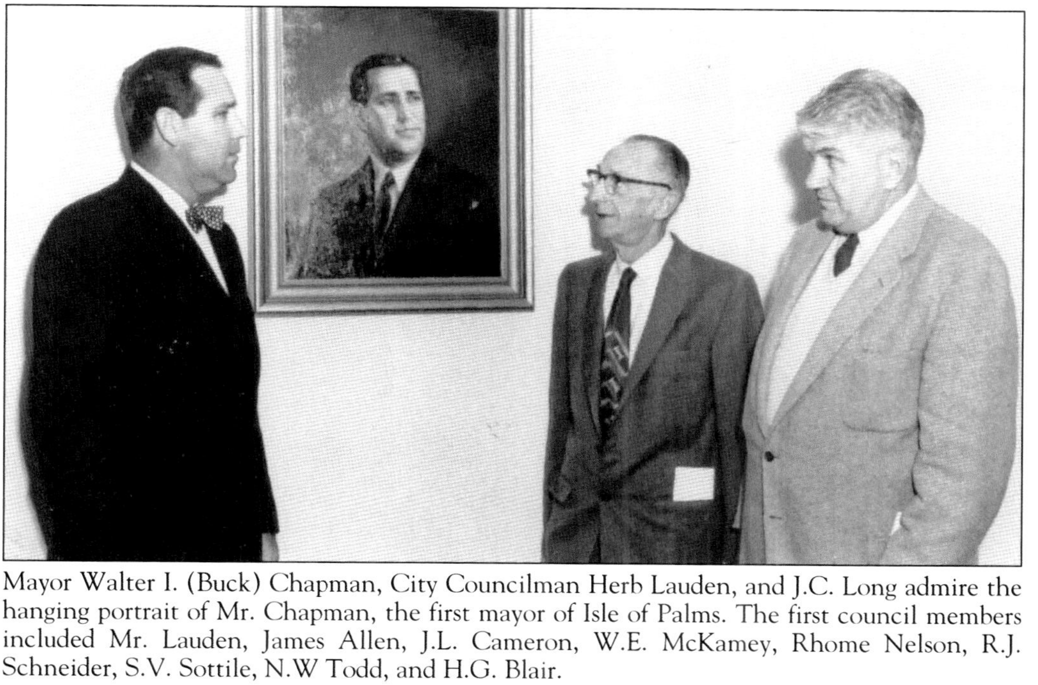

Mayor Walter I. (Buck) Chapman, City Councilman Herb Lauden, and J.C. Long admire the hanging portrait of Mr. Chapman, the first mayor of Isle of Palms. The first council members included Mr. Lauden, James Allen, J.L. Cameron, W.E. McKamey, Rhome Nelson, R.J. Schneider, S.V. Sottile, N.W Todd, and H.G. Blair.

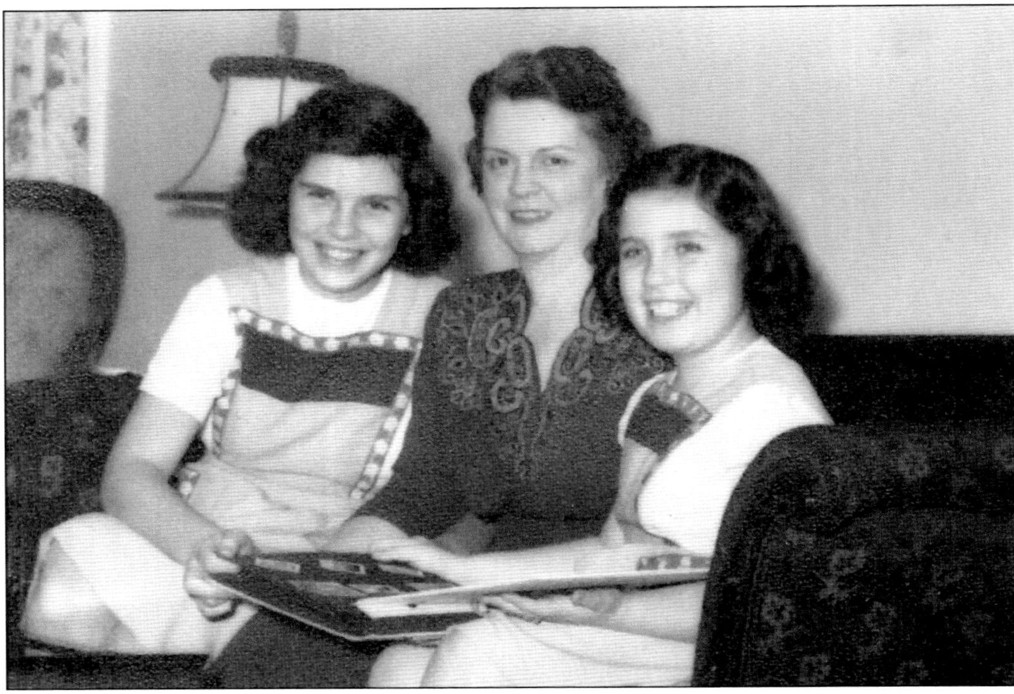

Joyce Long (Darby) and Mary Ellen Long (Way), daughters of J.C. Long, enjoy perusing old photos with their mother, Alberta Sottile Long. The album is most likely full of Sottile memories. Alberta is the daughter of Mary Ellen Hartnett and Albert Sottile.

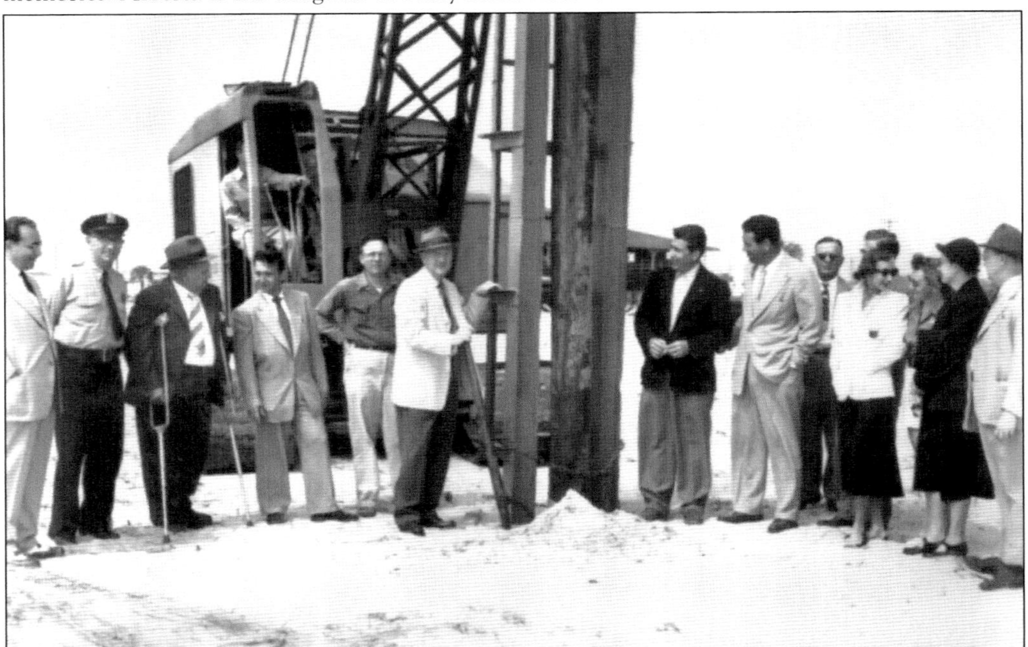

Johnnie Hartnett (center) and fellow island dignitaries watch the ceremonial first pile driving of the Isle of Palms fishing pier.

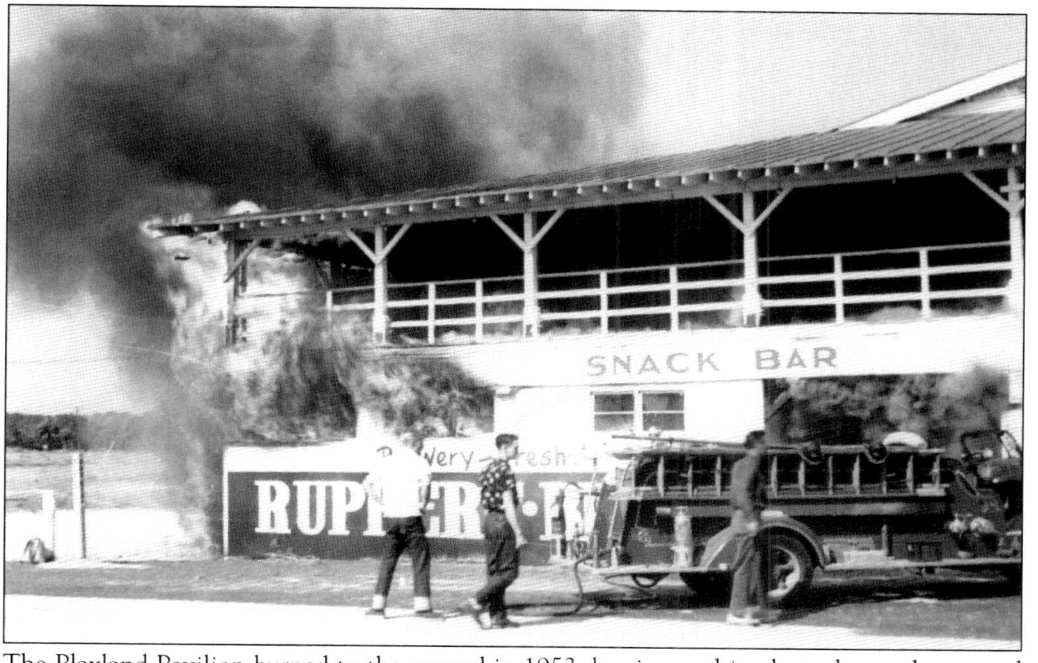

The Playland Pavilion burned to the ground in 1953, leaving nothing but ashes and scattered silverware behind. Volunteers from the fire department arrived on the scene, but there was little they could do with the equipment and one fire truck they had at the time. They could not get close enough to fight it, so they had to stand there and watch it burn to the ground.

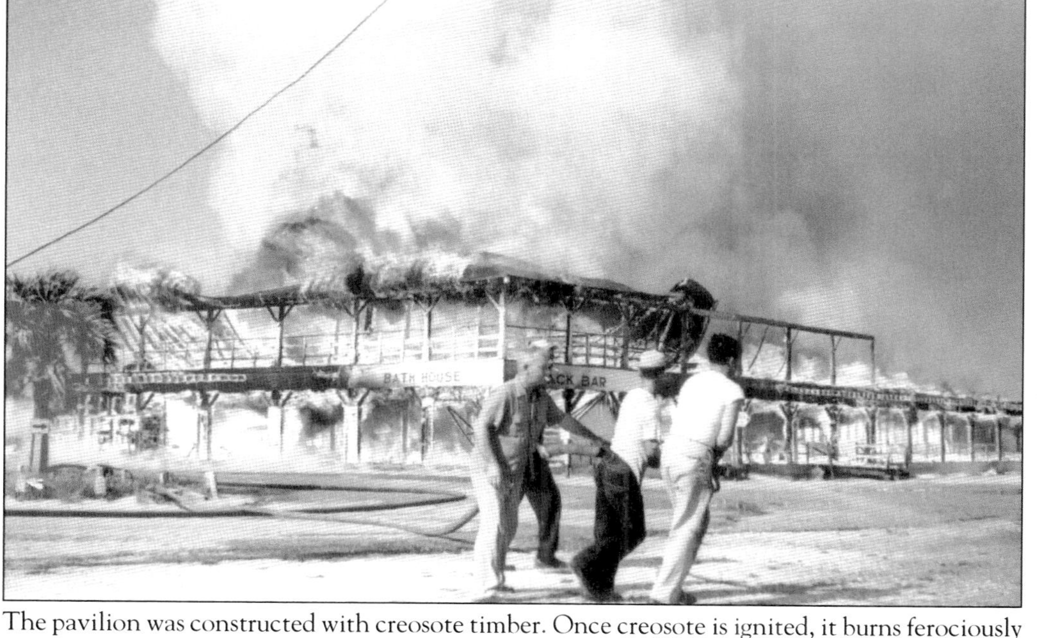

The pavilion was constructed with creosote timber. Once creosote is ignited, it burns ferociously at temperatures between 5,000 and 6,000 degrees. With the wind coming from the east, the popular dance pavilion burned in a matter of minutes. Its flames were so high they could be seen in Mt. Pleasant.

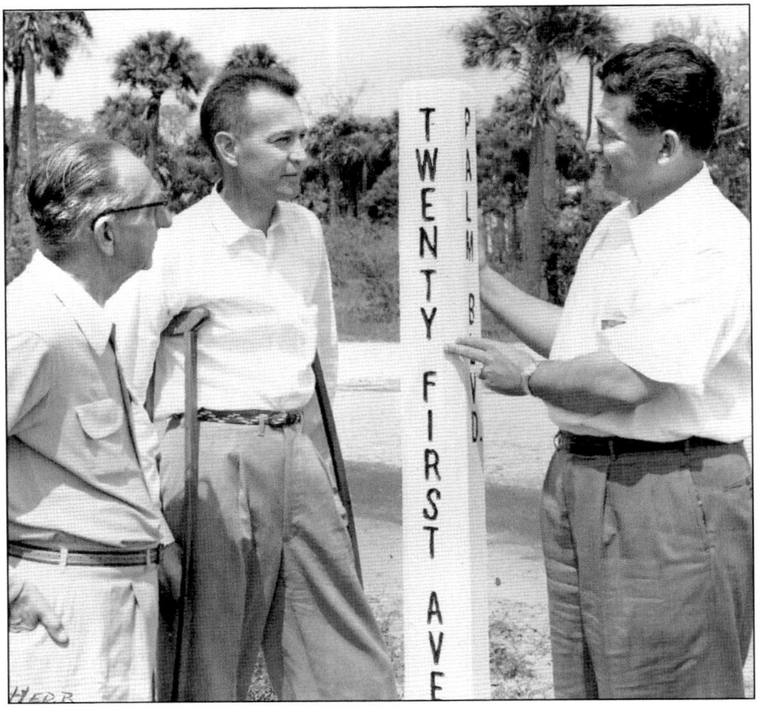

Mayor Herb Lauden, Councilman Howard Blair, and Mayor Sally Sottile plant the avenue markers that lined the island. Isle of Palms emulated the numbering system of streets from Myrtle Beach.

Mayor Herb Lauden and J.C. Long unveil Mr. Lauden's hanging portrait at city hall. Mr. Lauden served as mayor from 1955 to 1956.

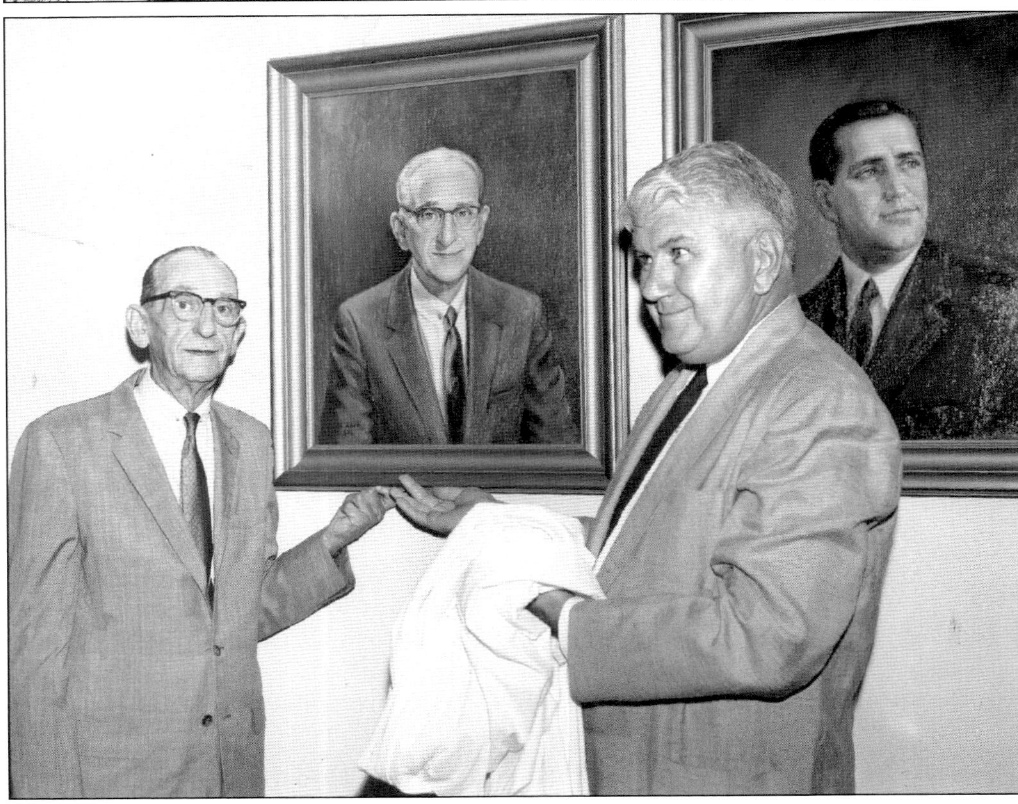

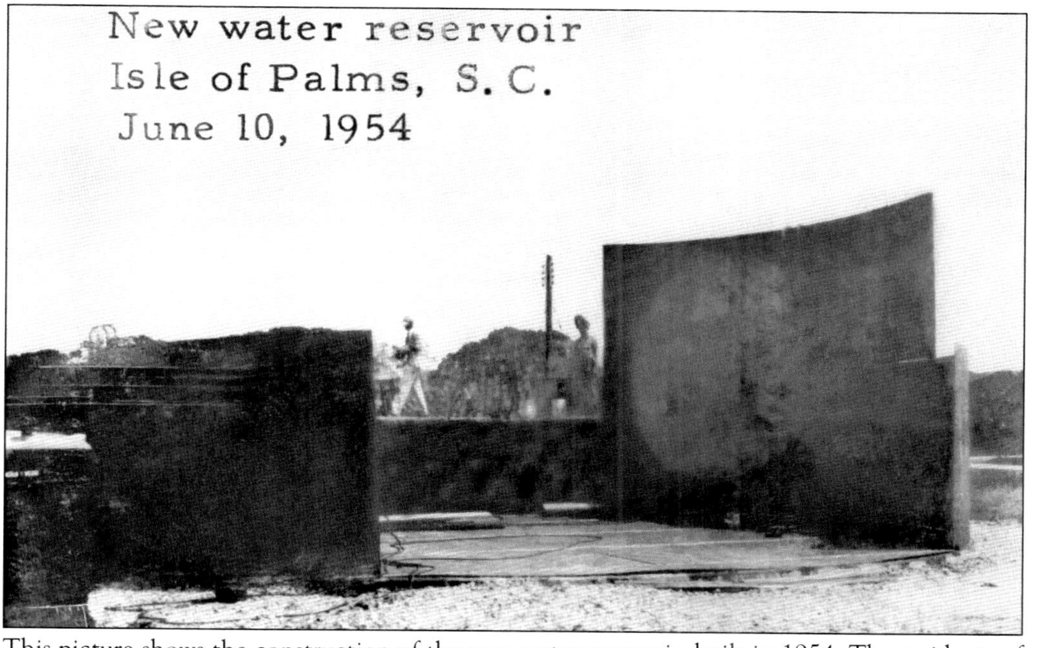

This picture shows the construction of the new water reservoir, built in 1954. The residents of Isle of Palms voted to purchase and operate the Isle of Palms Water Company in 1990.

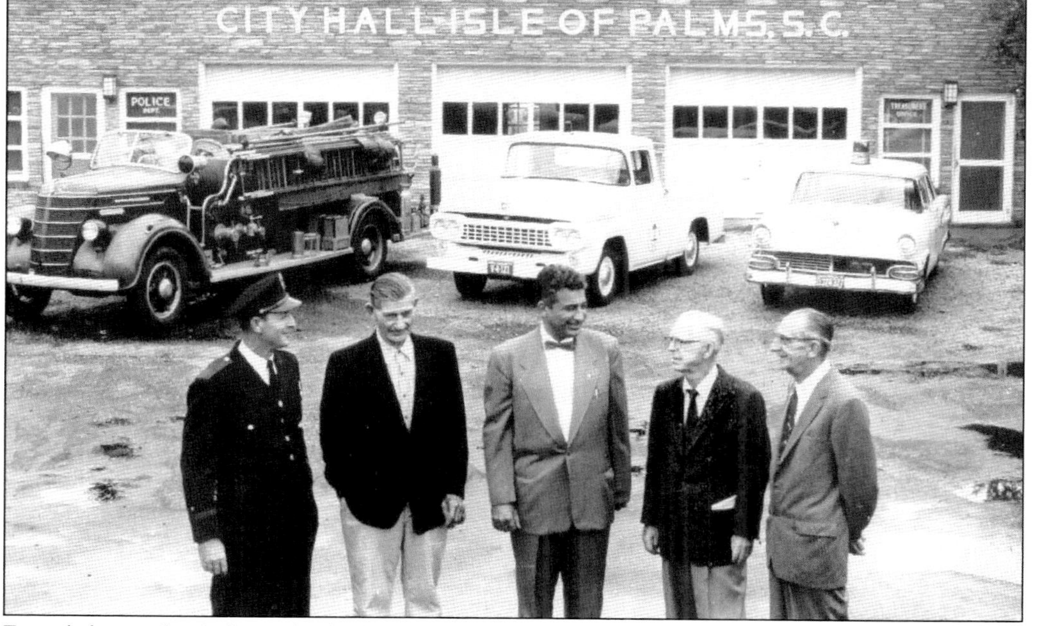

From left to right, Police Chief Eddie Walters, August W. Anderson, Councilman Sally Sottile, Wiley Horne, and Mayor Herb Lauden stand in front of the old city hall. The concrete-block building cost $13,000 to construct. It housed the fire station, the police station, the treasurer's office, and city hall. Shortly after Hurricane Hugo, the city undertook a capital improvement plan that called for the construction of a new municipal building to house police and city hall functions, two new fire stations, and a public works building for maintenance of vehicles.

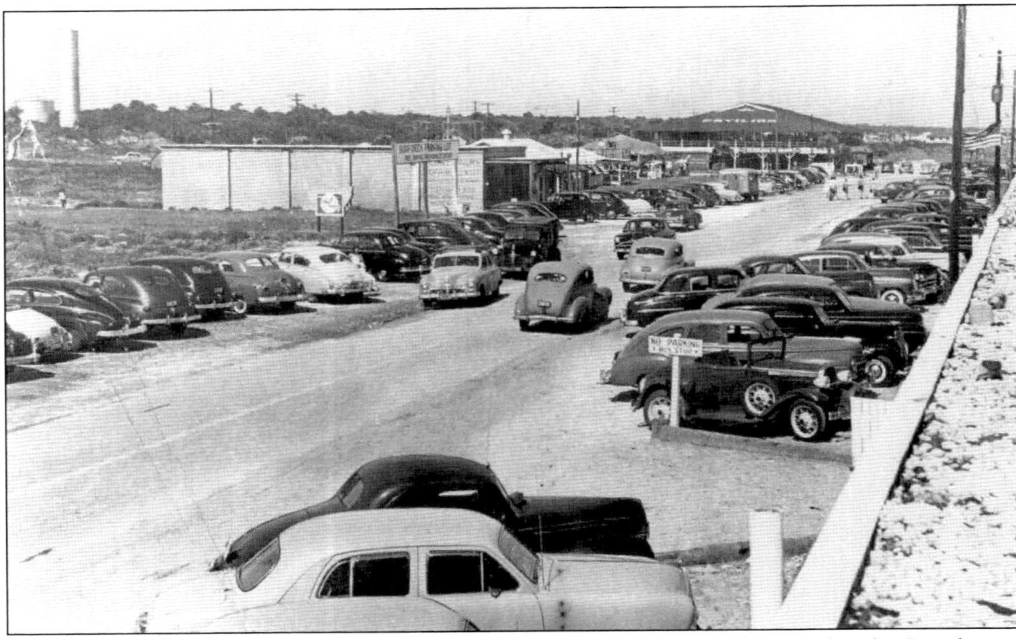

Front Beach was packed in the summer months, and parking was always a hassle. Beachgoers arrived as early as possible to get the perfect spot. In 2004, Isle of Palms completed a beautification project that alleviated some of the parking problems. The city constructed more multi-space parking areas with modern kiosk machines that distribute time-tracking tickets, allowing visitors to pay when they leave.

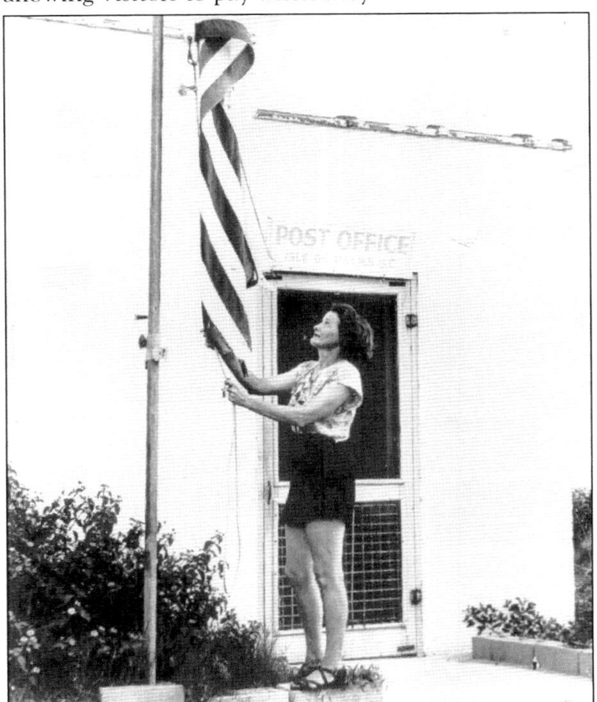

Postmistress Rita Clump hoists the American flag in front of the second post office on Isle of Palms. Mrs. Clump served in this position for 23 years. The first post office opened in 1913 in Hudson's Pavilion.

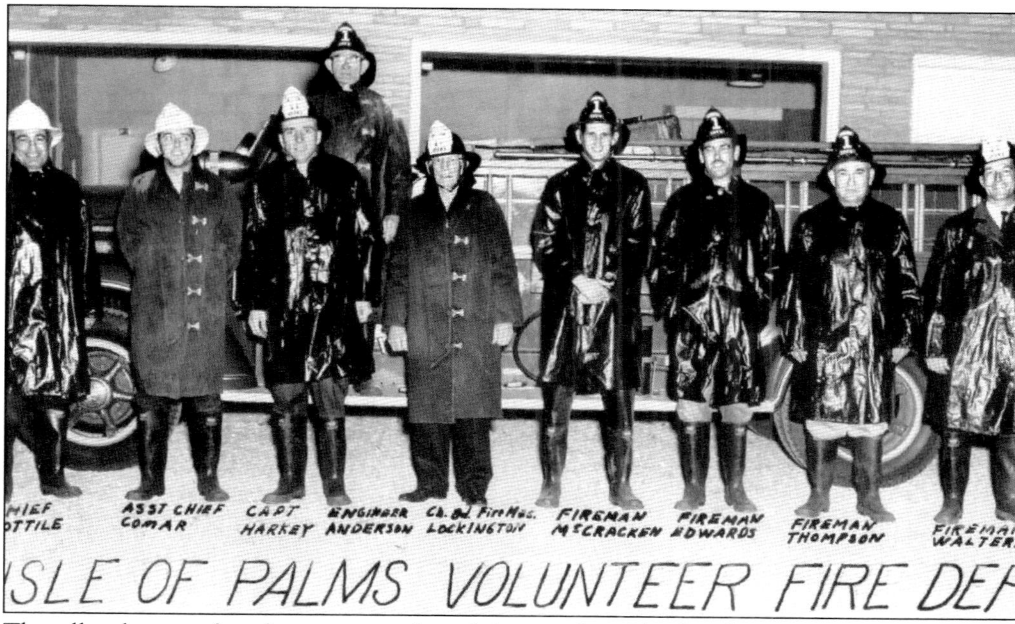

The all-volunteer fire department—from left to right, Chief Sally Sottile, Assistant Chief Eddie Comar, Capt. Harkey, Engineer Wally Anderson, Firemaster Herb Lockington, Fireman McCracken, Fireman Ralph Edwards, Fireman Thompson, and Fireman Eddie Walters—stand in front of a used 1929 American LaFrance 500-gallon pumper truck that Exchange Club president Clyde Dangerfield found in Eau Clair, South Carolina, for $4,500. This was the original wooden ladder truck.

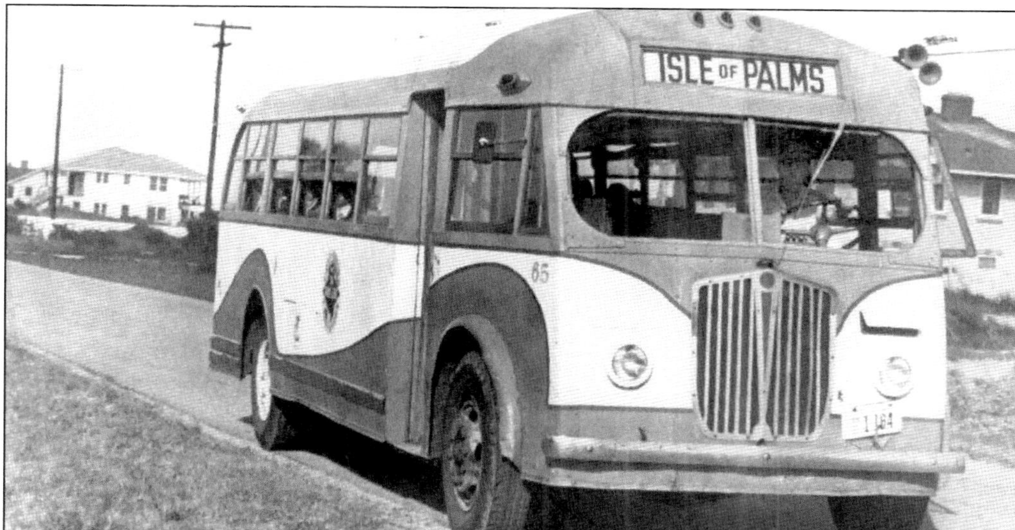

South Carolina Electric and Gas Company operated a commercial bus service that brought passengers from downtown Charleston to Isle of Palms. An ancestor of the company is Consolidated Railway Gas and Electric Company, presided over by Dr. Joseph S. Lawrence. Dr. Lawrence was credited for developing transportation to Long Island and renaming it Isle of Palms.

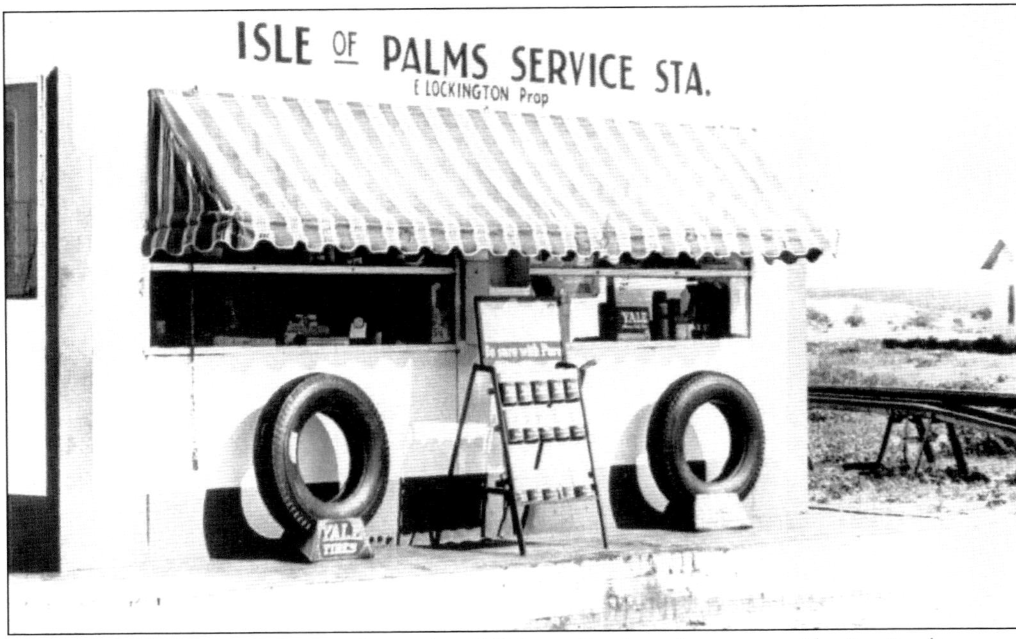

The Isle of Palms Service Station, located on J.C. Long Boulevard, was owned by Pop Lockington.

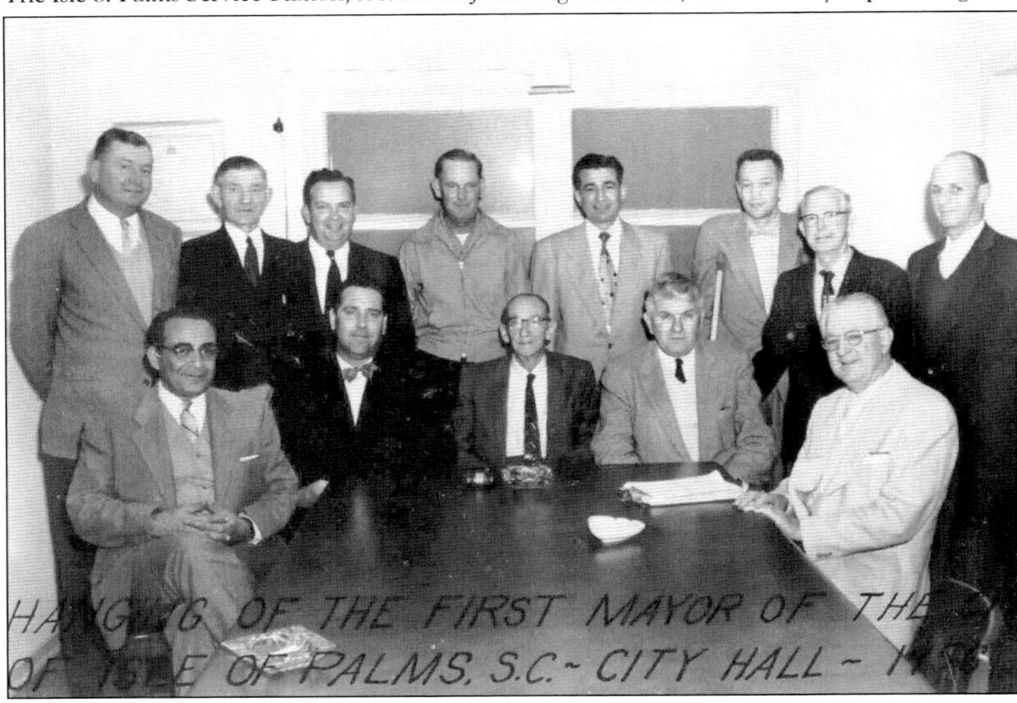

Exchange Club presidents, mayors, councilmen, and attorneys . . . these men made things happen on Isle of Palms. They are, from left to right, (front row) Frank Sottile, Mayor Buck Chapman, Mayor Herb Lauden, J.C. Long, and Johnnie Hartnett; (back row) Jimmy Bremer, Wally Anderson, Jabo Deans, Gene McKenney, Mayor Sally Sottile, Howard Blair, Wiley Horn, and Albion Johnson.

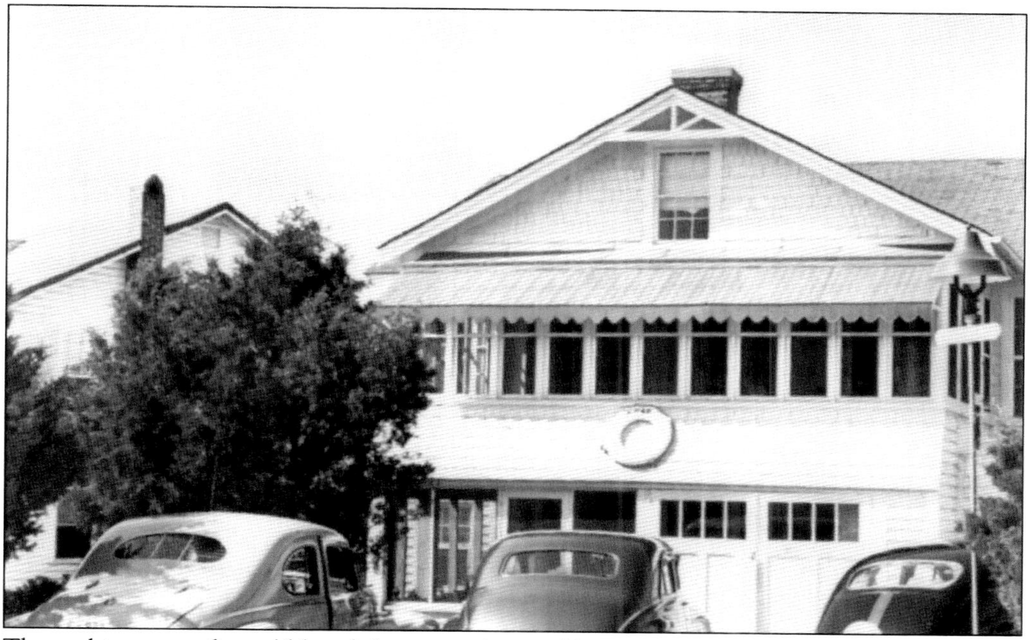

The architecture of an old beach house is classic. Always spacious, these quarters had simple floor plans that could accommodate huge family gatherings. And don't worry about tracking in sand; these cottages were minimally decorated, because relaxing was the main objective!

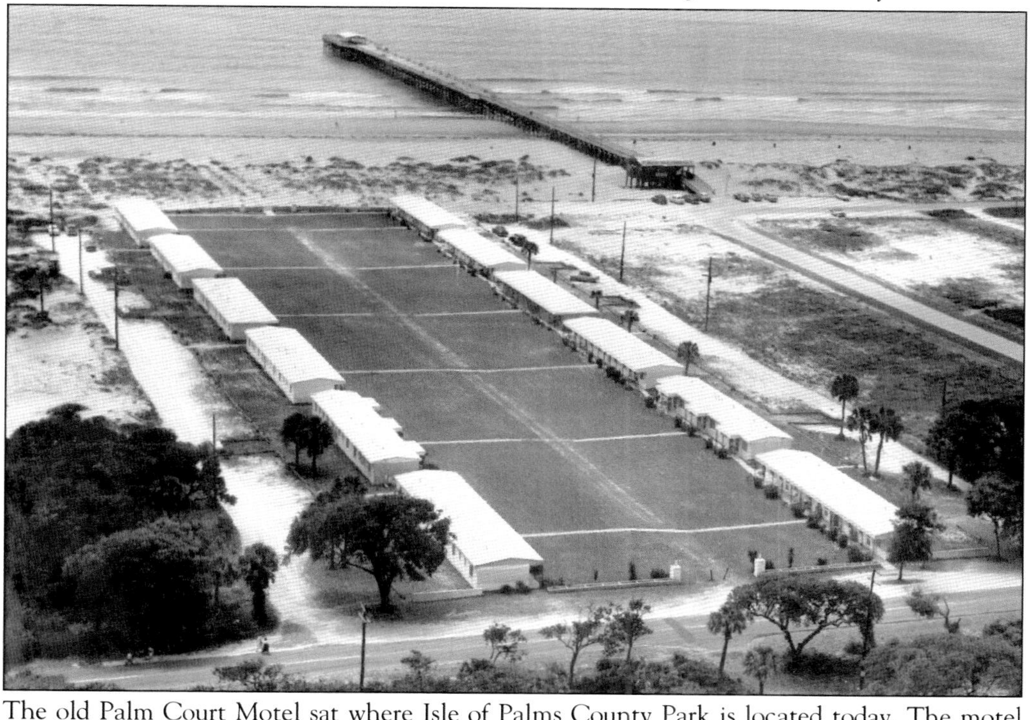

The old Palm Court Motel sat where Isle of Palms County Park is located today. The motel offered affordable rates with a beachfront view for people vacationing on the island. Its proximity to the fishing pier attracted visiting anglers from across the state.

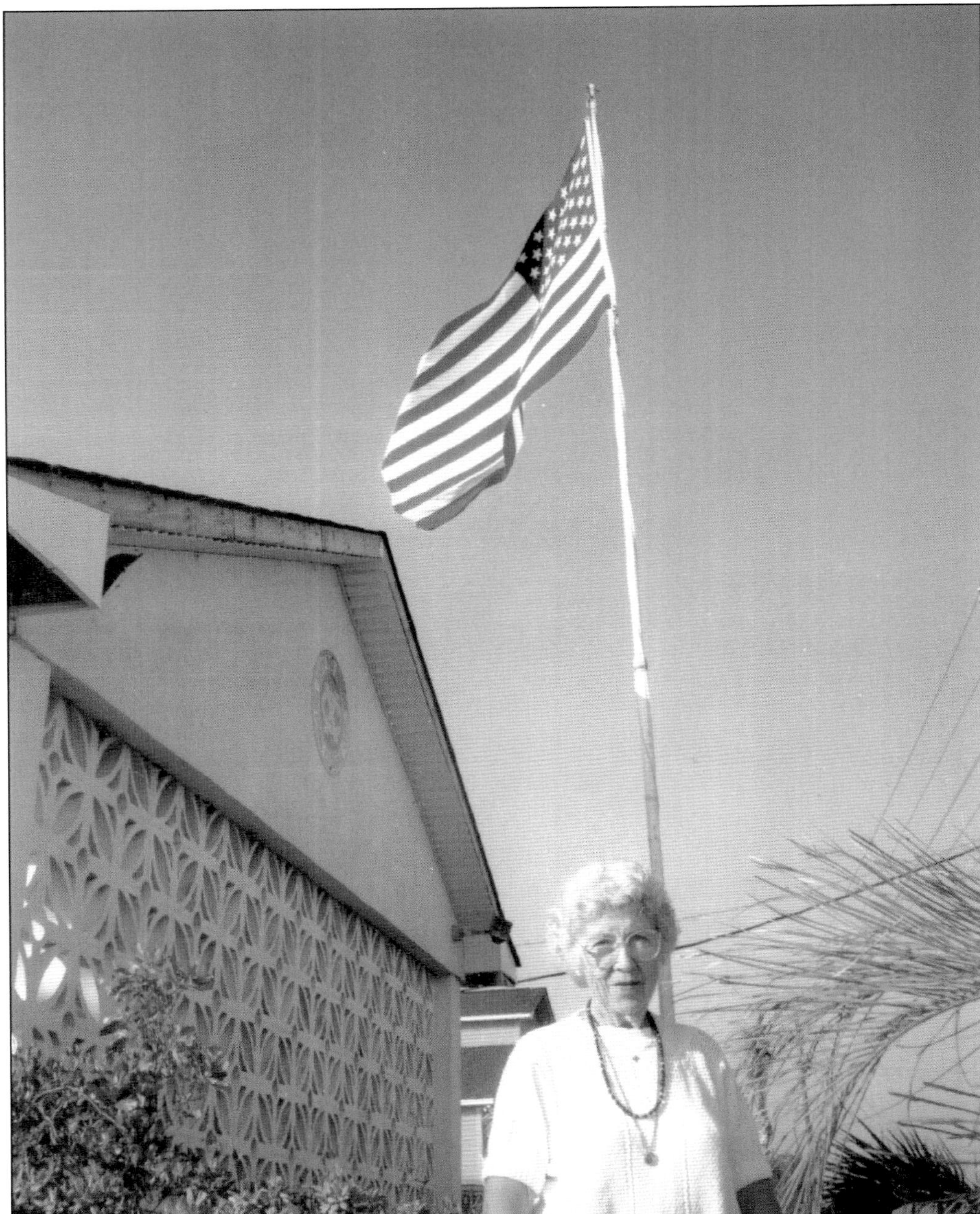

Eleanor Sottile, wife of John Sottile, donated a five-foot by seven-foot flag—presented to her at her husband's funeral by his veterans' group—to the Exchange Club to be flown on national holidays. John Sottile served as the Exchange Club president in 1963. When asked how to run the island's playground, he famously said, "turn it over to the women." Eleanor helped form the Playground Auxiliary and raised funds to purchase a recreation building. She served as chairwoman of ways and means for the Playground Auxiliary, the Exchange Club Auxiliary, and the Garden Club.

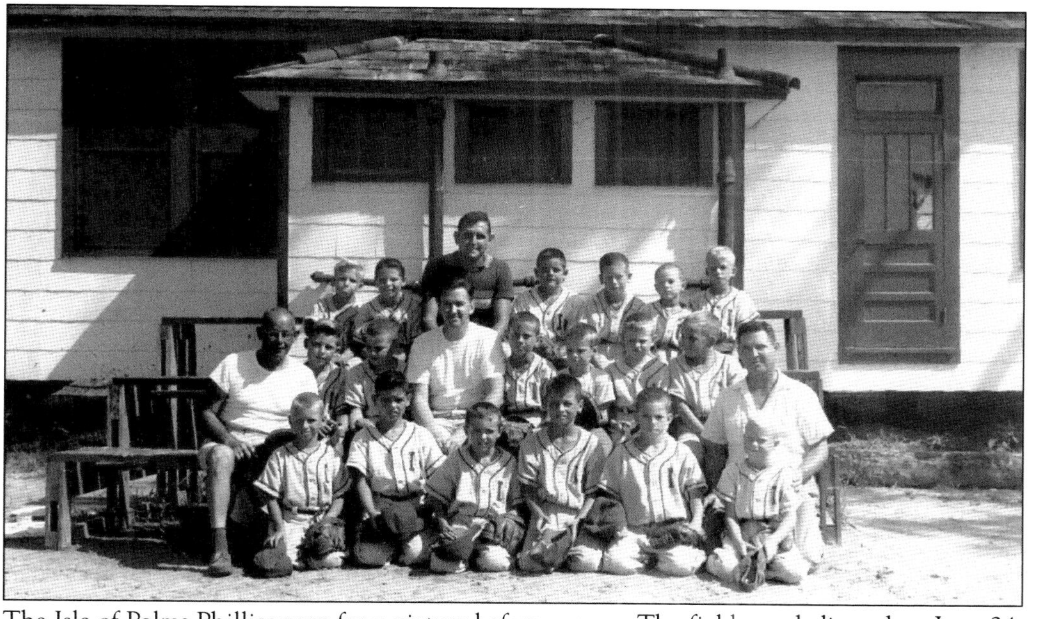

The Isle of Palms Phillies pose for a picture before a game. The field was dedicated on June 24, 1959, to Rudy Montsko, the town's first assistant fire chief. Mr. Montsko organized teams for the East Cooper Little League before the city even had a site for a playground. The Playground Auxiliary purchased and moved the old cafeteria building at Sullivan's Island Elementary, seen in the background, from Sullivan's Island to Isle of Palms. Isle of Palms baseball teams included the Sandcrabs, the White Sox, the Panthers, and the Phillies. The Beachcombers and the Sharks were the girls' softball teams.

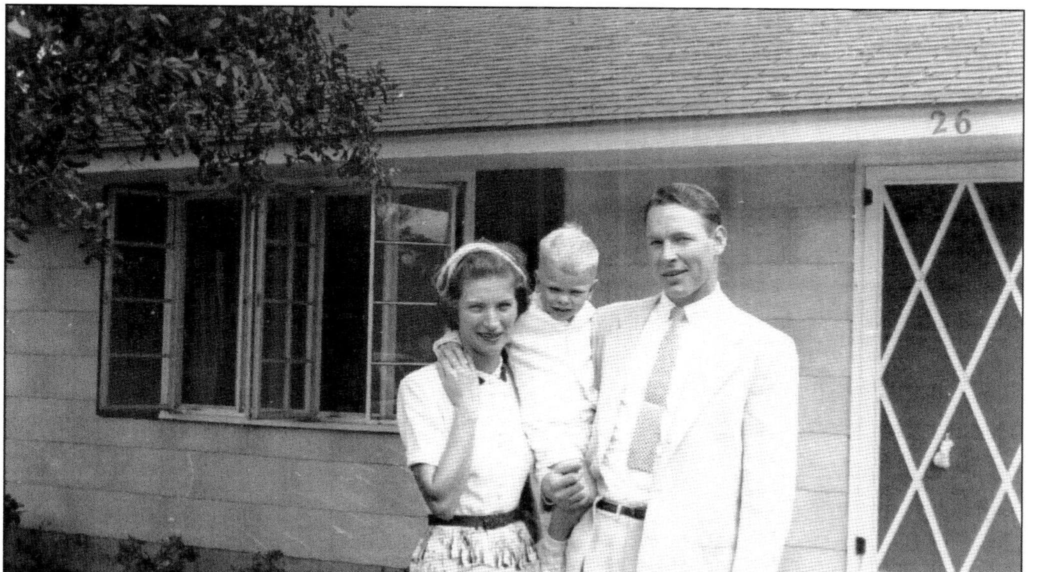

Anne, Skipper, and Henry Shaffer stand in front of their first home on Isle of Palms at 26 Beach Drive, which is now Twenty-first Avenue. They bought this house for $8,500 with $500 down and payments of $48 per month.

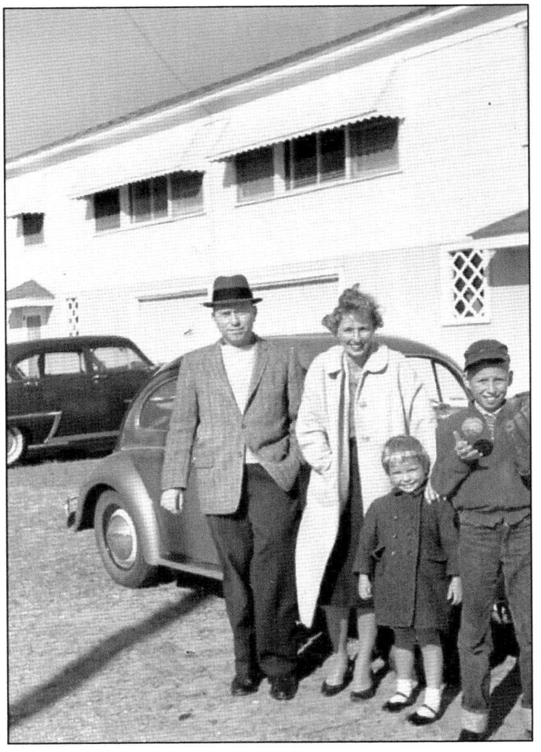

Jim, Marge, Sally, and Jimmy Sexton stand in front of their house on Fifth Avenue. The Sextons first moved to the island in 1956.

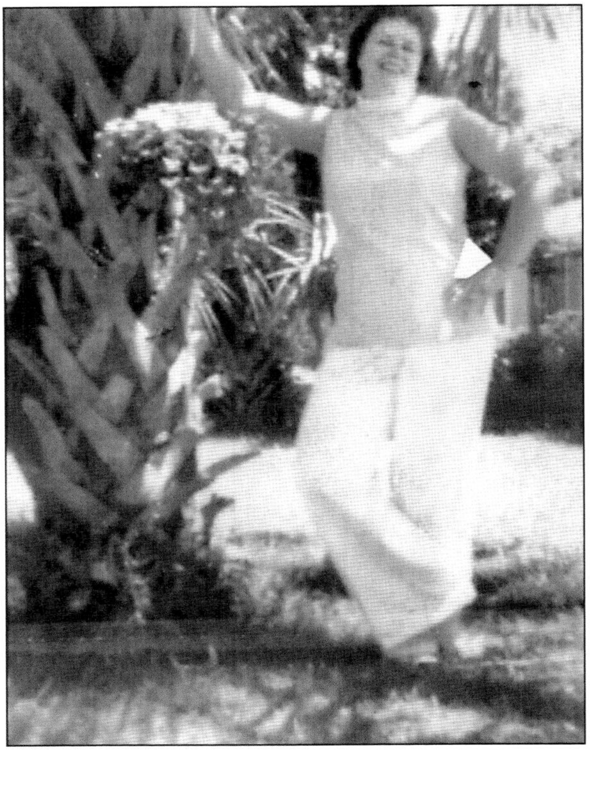

Like so many island residents, Lillian Nilsen moved to Isle of Palms in the 1960s, when development was really gaining momentum. She and her husband, Stanley "Swede," bought a ranch-style home on the corner of Twenty-eighth and Waterway Boulevard. Her family saw the island grow exponentially during the next two decades. In 1989, the Nilsens and 95 percent of the families on Isle of Palms lost everything to Hurricane Hugo. They rebuilt, like most residents did, while living in a small trailer on their lot. Now, the house on Twenty-eighth and Waterway is elevated on 10-foot piers, as required by most insurance companies.

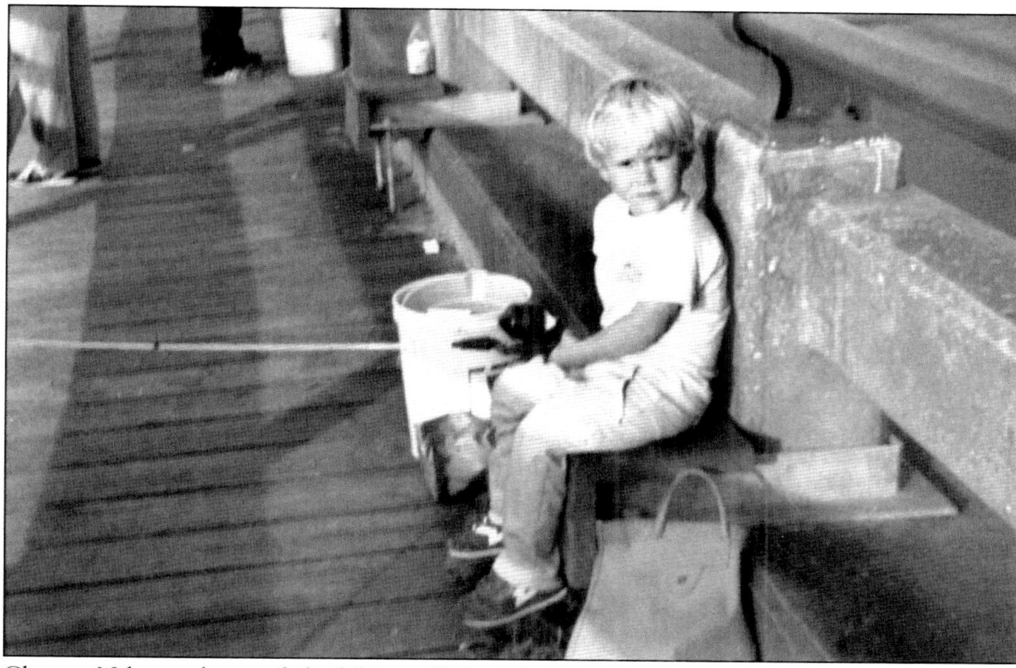

Chance Nilsen relaxes while fishing off the Thomson Memorial Bridge. Built in 1956, the overpass replaced the 30-year-old wooden bridge that linked Sullivan's Island and Isle of Palms. Sidewalks four and a half feet wide were built for fisherman like Chance to enjoy.

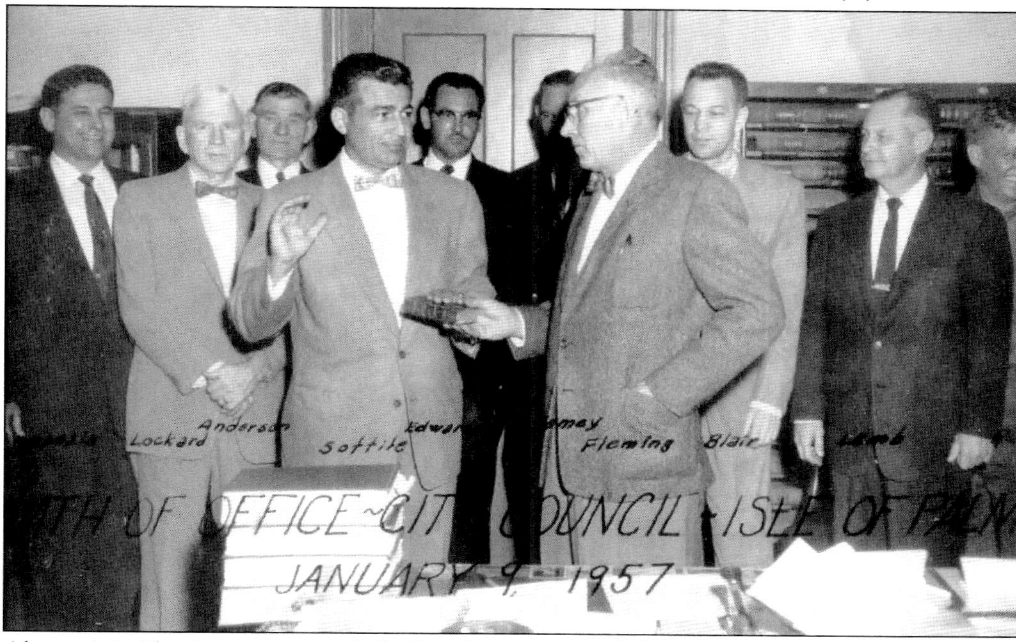

Above, Mr. Fleming swears in Sally Sottile as mayor of the Isle of Palms in 1957. The city councilmen standing behind them are, from left to right, J. Louis Lempesis, Claude W. Lockard, A.W. Anderson, Ralph P. Edwards, W.E McKamey, Howard G. Blair, James J. Lamb, and Wilson P. Rumph.

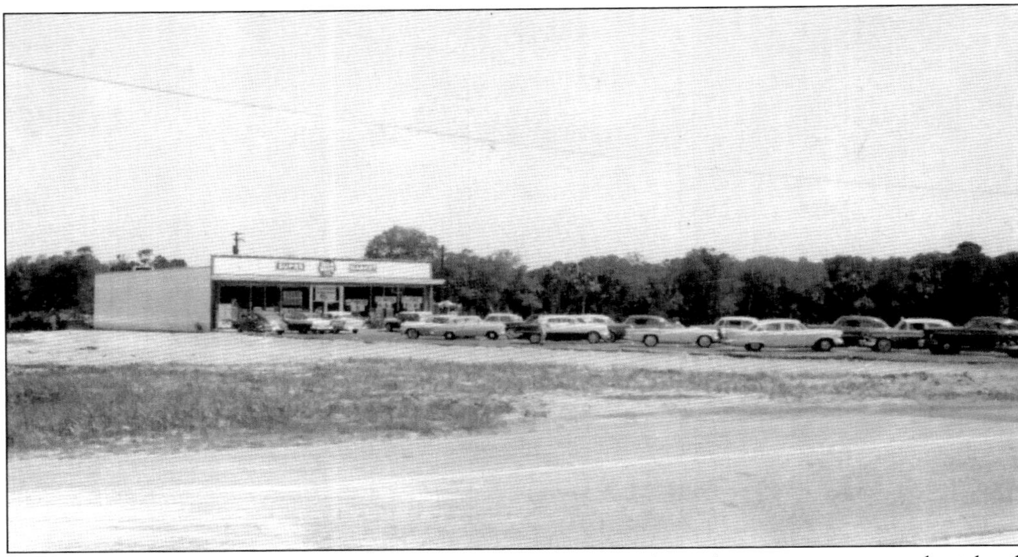

The Isle of Palms Red and White opened on June 5, 1958. The only grocery store on the island, it was owned and operated by Wade Kincaid. The store's meat department was managed by J.T. Forbes.

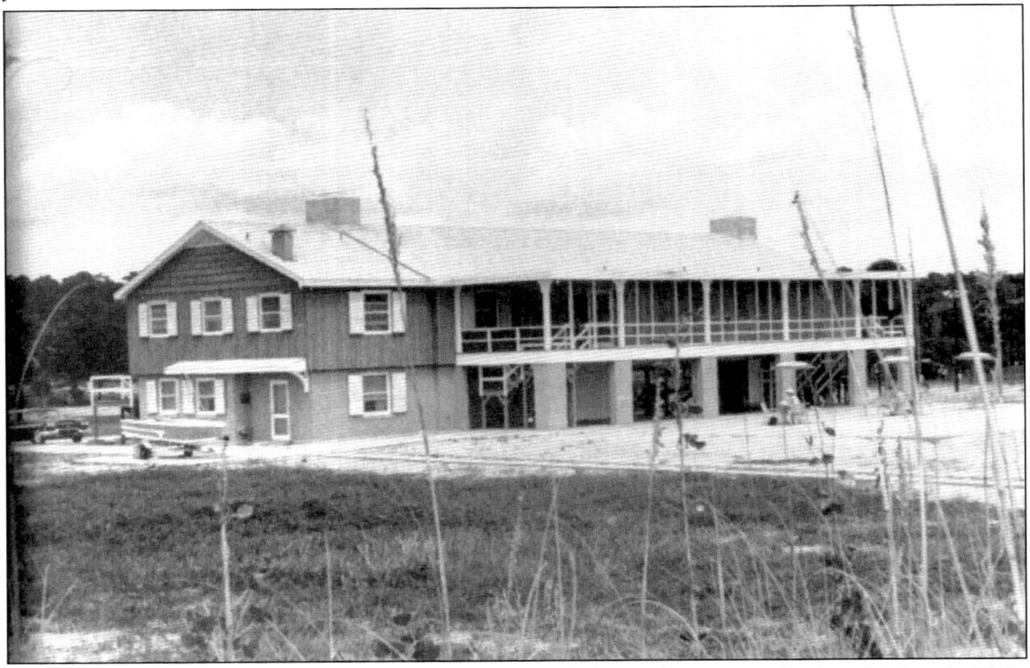

The Citadel's Col. Robert R. McCormick Beach Club, better known as the Citadel Beach Club, opened on November 30, 1958. In 1941, Colonel McCormick deeded Whitehall Plantation in Aiken, South Carolina, to The Citadel, with the stipulation that the property be Gen. Charles P. Summerall's home for life. Colonel McCormick's admiration for General Summerall started when they served in the First Division during World War I. General Summerall lived at Whitehall until his death. Funds from the sale of this estate started the construction of the Citadel Beach House. (Photo courtesy of The Citadel Archives and Museum.)

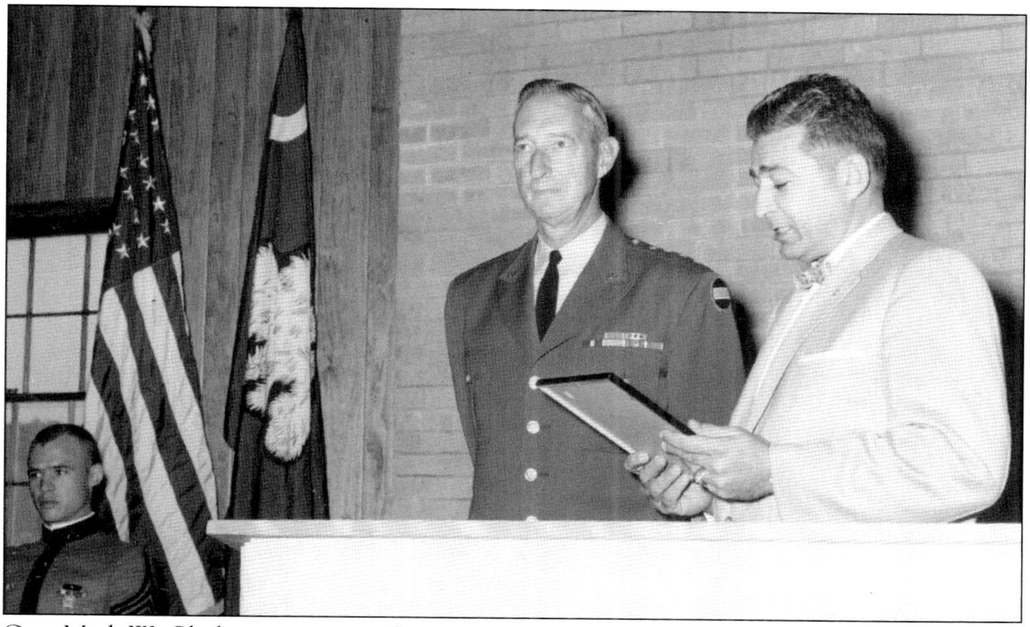

Gen. Mark W. Clark accepts a certificate of honorary citizenship from Mayor Sally Sottile. To the left of General Clark is Cadet Col. T.L. Avant, who was there to accept a similar certificate for the Corp of Cadets. The presentation was made at the dedication ceremonies of the Citadel Beach Club in 1958. (Photo courtesy of The Citadel Archives and Museum.)

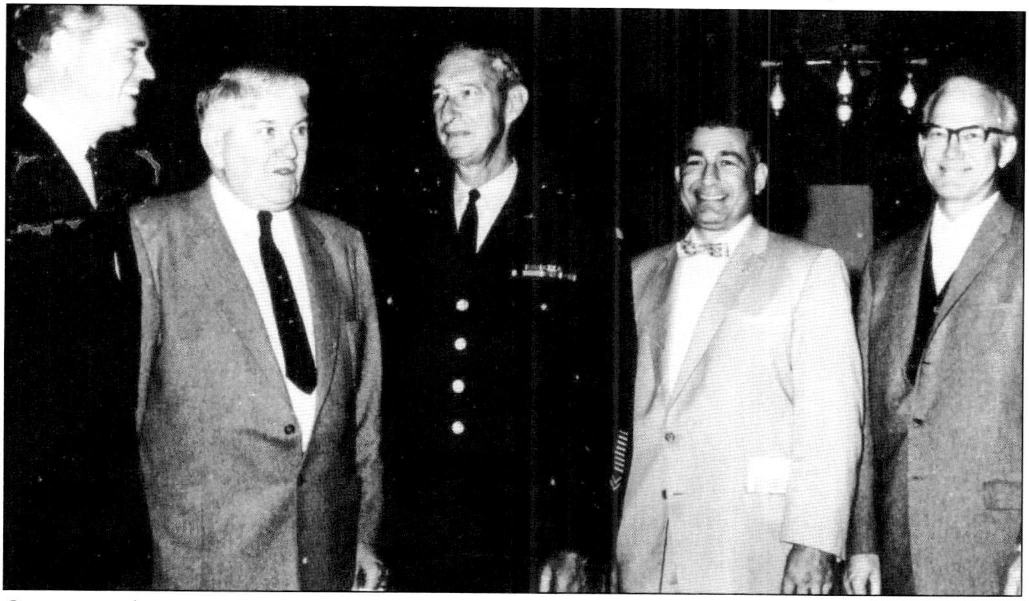

Governor elect Ernest "Fritz" Hollings (South Carolina governor 1959–1963; U.S. Senate 1966–2005), J.C. Long (Isle of Palms developer and state senator), Gen. Mark Clark (Citadel president and military hero), Sally Sottile (Isle of Palms mayor 1957–1961), and Rep. L. Mendel Rivers (U.S. House of Representative 1941–1970) chat at the dedication ceremony of the Citadel Beach Club on November 30, 1958. (Photo courtesy of The Citadel Archives and Museum.)

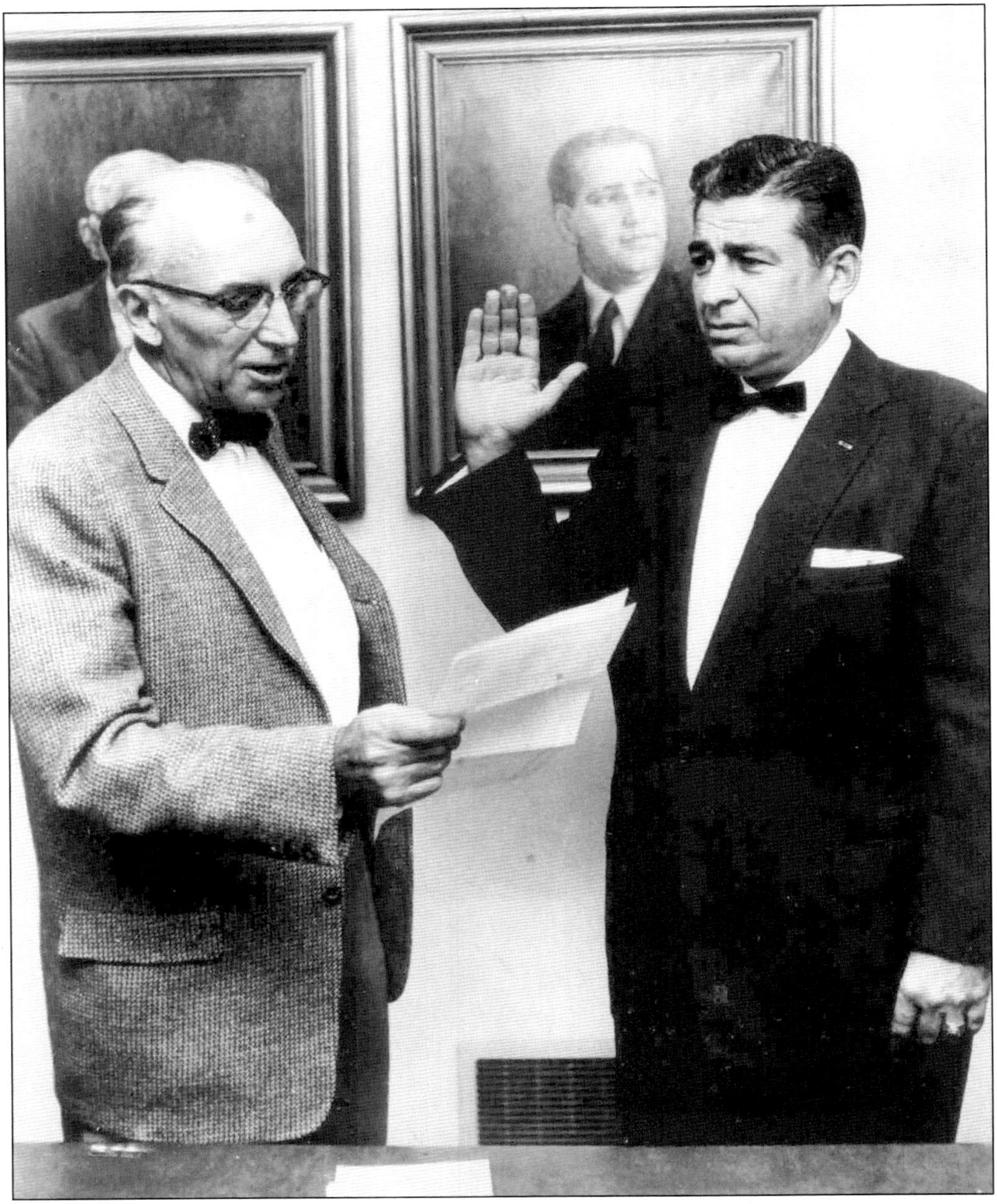

Mayor Sally Sottile gets sworn in for a second term. Mr. Sottile served two consecutive terms before he self-imposed mayoral term limits.

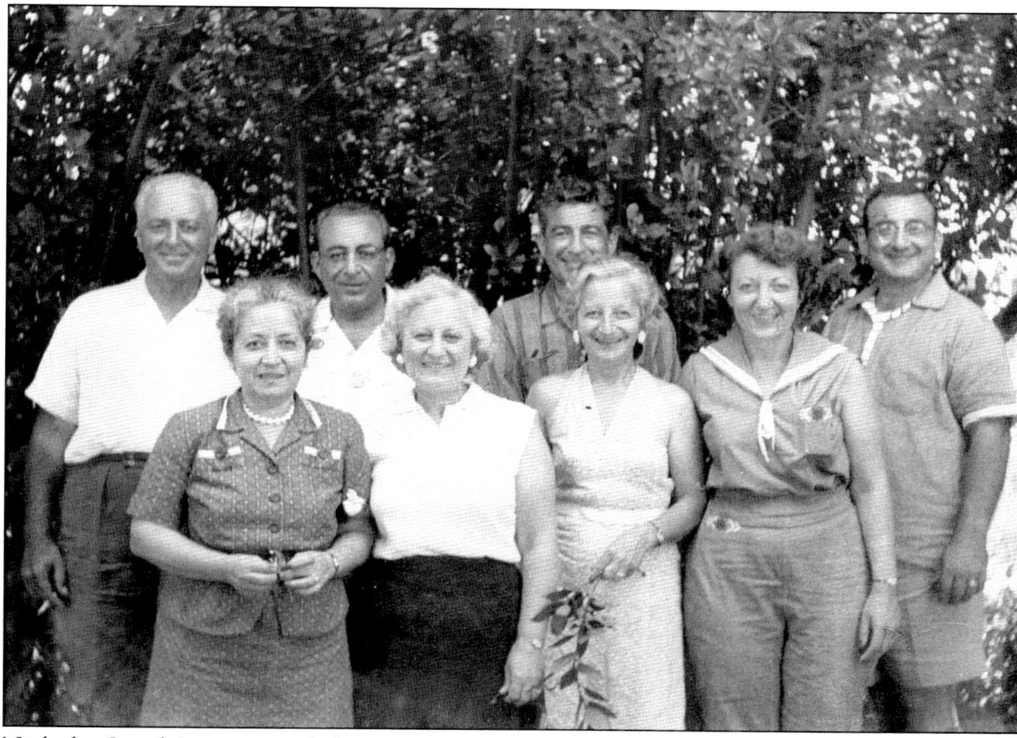

Nicholas Sottile's civic-minded sons, Nicholas, Frank, Sally, and Vincent, stand behind their equally benevolent sisters, Rosina (Kennerty), Lucille (Conlon), Marie (Daley), and Josephine Sottile.

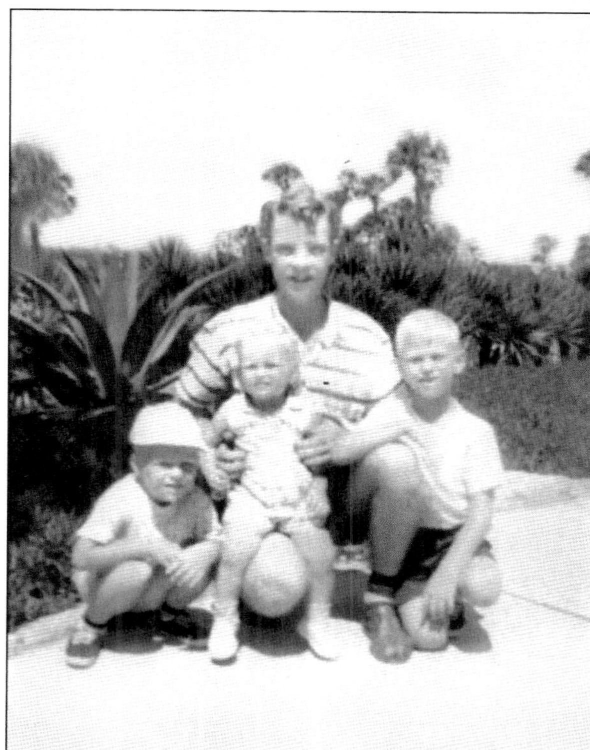

Stanley "Swede" Nilsen kneels with his three children, Lance, Carol, and Stewart. Stanley, a retired inspector for the Town of Mt. Pleasant, still lives on Twenty-eighth Avenue. Lance and Stewart live in Mt. Pleasant and both own their own businesses, while Carol works for the Isle of Palms Fire Department. The family moved to the island in 1968.

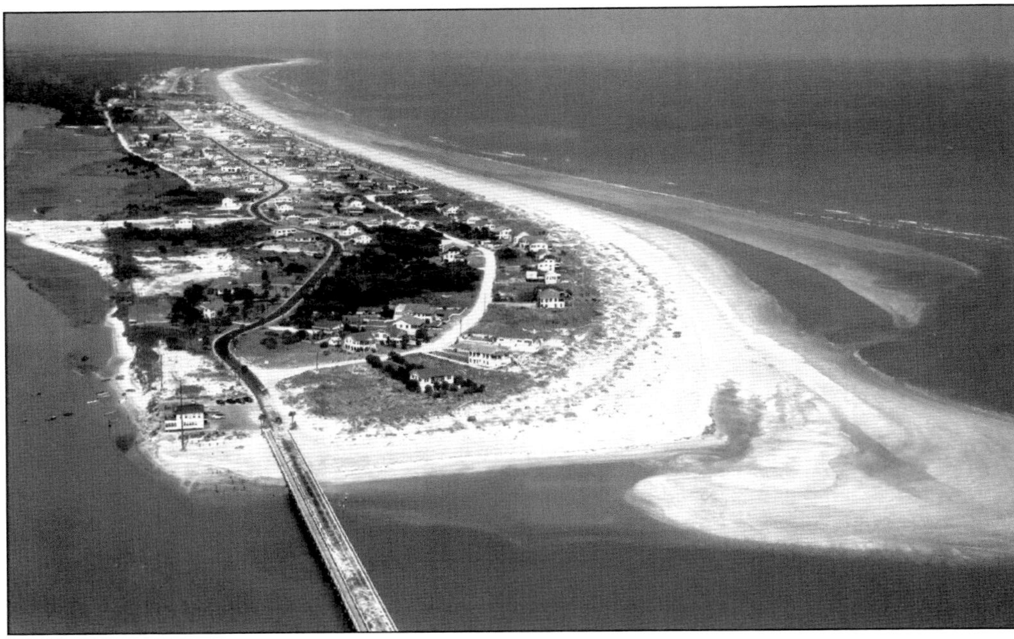

Isle of Palms is generally accretive, because the downdrift Charleston Harbor jetties interrupt the flow of sand from north to south. As this picture indicates, the area between Breach Inlet and Third Avenue has quite an accumulation of sand. The long-term accretion is influenced by the inlet's channels and shoals and is more dynamic than the central portion of the island. The more stable portion of the shoreline, between Fourth and Fiftieth Avenues, is a well-defined primary sand dune and has only minor to moderate yearly variations.

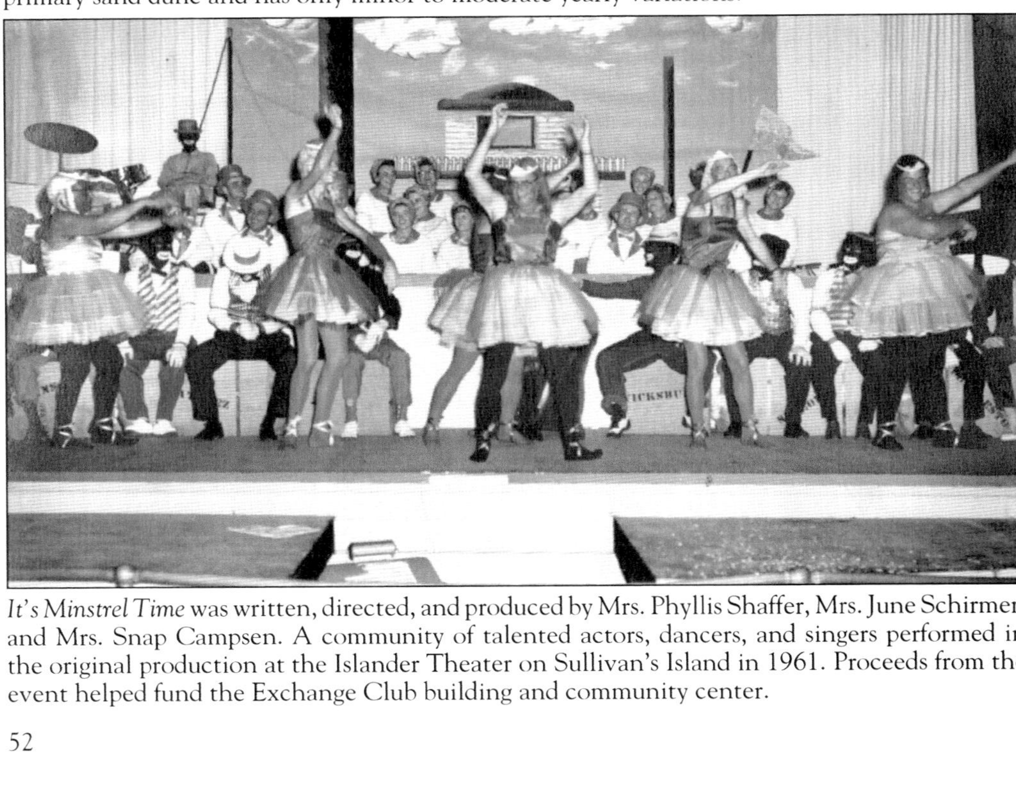

It's Minstrel Time was written, directed, and produced by Mrs. Phyllis Shaffer, Mrs. June Schirmer, and Mrs. Snap Campsen. A community of talented actors, dancers, and singers performed in the original production at the Islander Theater on Sullivan's Island in 1961. Proceeds from the event helped fund the Exchange Club building and community center.

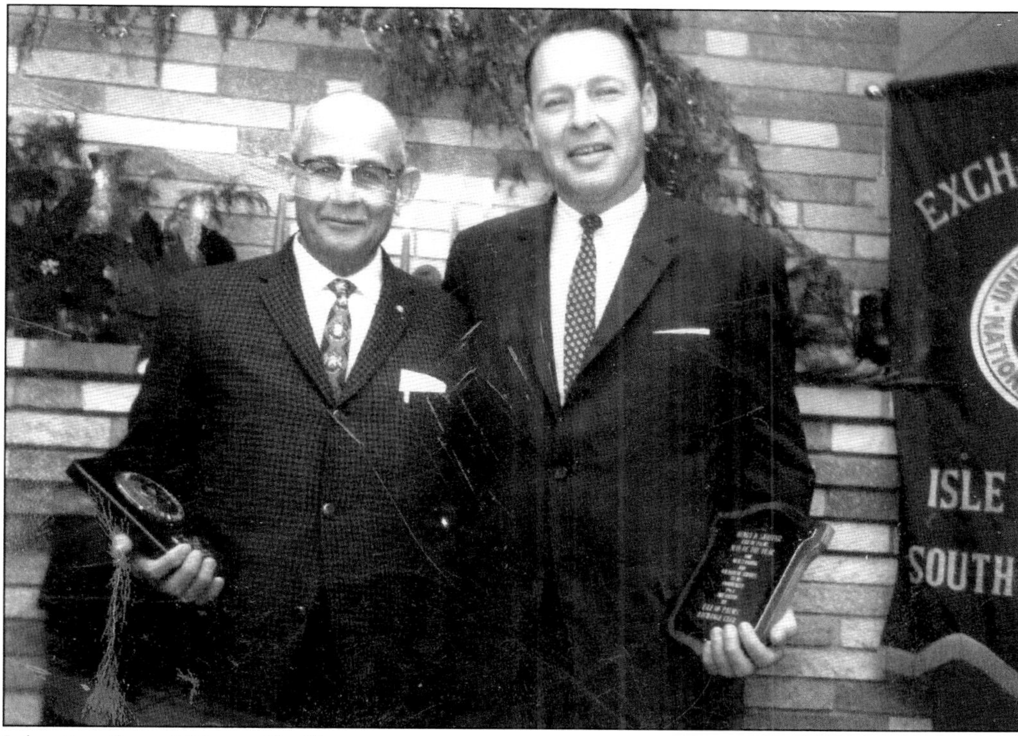

John Sottile and Henry Shaffer smile as they show off awards given to them by the Isle of Palms Exchange Club. Henry served as the club's president in 1962 and John in 1963.

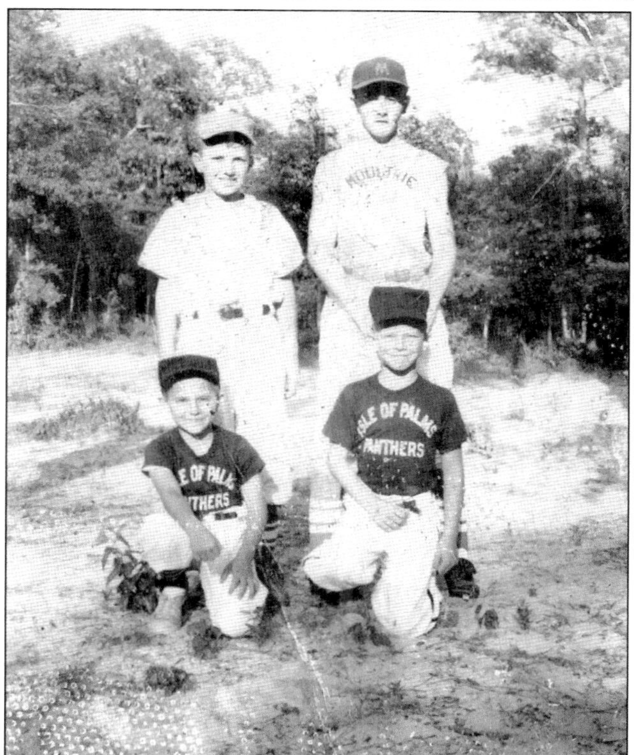

Paul and Clarisse Pearson bought a house on 23rd Avenue in 1962 and raised four boys. Frank, Ronnie, and Stan Pearson pose in their Isle of Palms baseball uniforms, while Wayne Pearson sports his Moultrie High School uniform.

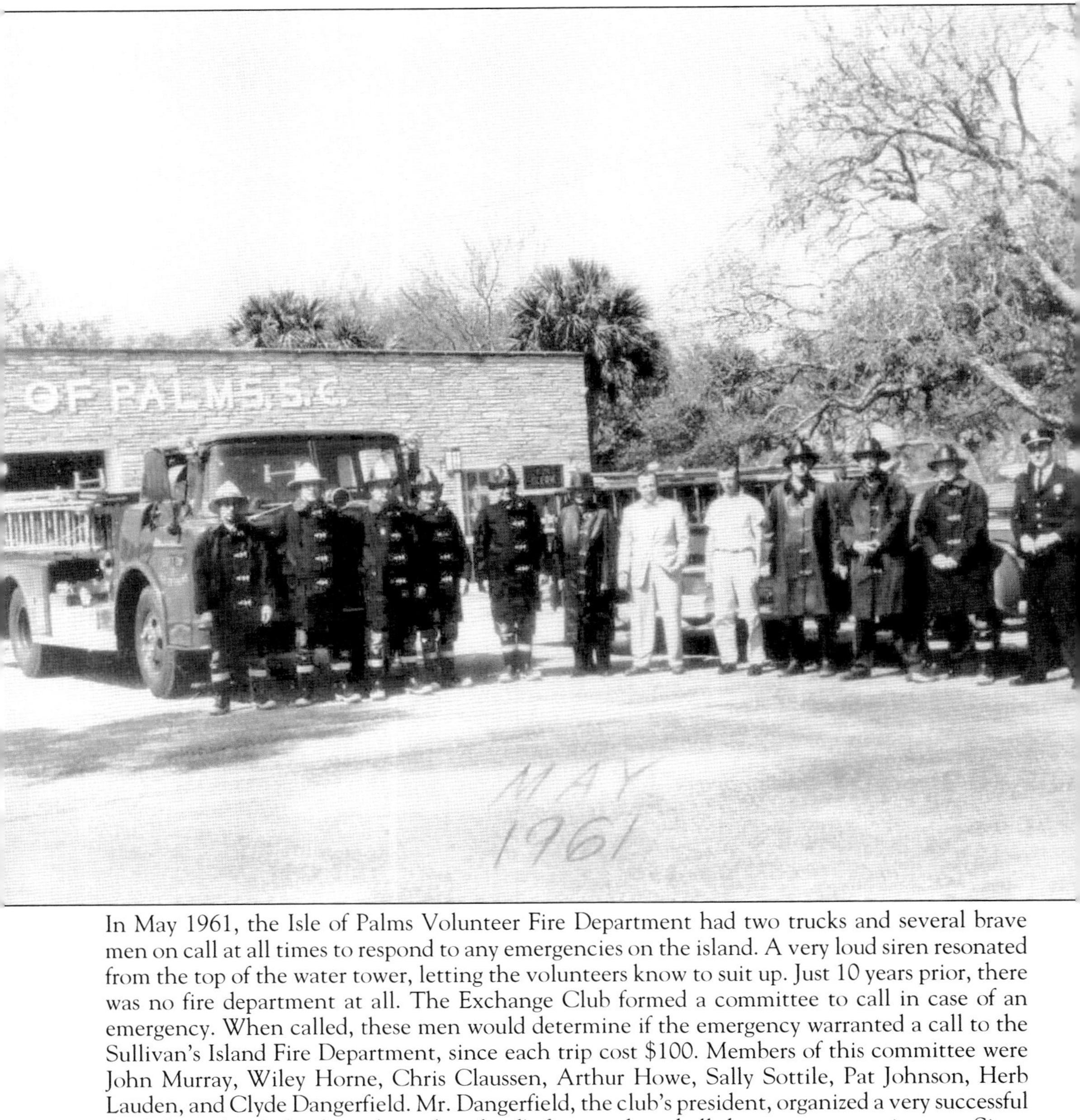

In May 1961, the Isle of Palms Volunteer Fire Department had two trucks and several brave men on call at all times to respond to any emergencies on the island. A very loud siren resonated from the top of the water tower, letting the volunteers know to suit up. Just 10 years prior, there was no fire department at all. The Exchange Club formed a committee to call in case of an emergency. When called, these men would determine if the emergency warranted a call to the Sullivan's Island Fire Department, since each trip cost $100. Members of this committee were John Murray, Wiley Horne, Chris Claussen, Arthur Howe, Sally Sottile, Pat Johnson, Herb Lauden, and Clyde Dangerfield. Mr. Dangerfield, the club's president, organized a very successful fund drive that helped purchase the island's first truck and all the necessary equipment. Since the island was not yet incorporated and had no tax base, the community pooled their own money together to establish one of the finest departments on the East Coast.

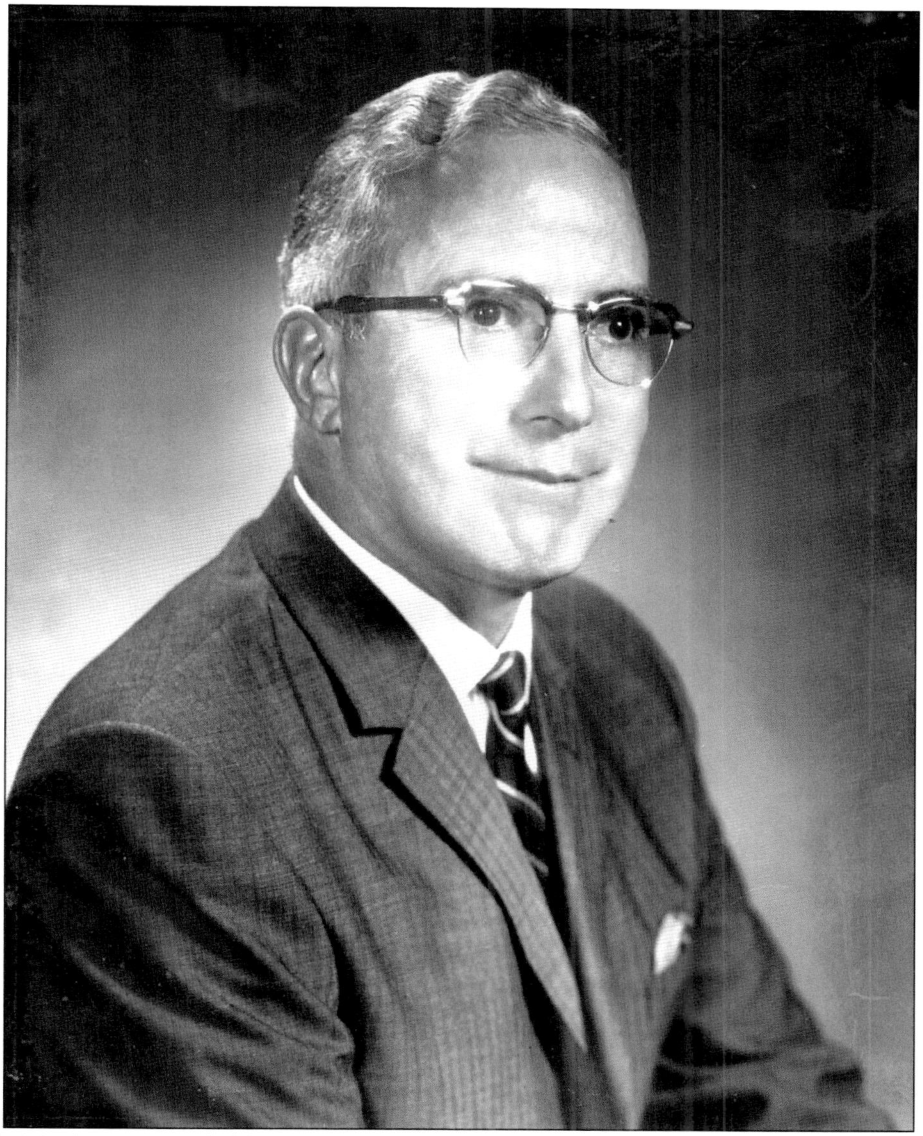

Clyde Moultrie Dangerfield was president of the Exchange Club in 1952, founder of the First United Methodist Church, and member of the South Carolina House of Representatives. A quiet man, Mr. Dangerfield got things done behind the scenes. He helped establish the first fire department on Isle of Palms and lobbied tirelessly for the Isle of Palms Connector. Sen. Ernest Hollings gave this tribute to Clyde Dangerfield on the Senate floor on June 24, 1996:

> Mr. President, I would like to say a few words about a man from my home State who, in his work and his life, set an example for us all. Clyde M. Dangerfield died on June 19 at the age of 81. He served 35 years in the South Carolina House of Representatives, and was responsible for improving the lives of citizens all over Charleston County. His concern, persistence, and integrity made him one of the finest public servants South Carolina has known. He was a good friend, a credit to his county, and I can say, without exaggeration, that the State is a better place because of him.

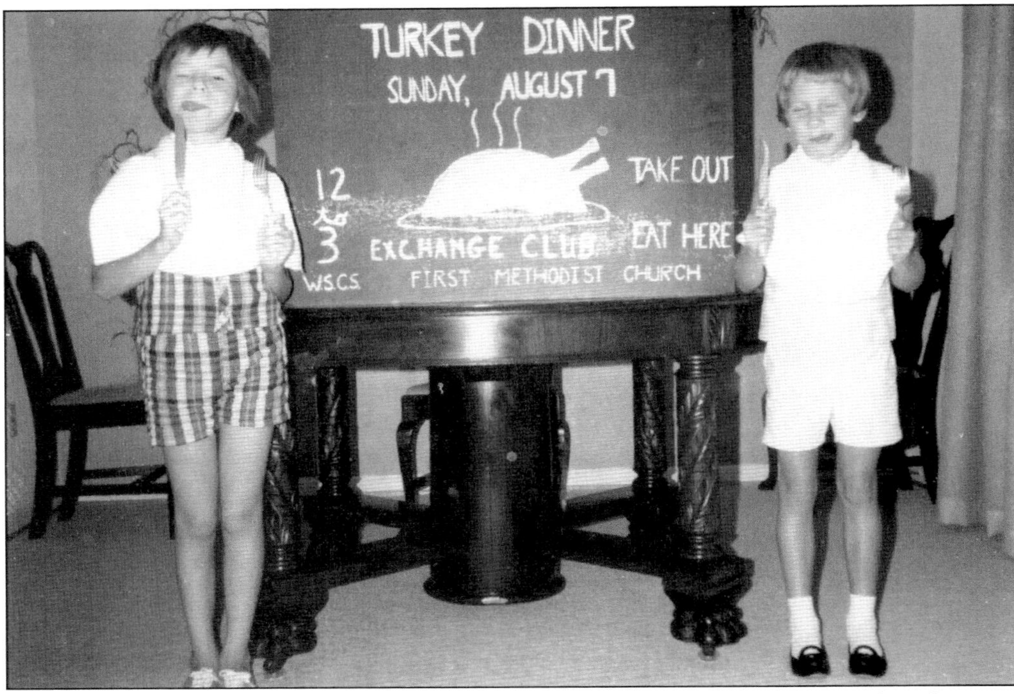

Sandy Simpson and Susan Shaffer promote the Exchange Club's Auxiliary turkey dinner in August 1963. They sure do look hungry!

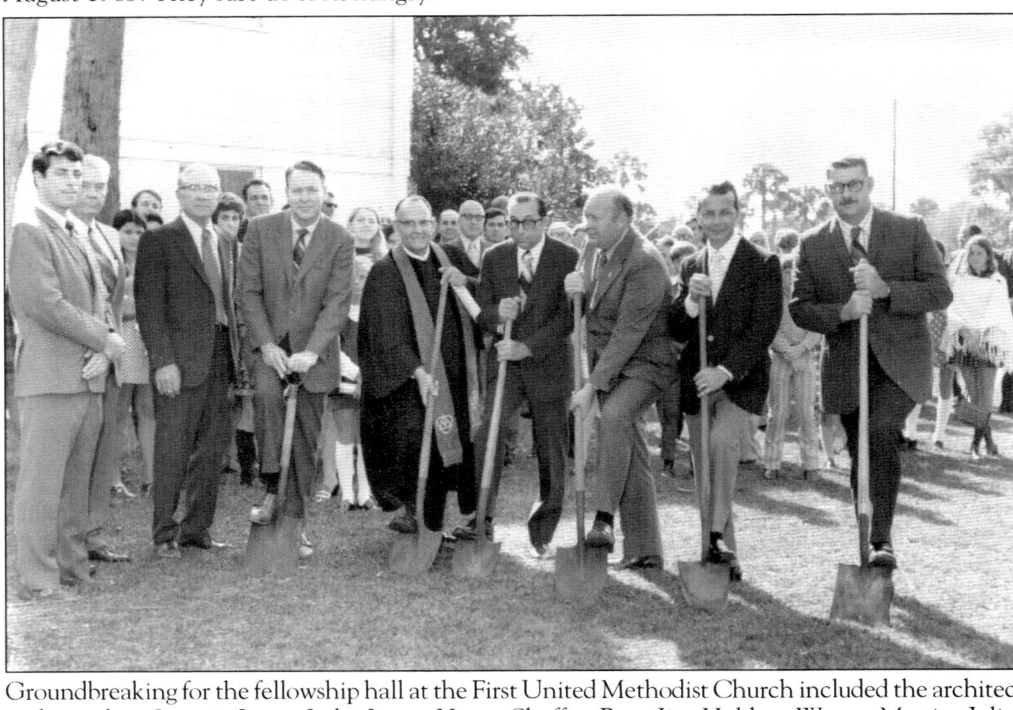

Groundbreaking for the fellowship hall at the First United Methodist Church included the architect and members Lonnie Long, Luke Lupo, Henry Shaffer, Rev. Jim Holden, Wayne Martin, Julius Wannamaker, Jim Berry, and Will Walters. The fellowship hall is named after Luke Lupo.

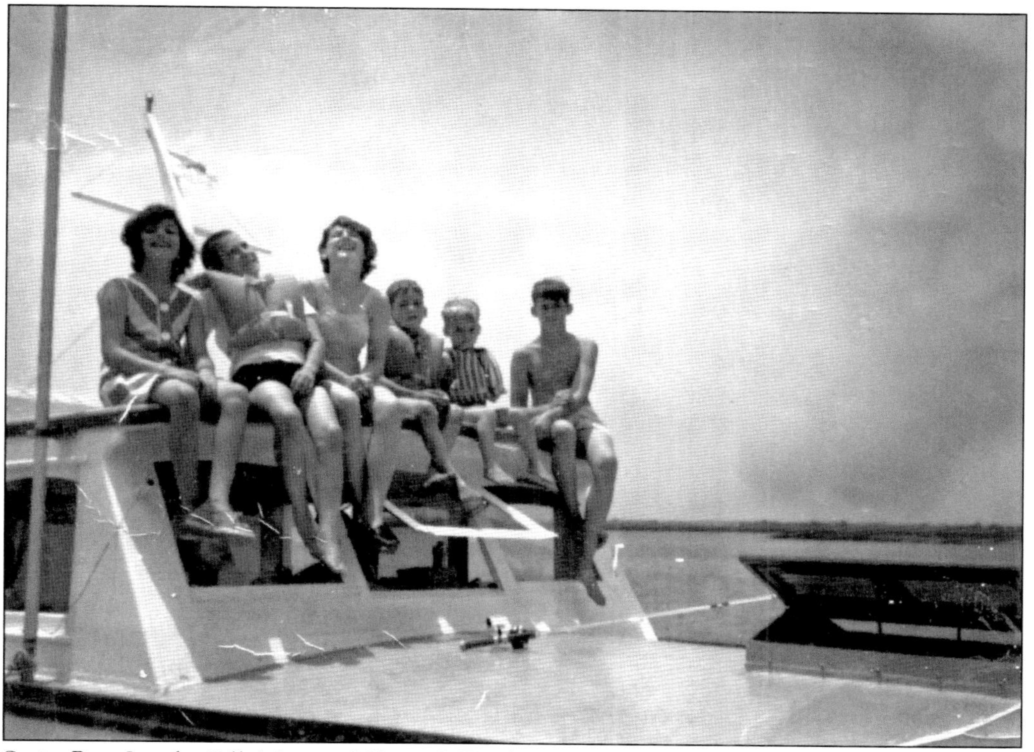

Susie, Ray, Lynda, Bill, Mac, and Henry J. Finch sit aboard the *Colonial Queen* at the Esso dock on Breach Inlet.

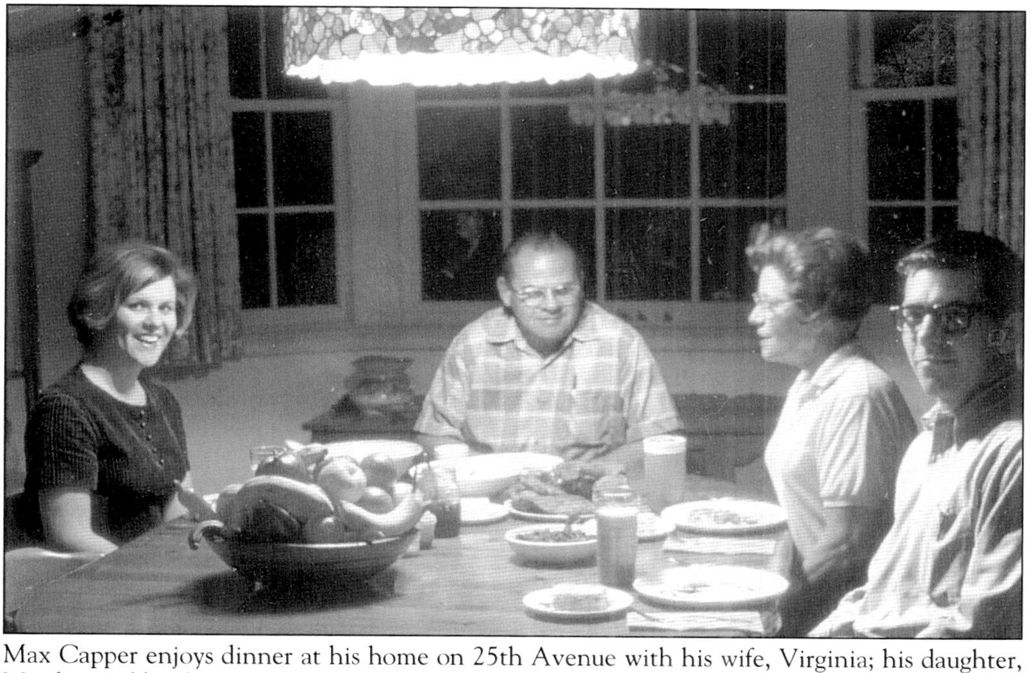

Max Capper enjoys dinner at his home on 25th Avenue with his wife, Virginia; his daughter, Martha; and his future son-in-law, Roger Sparwasser.

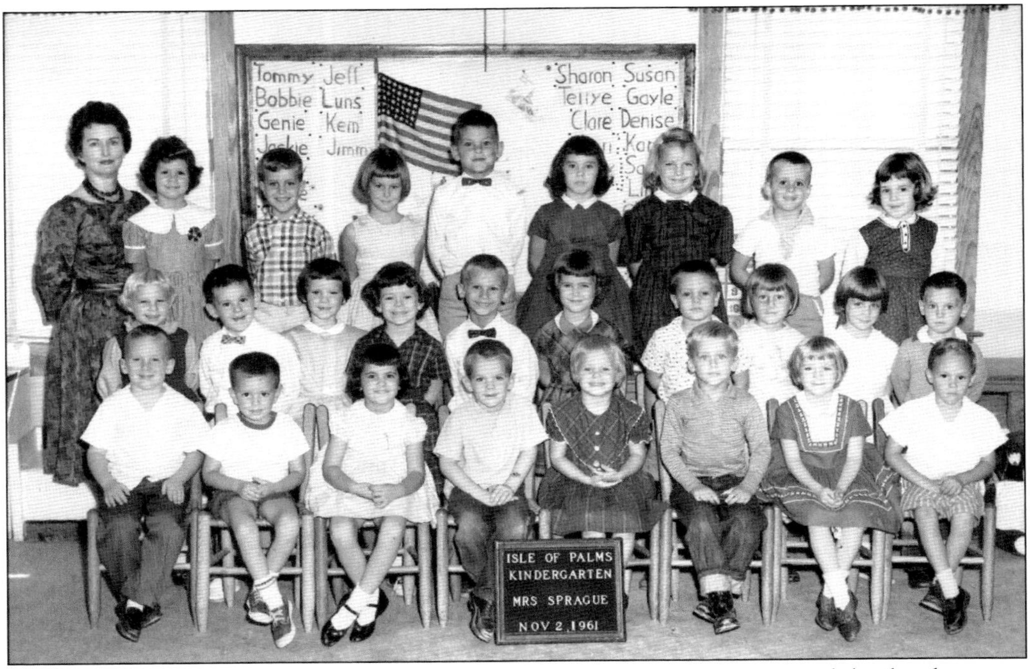

In 1953, the First United Methodist Church on Isle of Palms began a weekday kindergarten program. Mrs. Leila Sprague was the first director of the program. She is seen here with her class of 1961, many of whom still live on the island.

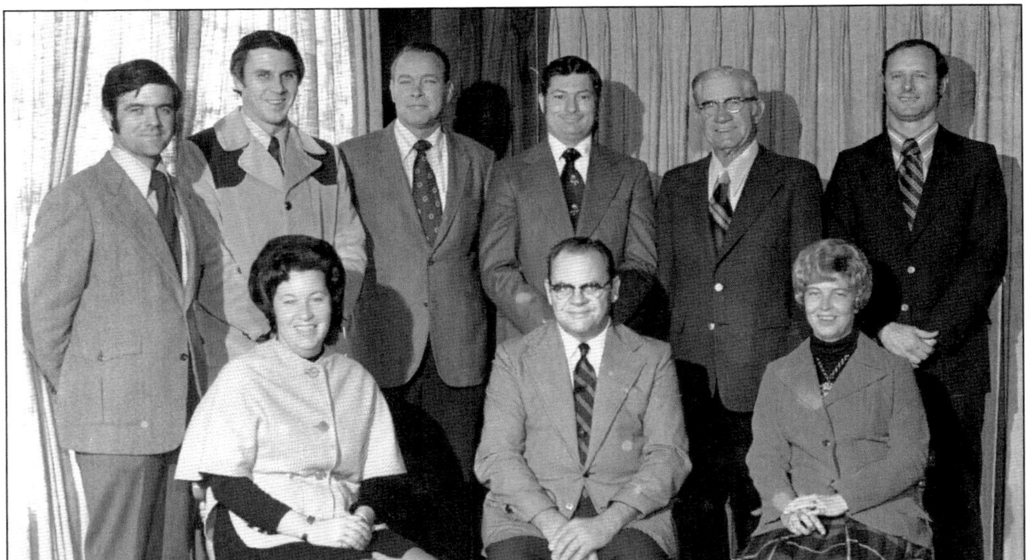

One slate of candidates for the Isle of Palms City Council in 1974 was the Capper Team: Joyce Baxter, Max Capper, Nancy Preston, Bill Casey, Dick Marsh, Henry Shaffer, Bill Lee, Luke Lupo, and Ted Guerard. In 1974, the city operated under a mayor-council form of government. In 1992, the municipality voted to adopt a strong-council form of government, consisting of a mayor and eight council members. Candidates run in non-partisan, at-large elections for staggered four-year terms.

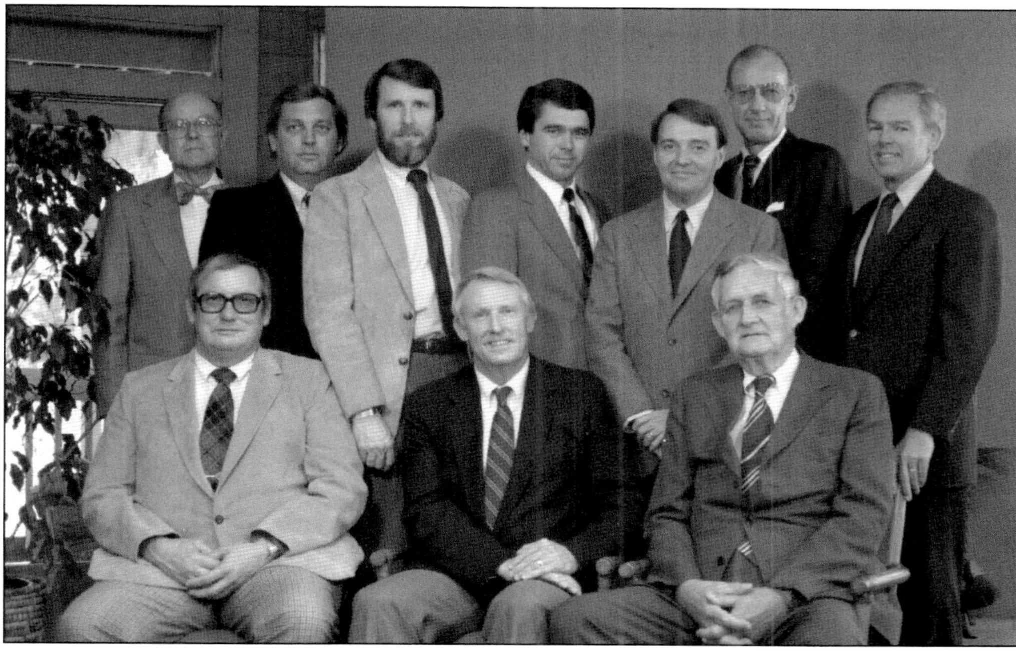

The development of Isle of Palms Beach and Racquet Club (Wild Dunes) began in 1972, when Finch Properties purchased the site from developer J.C. Long. Serving on the resort's first board of directors were the following, pictured from left to right: (front row) Henry Finch, Raymon Rinch Jr., and Wilbur Smith; (back row) Cleveland Putnam, Dave Carr, Mike Finch, Pat McKinney, Frank Brumley, Charlie Way, and Dr. Charles Darby. In a letter written to Henry Finch by Mr. Long, he writes:

Dear Henry,

A month ago, it was a beautiful day, and Charlie Way called me up and asked if I would like to go riding. I accepted his kind invitation, and he drove me through the Beach and Racquet Club. Henry, I am completely at a loss for words to express to you and to the others who have participated in the development of the Beach and Racquet Club, what a magnificent job I think has been accomplished.

It is something that I believe surpasses the dreams of anybody. I know it surpasses any dreams I ever had of how beautiful a development could be made of the property. The development that you folks have made is something that I would have never attempted to accomplish. I would not have had the courage to borrow the money necessary to do what has been done, and of course I know that the mortgage given for the development of the property has been liquidated.

I want to take credit for having sold the property to the Finch Properties, for it was through Finch Properties that means, I feel, so much not only to Charleston County, but to the State of South Carolina at large, has taken place. I want to say that I don't have one minute's regret in the sale of the property. I am really proud of what all of you have accomplished.

I am sending you two extra copies of this letter as I would like you to send one to your Dad and give one copy to Raymon, Jr.

Regards and best wishes,
J.C.

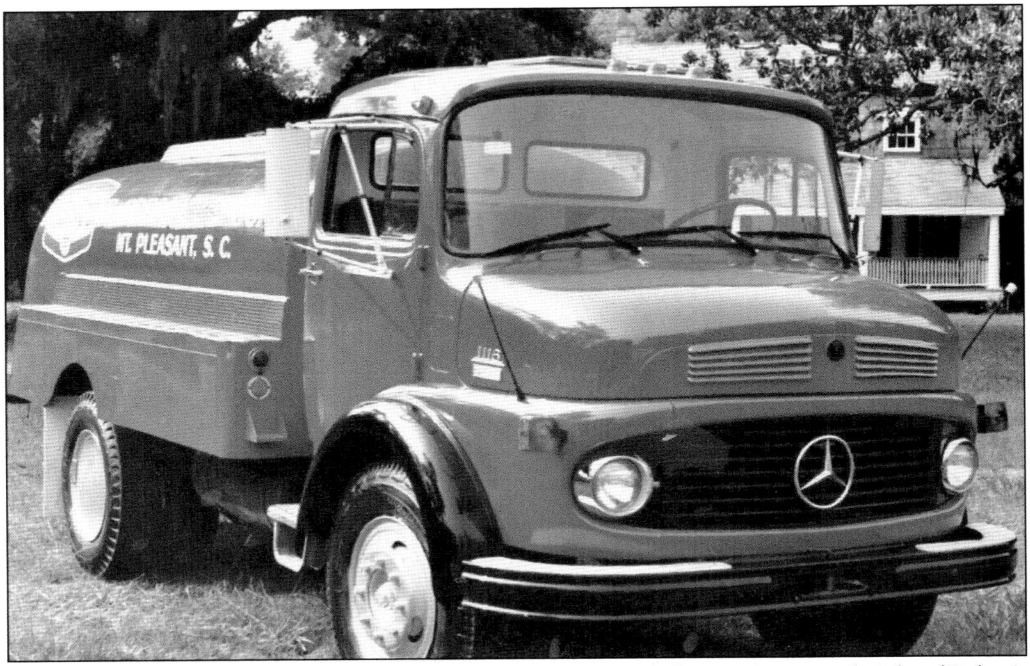

Before residents had electric heat, F. Gregorie and Sons used this truck to supply Isle of Palms's tanks with fuel oil.

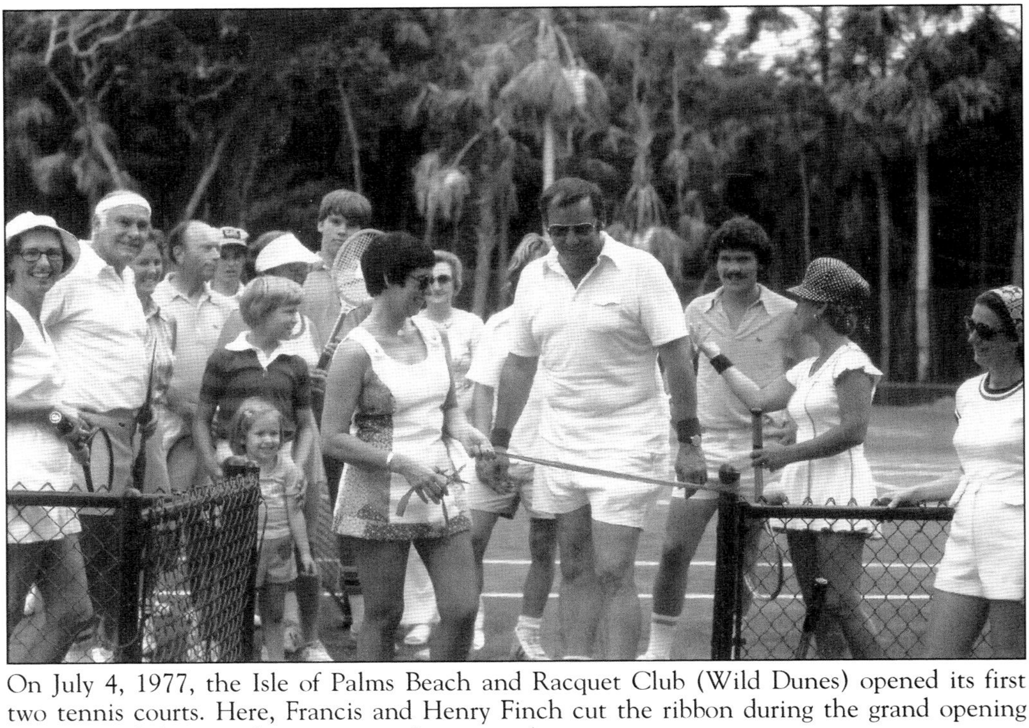

On July 4, 1977, the Isle of Palms Beach and Racquet Club (Wild Dunes) opened its first two tennis courts. Here, Francis and Henry Finch cut the ribbon during the grand opening ceremony while an enthusiastic crowd waits to play.

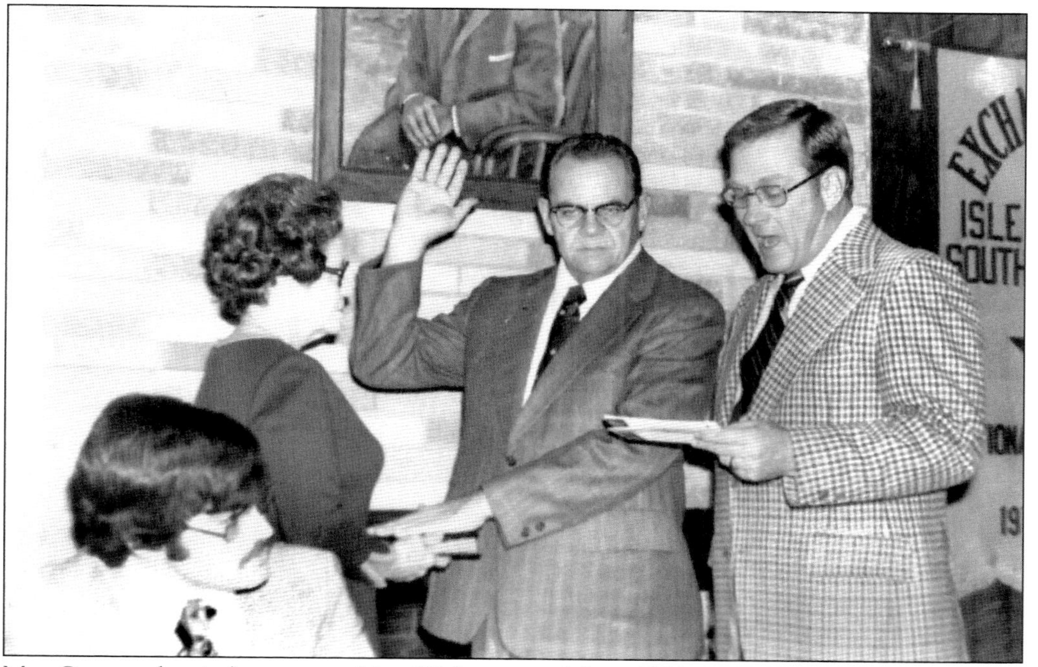

Max Capper, the sixth mayor on Isle of Palms, served from 1978 to 1981. He is seen here taking the oath of office. Holding the bible is his wife, Virginia Capper.

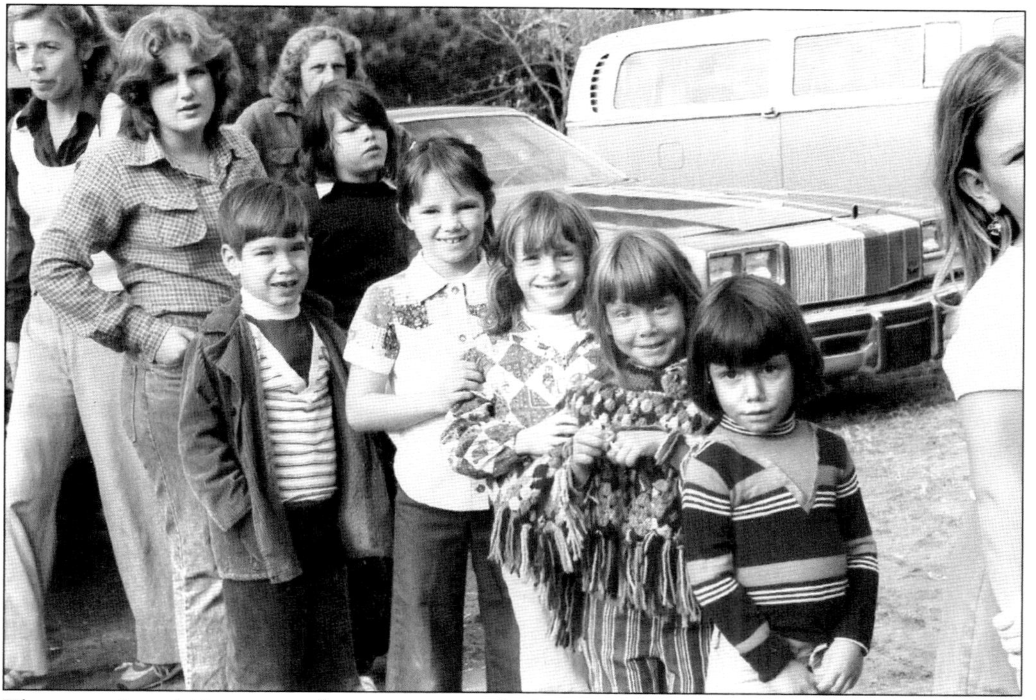

These anxious kids wait in line to visit with Santa Claus at the Isle of Palms Children's Christmas Party in 1979. Bill Casey organized the event at the playground.

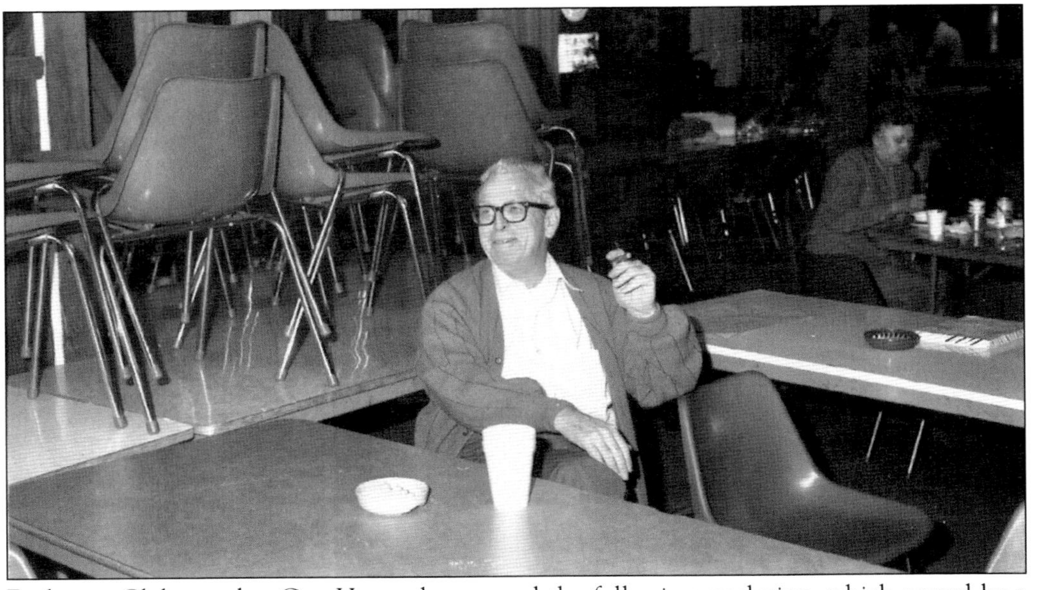

Exchange Club member Guy Hancock proposed the following resolution, which passed by a majority vote at the Exchange Club's January meeting in 1980. It was conveyed to President Jimmy Carter. It read:

> We, the Exchange Club of Isle of Palms, South Carolina, support the complete removal of athletes from the Olympics if they are held in Russia.
>
> We are completely in favor of our athletes entering and competing in the Olympics if they are held in a country not involved in international aggression.

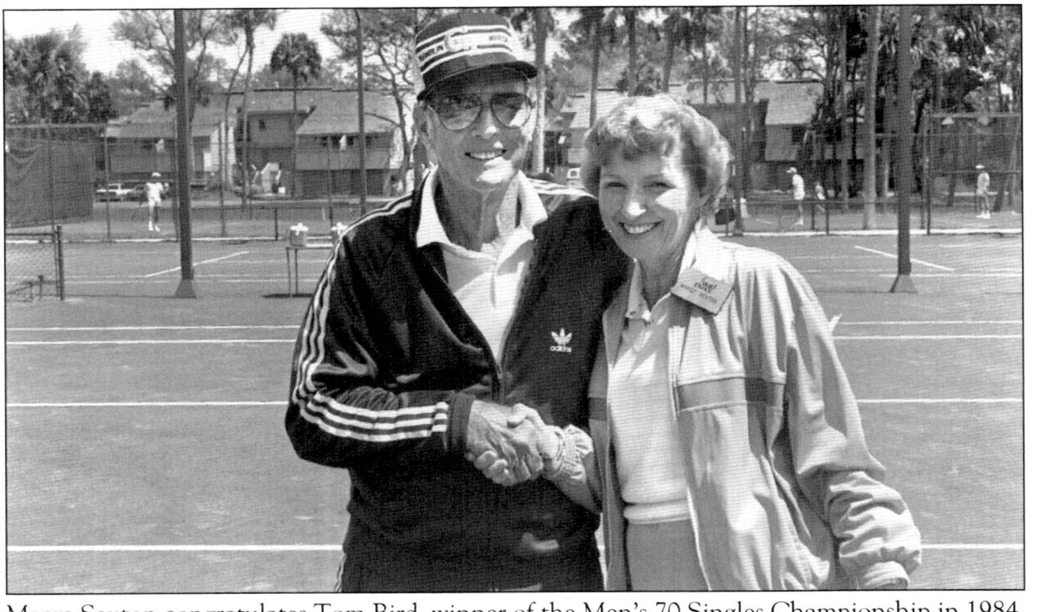

Marge Sexton congratulates Tom Bird, winner of the Men's 70 Singles Championship in 1984. Isle of Palms Beach and Racquet Club hired Marge as the director for club membership in 1977. Still with Wild Dunes after 28 years, she is a real-estate agent for the company.

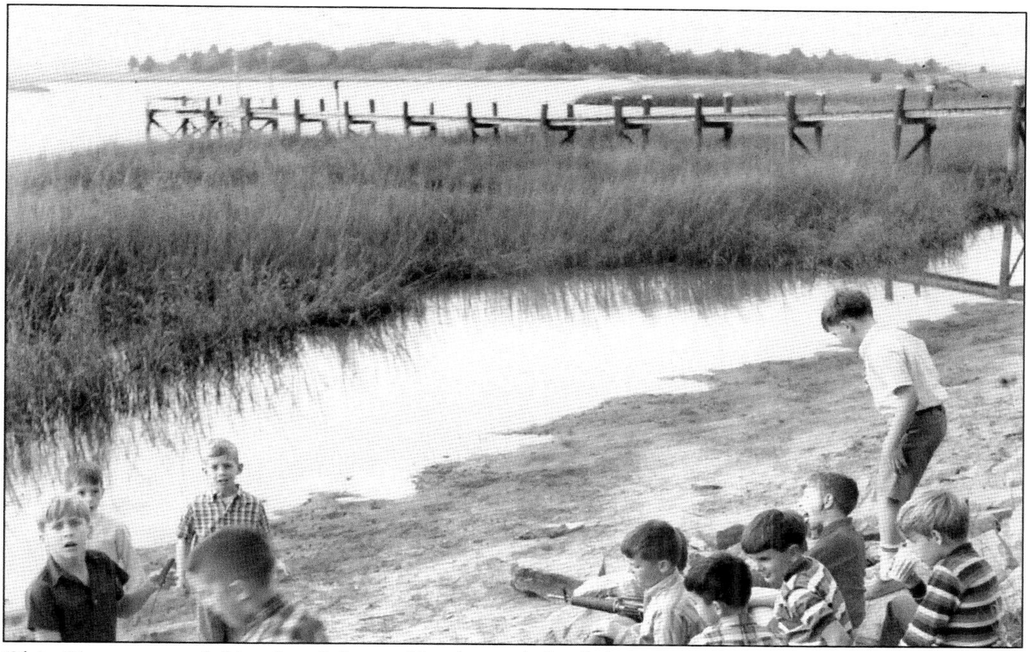

Chip Campsen and friends celebrate Chip's ninth birthday in 1968 on Hamlin Creek.

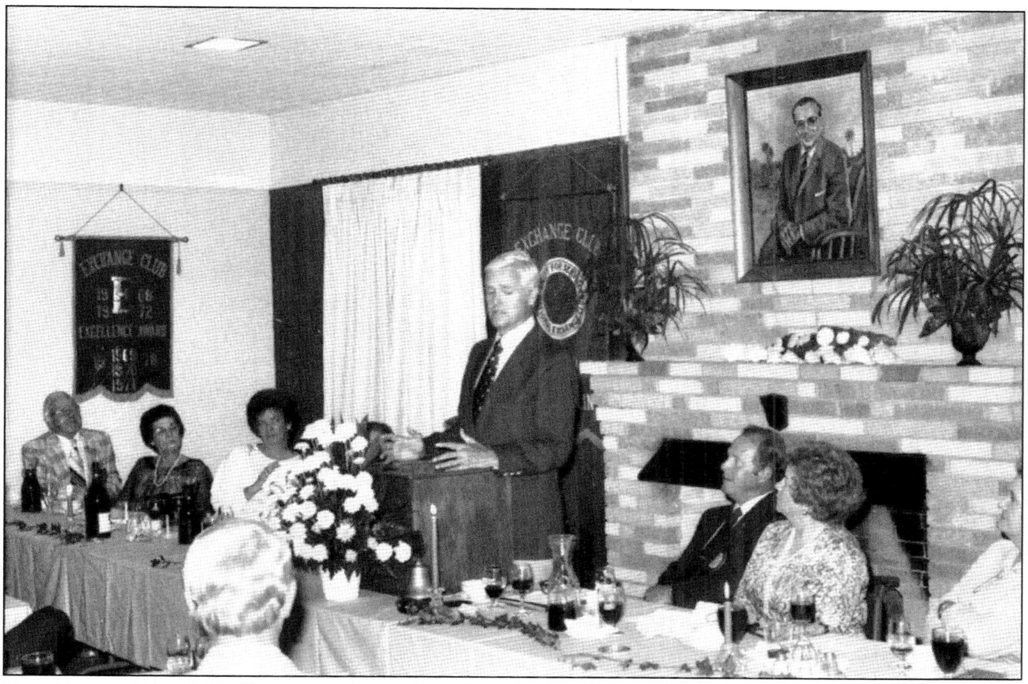

Sen. Ernest "Fritz" Hollings speaks at the 32nd Annual Awards and Installation Banquet at the Exchange Club. Senator Hollings served as South Carolina's senator from 1966 to 2005. An army veteran, he is a graduate of The Citadel and the University of South Carolina School of Law. Senator Hollings is one of many politicians who reside on Isle of Palms. He is an honorable statesman and an exemplary South Carolinian.

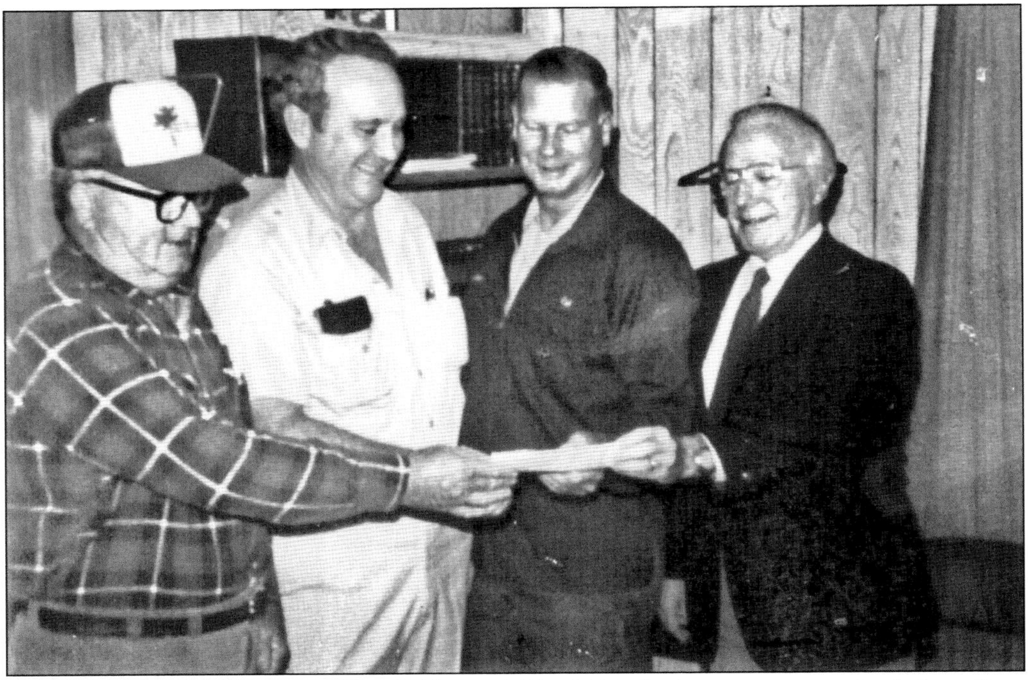

"Sarge" Andy Parrish, Mayor Clay Cable, and Chief Cal Cochrane accept a check from Rep. Clyde Dangerfield for the purchase of an emergency vehicle in 1985.

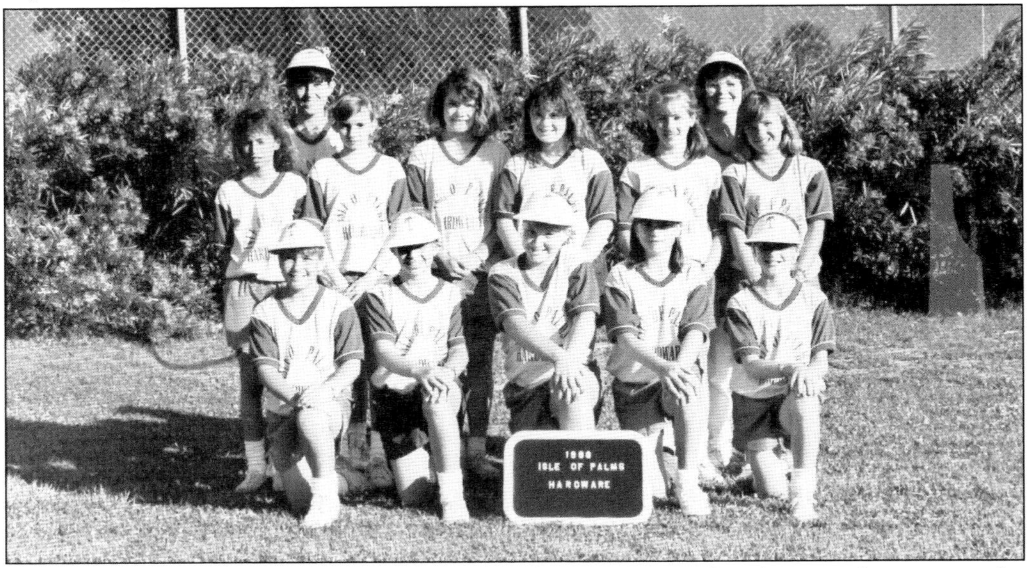

Isle of Palms teams, like this group of softball players, competed with teams from across the bridge. The Isle of Palms Recreation Department and the Mt. Pleasant Recreation Department worked together to schedule games for all of East Cooper's youth. Pictured here, from left to right, are (front row) Hollis Parks, Stephanie Mitchell, Christy Nations, Wendy ?, and Callie Jenkins; (back row) Stephanie Avery, and unidentified Isle of Palms Hardware player, Clancy Bessinger, Ashley Rowe, Heather Holmquist, and Robin Potter. In the very back are Coach Bessinger and her assistant.

A miniature golf course occupied a small section of Front Beach for amateur putt-putt enthusiasts. The pros, of course, headed to Myrtle Beach for the more elaborate courses.

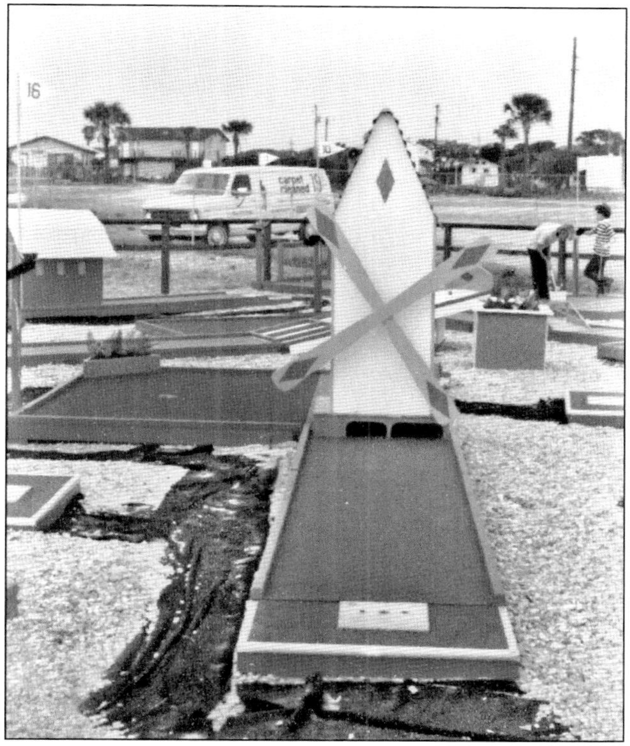

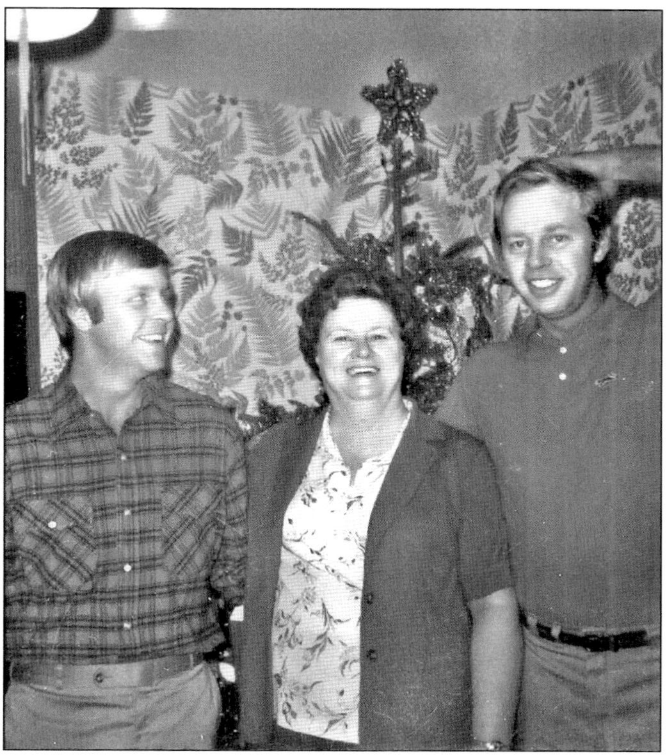

Lance and Stewart Nilsen's love for Isle of Palms began when their mother, Lillian, and father, Stanley, brought them to the Sand Dollar Campground in the early 1960s. Lillian loved the island so much that she moved her family there in 1968. The boys share a hug with mom, thanking her for her wise decision.

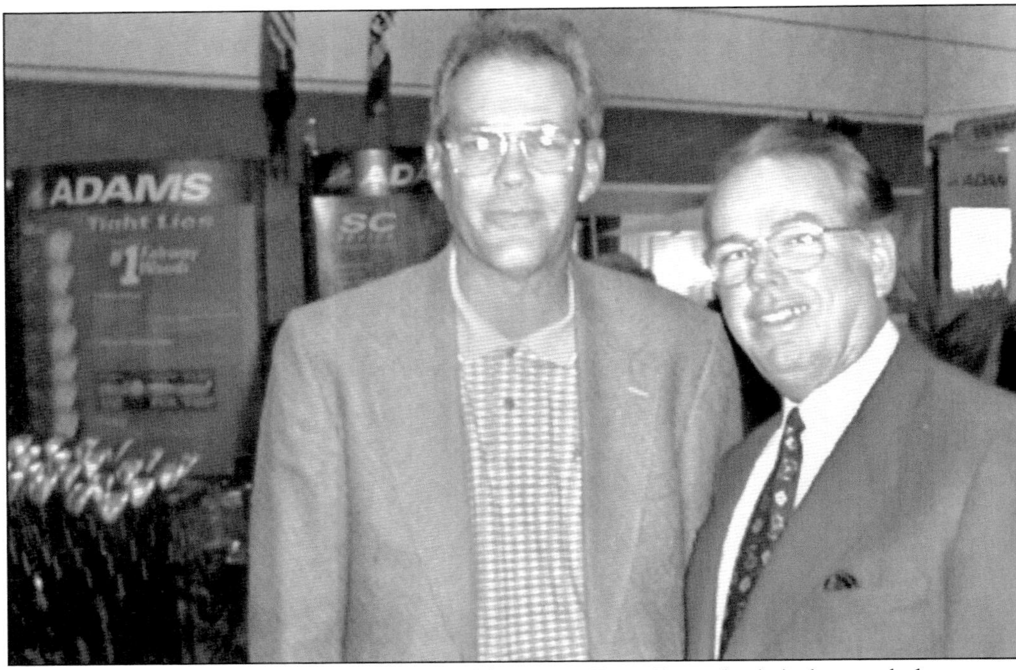

In 1980, the Links Course opened at Wild Dunes. Tom Fazio (right) designed the course, incorporating the dunes, marsh, and oceanfront at the northeast end of the island into the layout. The natural terrain and Fazio's artistic planning created a course that immediately vaulted into every top 100 poll. Wild Dunes hired Terry Florence (left) as its director of golf, and he played an integral part of the resort's climb to international recognition. Terry was with Wild Dunes for over 20 years before he joined the PGA Senior Tour.

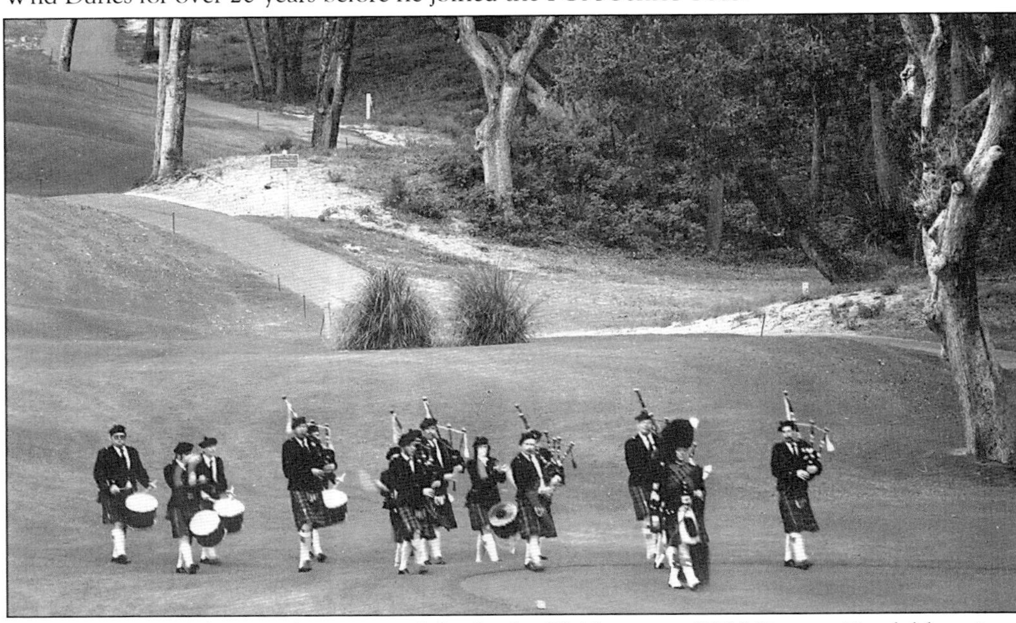

In celebration of the grand opening of the Links Clubhouse at Wild Dunes, Citadel bagpipers march from the 10th hole to the clubhouse in June 1985.

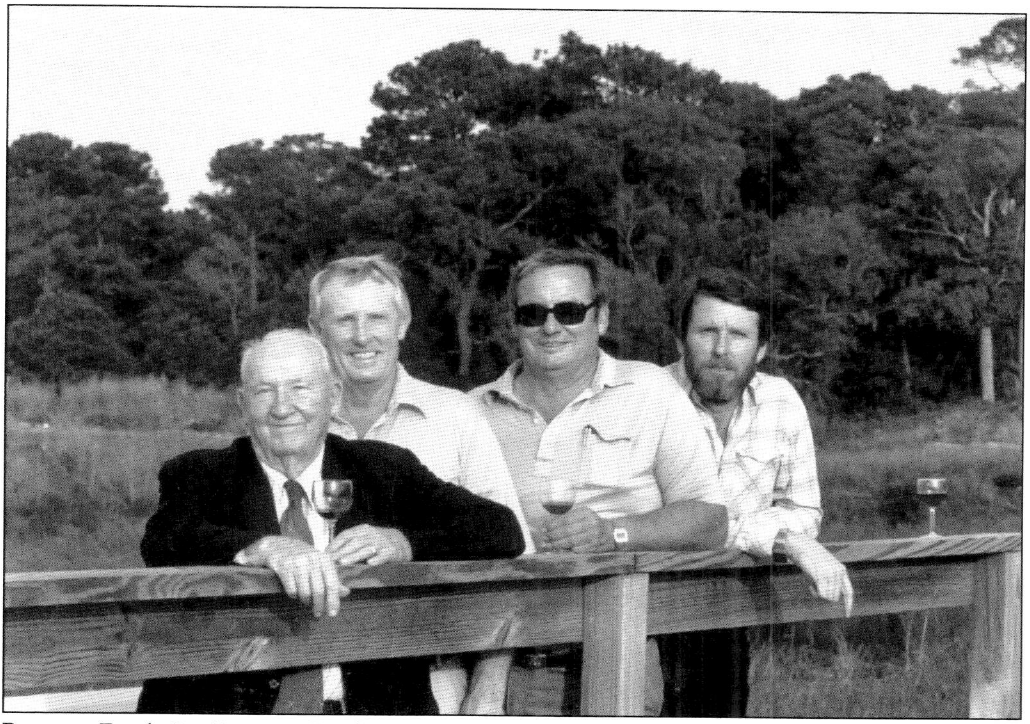

Raymon Finch Sr., Raymon Finch Jr., Henry Finch, and Mike Finch gather on the bridge named in honor of Raymon Finch Sr. The bridge crosses Morgan Creek to Waterway Island in Wild Dunes.

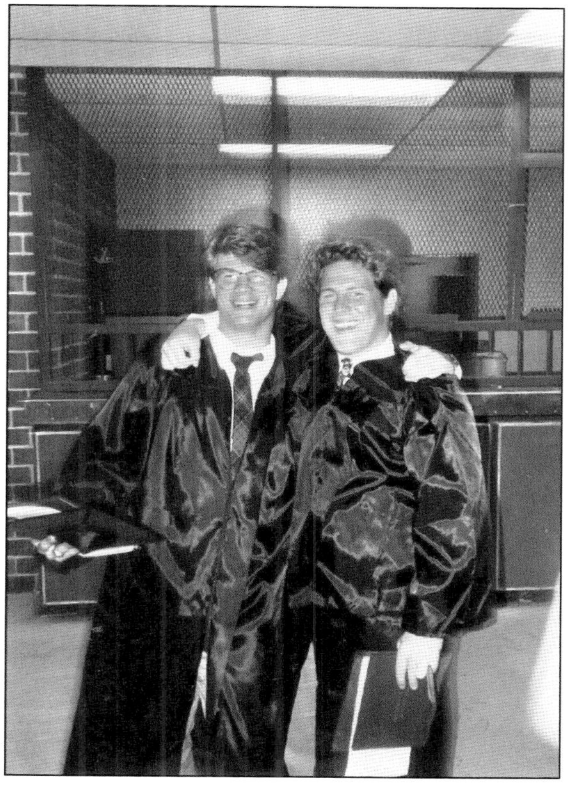

Isle of Palms students Rhett Reidenbach and Kyle Crout share a deserving hug upon graduating from Wando High School in Mt. Pleasant. Since there are no public schools on the island, students were subject to a minimum 45-minute bus ride to Wando before the connector was built. Most students, however, opted to drive or ride with friends.

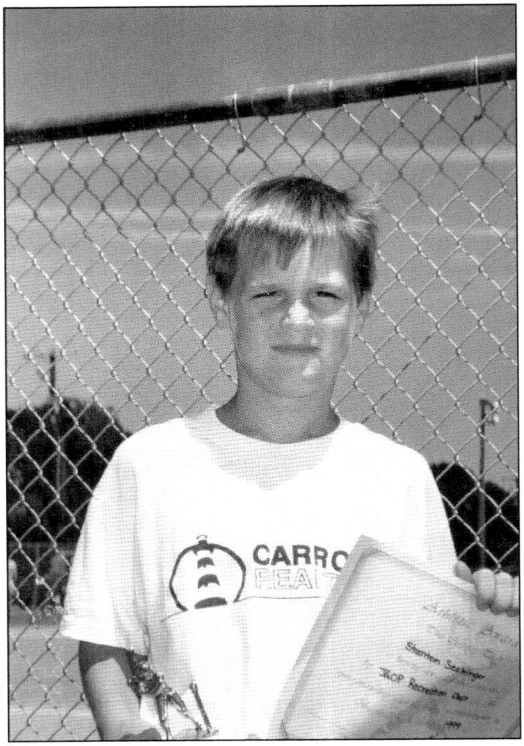

Stanton Seckinger shows off his athletic award and trophy given to him by the Isle of Palms Recreation Department. J.C. Long donated the land between 27th and 28th Avenues to be used as a playground. The City of Isle of Palms hired Katherine Carroll to serve as the first recreation director; she held the position for six years. Ironically, Stanton poses in a T-shirt advertising Carroll Realty, a firm once brokered by Mrs. Carroll.

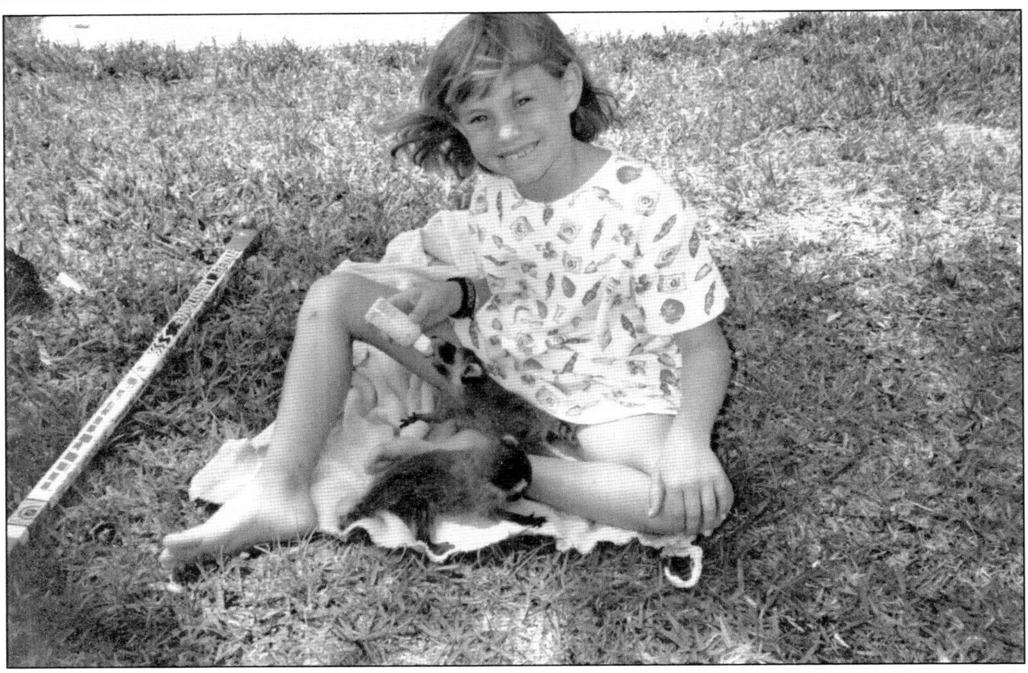

Brooke Mosteller nurses two baby raccoons. It must be in her genes; her mother, Cyndi Campsen (Mosteller) grew up in a family dedicated to nurturing injured or disoriented wildlife on the island.

Three

LEISURELY LIVING

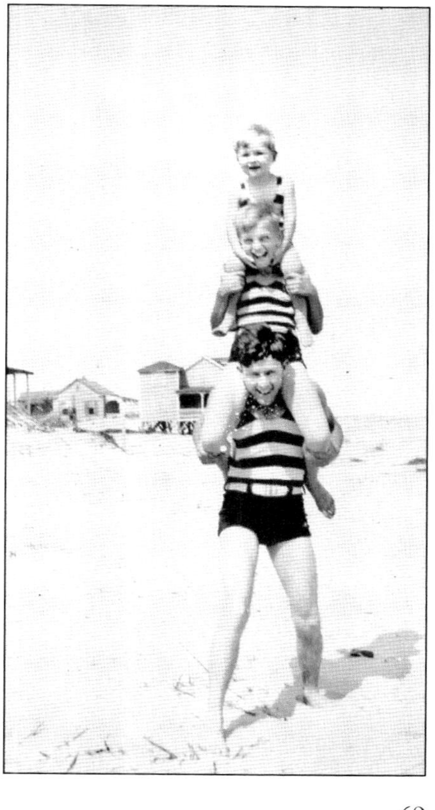

Henry Shaffer, Wally Shaffer Jr., and Wally Shaffer Sr. build a three-man shoulder pyramid. Their striped tank suits were the appropriate attire for bathing at the beach in the 1930s.

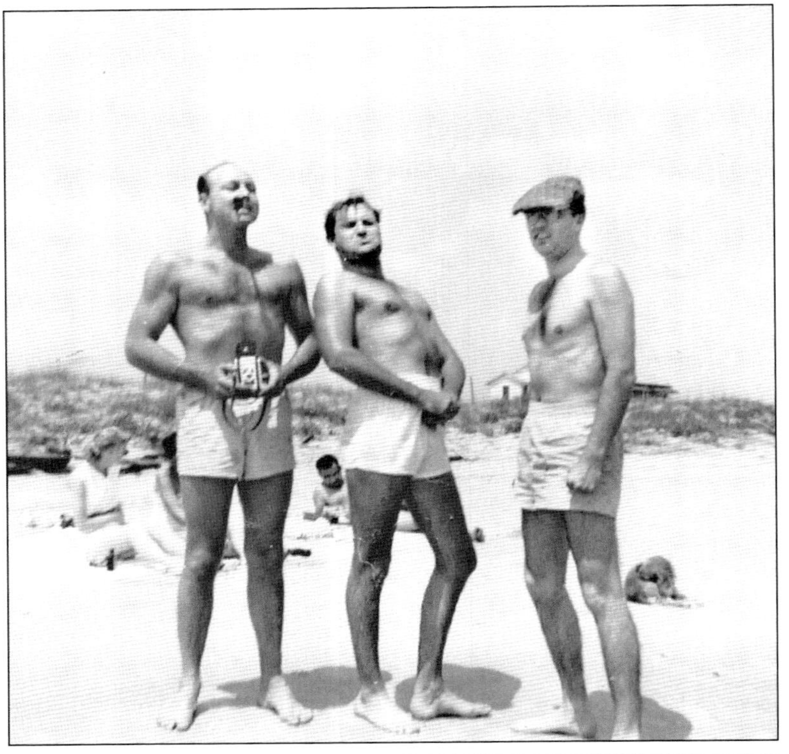

These handsome muscle men flirt with the camera. It is probable that they were covered with baby oil or iodine to enhance their tan. Sunscreen was not yet available.

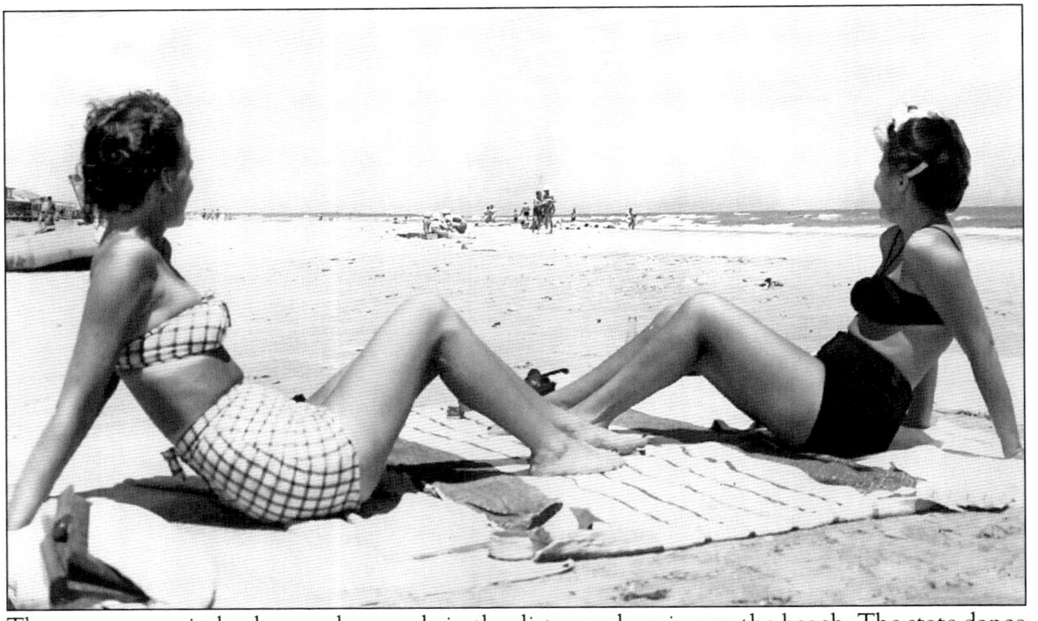

These women quietly observe the couple in the distance shagging on the beach. The state dance originated in Myrtle Beach, where carefree teenagers flocked to the beach to hear R&B groups perform live or on the jukebox. "Beach music," as it is called, comes from the act of dancing in the sand. It is not necessarily a genre of music, it is a mood—a Lowcountry institution. And there is no better place to shag than on the beach!

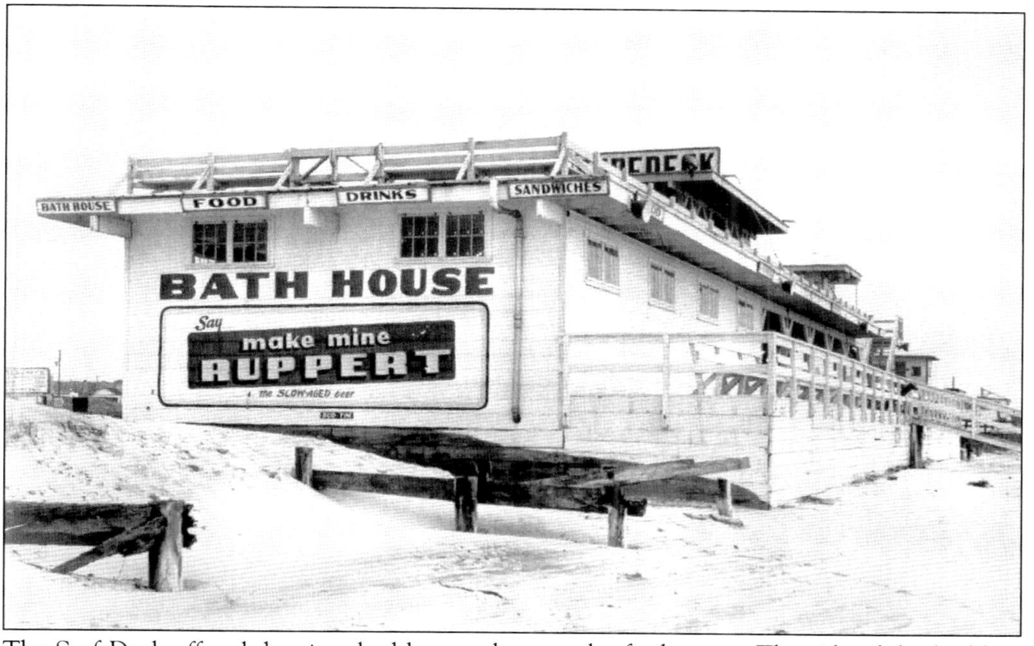

The Surf Deck offered dancing, bathhouses, beer, and refreshments. The side of the building advertised products like Ruppert Beer. The Surf Deck was owned and operated by W. Lee Hartmann, and it was later run by part-time police chief Eddie Walters and his wife. The Windjammer now sits on the site of the original Surf Deck.

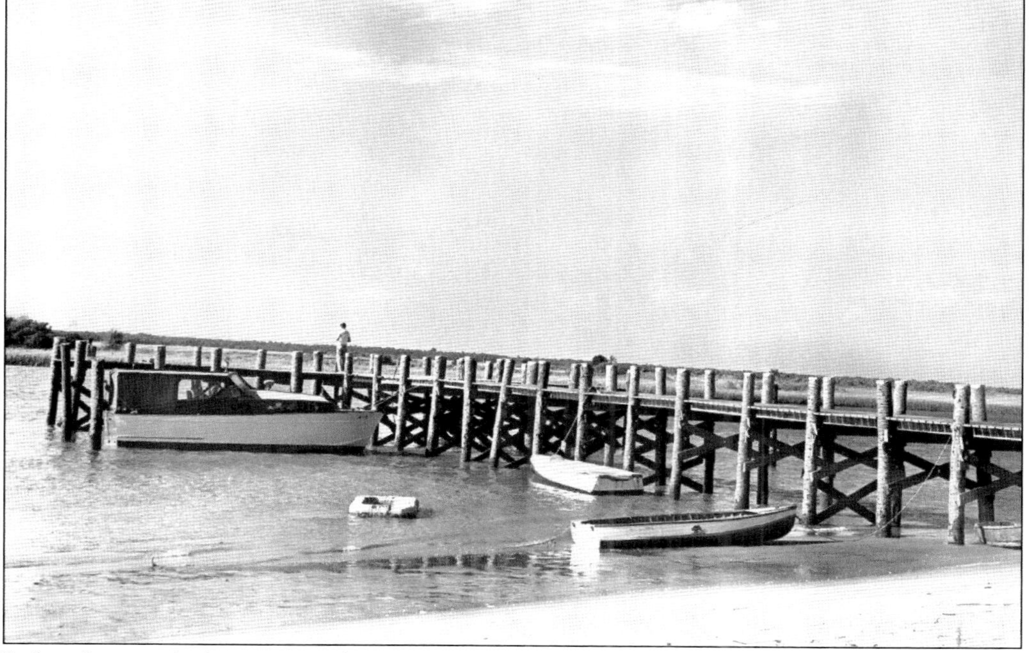

Before floating docks were popular, cruisers and dinghies tied up to the pilings. This classic dock was located on the back side of Breach Inlet. The pilings were actually palmetto logs, abundant on the island and useful for various types of construction.

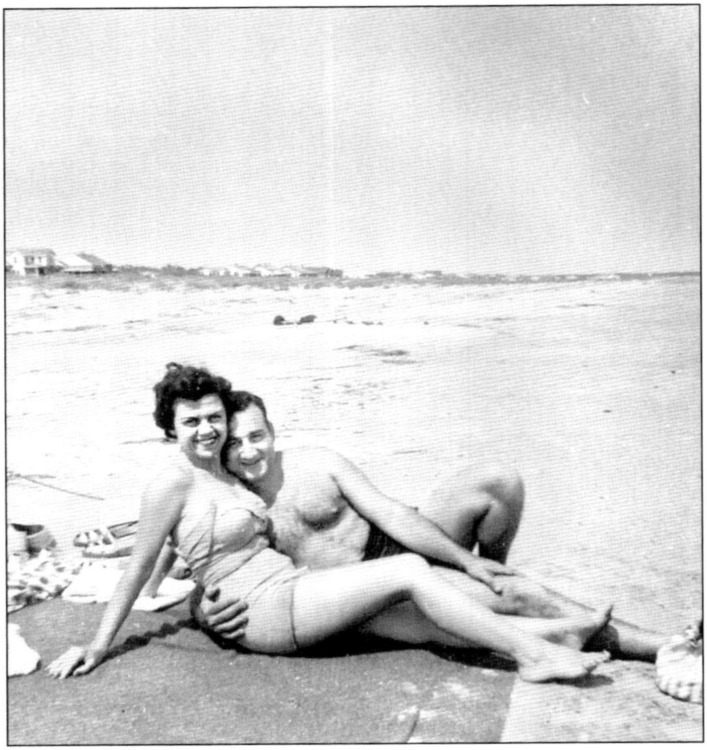

Pauline and Vincent Sottile cuddle on the beach. The two wed in 1953 and later had twins, Vincent Jr. and Mary. Vincent was a property manager with the Worth Agency and director of the Charleston Junior Chamber of Commerce. He built Charleston's first Tourist Information Center. Like his father and uncles, Vincent made hospitality his business!

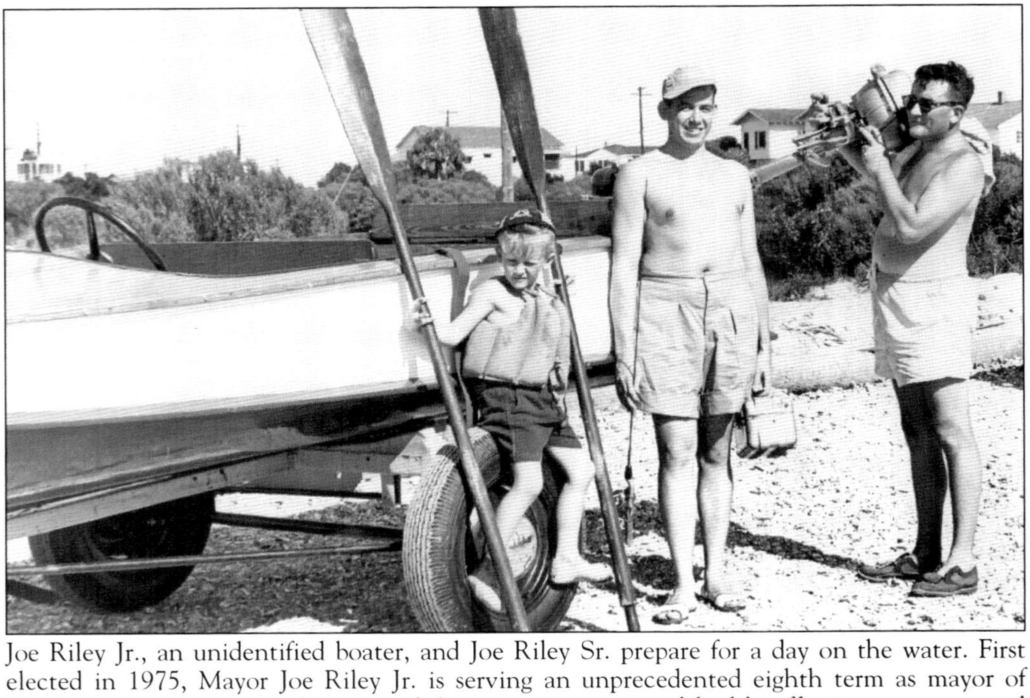

Joe Riley Jr., an unidentified boater, and Joe Riley Sr. prepare for a day on the water. First elected in 1975, Mayor Joe Riley Jr. is serving an unprecedented eighth term as mayor of Charleston. He is regarded as one of the most visionary and highly effective governmental leaders in the country.

A young woman looks on as an Isle of Palms lifeguard places a bandage on the ankle of an injured sunbather. The lifeguard stations lined the beach, and the guards were certified by the American Red Cross.

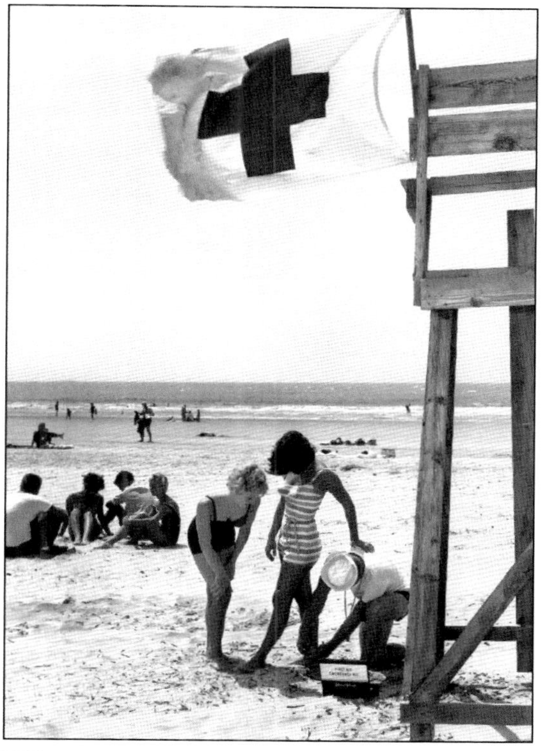

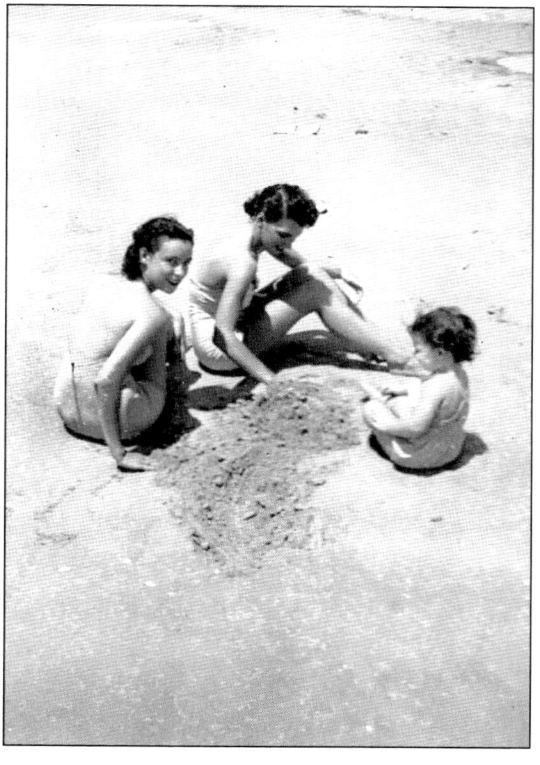

Frances, Nan, and Lynda Finch play in the sand in 1952. Bikinis had just been introduced a few years prior, and they were taking the world by storm! Wartime rationing ordered a reduction of fabric in the manufacturing of garments, giving yet another reason to thank our soldiers from the "Great Generation."

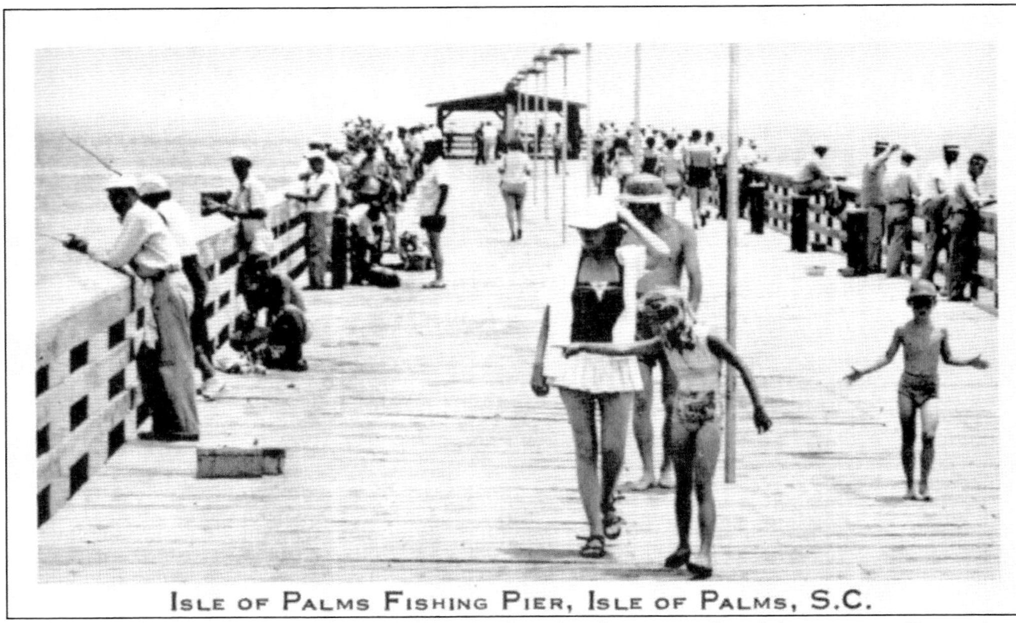

One of the most popular attractions on Isle of Palms was the fishing pier. Opened in 1953, it was the longest in South Carolina, stretching 1,000 feet into the Atlantic. Fishing on the pier cost 65¢ a day. It featured a snack bar, restrooms, and fishing equipment for rent or purchase. The pier was also furnished with sinks and cleaning counters so that fisherman could clean their catch.

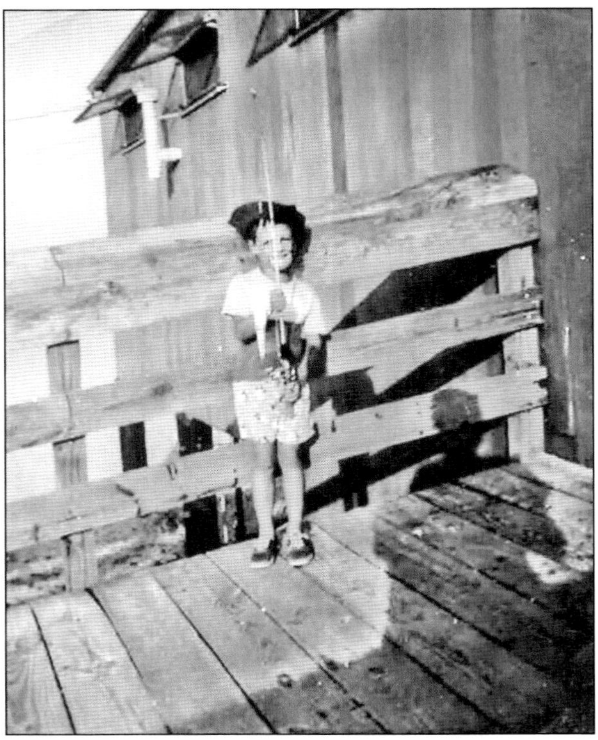

A young Mike Sottile stands, rod in hand, on the fishing pier. Mayor Sottile was elected in 2001 after serving 11 years on Isle of Palms City Council. His Uncle Sally, the island's third mayor, would be mighty proud!

It must have been a full moon on this October night in 1953 at the Exchange Club's annual costume party. Future club president John Sottile entertains fellow Exchange Club members.

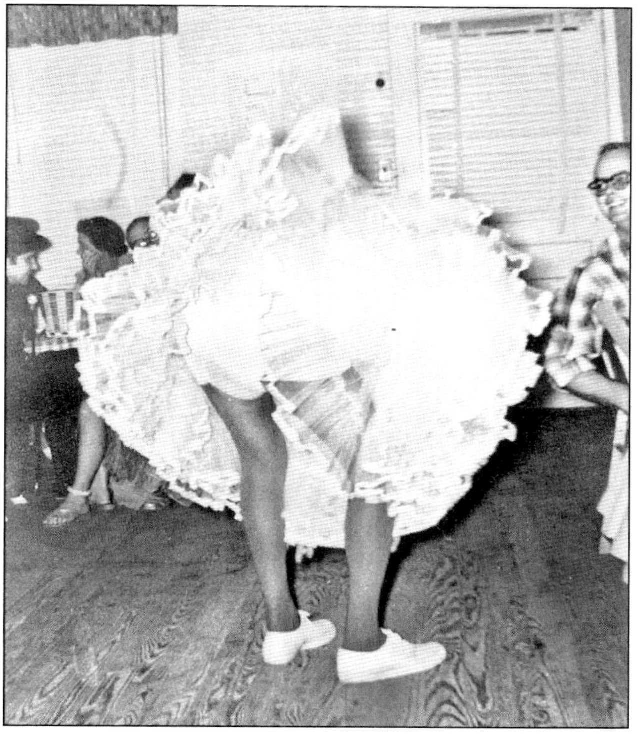

The amusement park was complete with a carousel for the children to ride when the beach water was a little too chilly. Round and round, up and down they go!

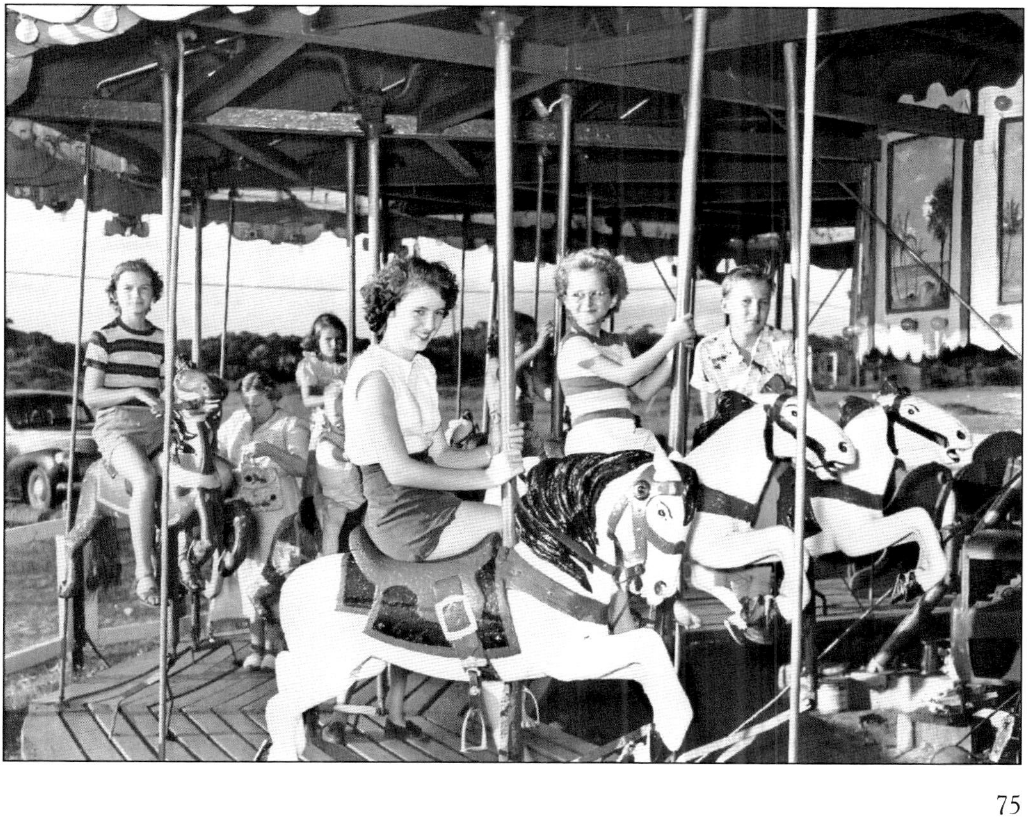

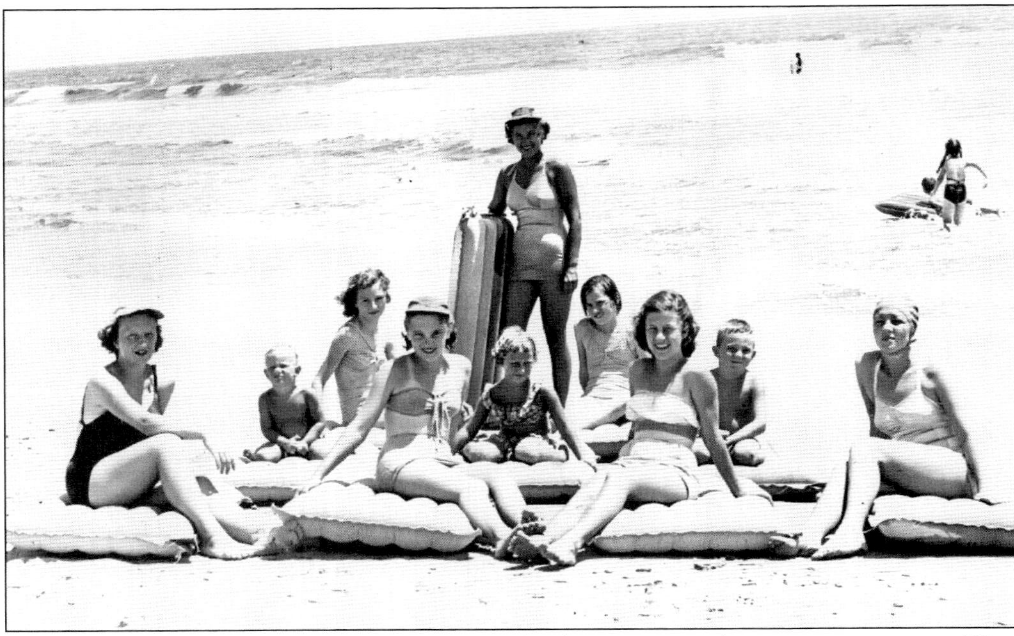

This picture-perfect group of beachgoers poses for the camera in their swimming attire. Wave riding, known today as boogie boarding, was and still is a favorite pastime on Isle of Palms.

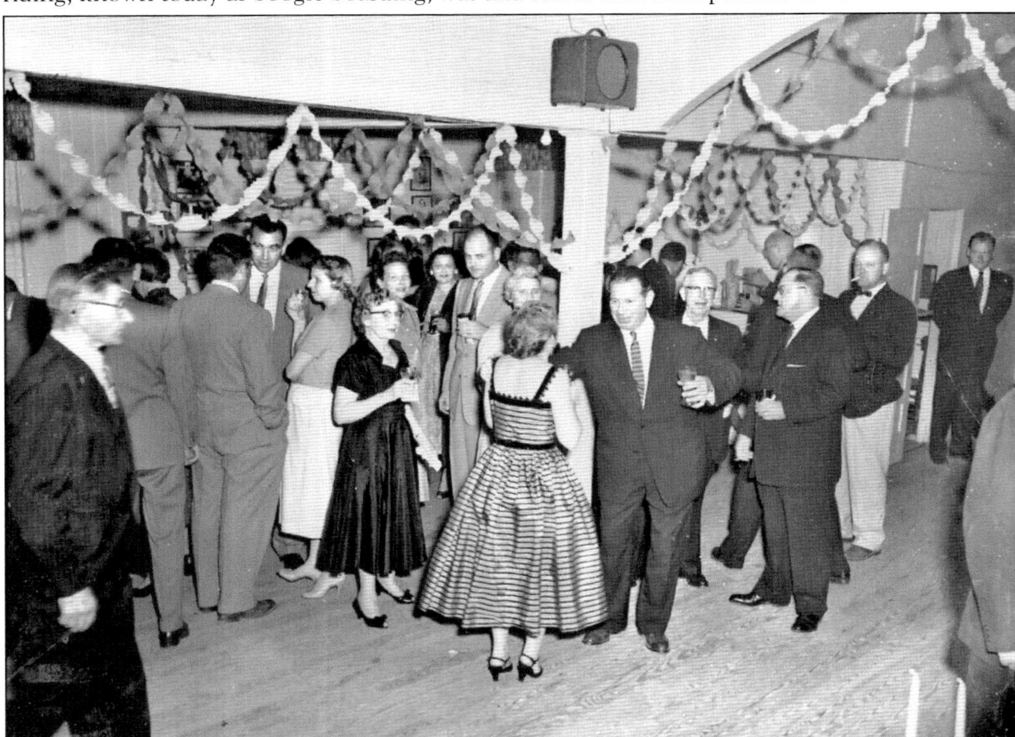

A dance was held at the Playland Pavilion for the Exchange Club's ninth anniversary party on March 30, 1957.

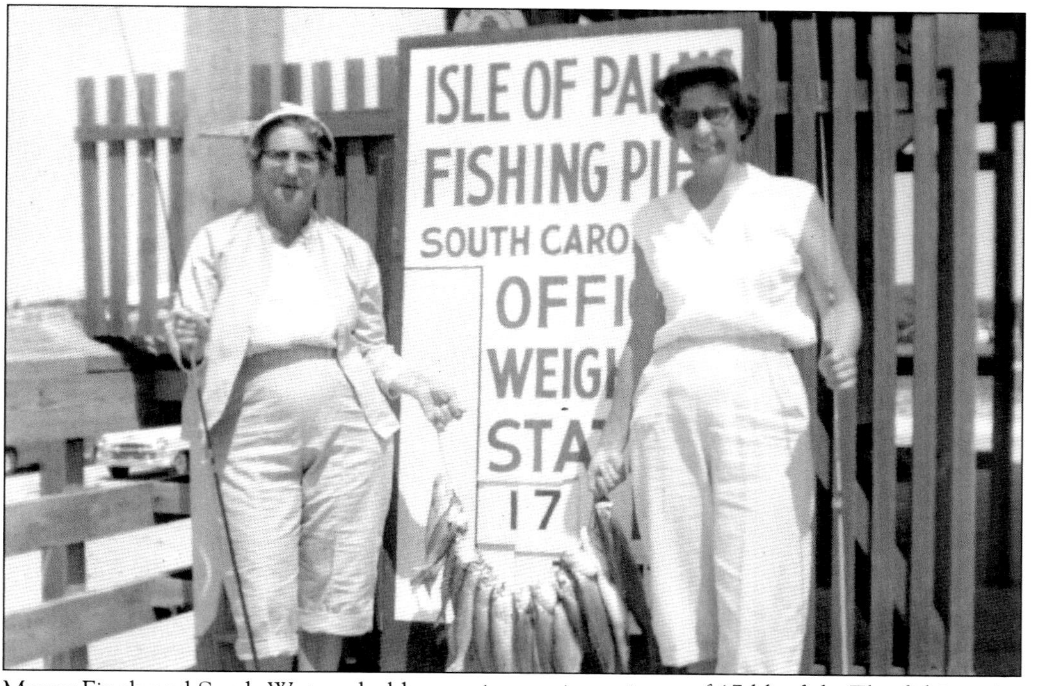

Maxcy Finch and Sarah Watson hold up an impressive stringer of 17 bluefish. The fishing pier allowed anglers to cast a further distance into the Atlantic, hooking fish that waders in the surf could not reach.

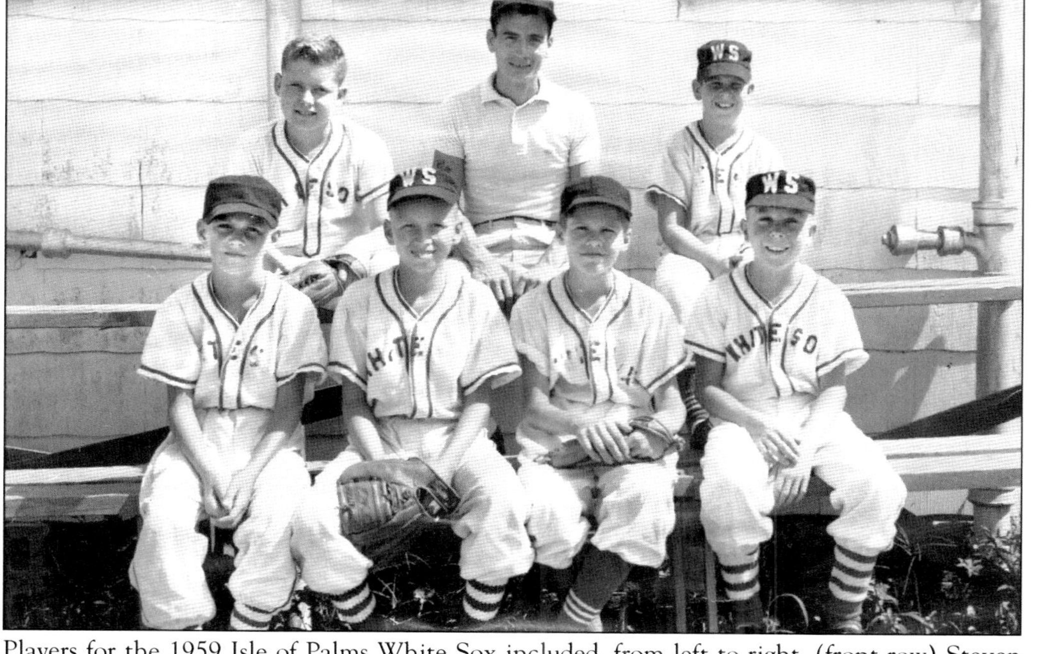

Players for the 1959 Isle of Palms White Sox included, from left to right, (front row) Steven Kibbey, Jimmy Sexton, John May, and Frank Haupt; (back row) Kerry May, the White Sox coach, and Jimmie Sahlman.

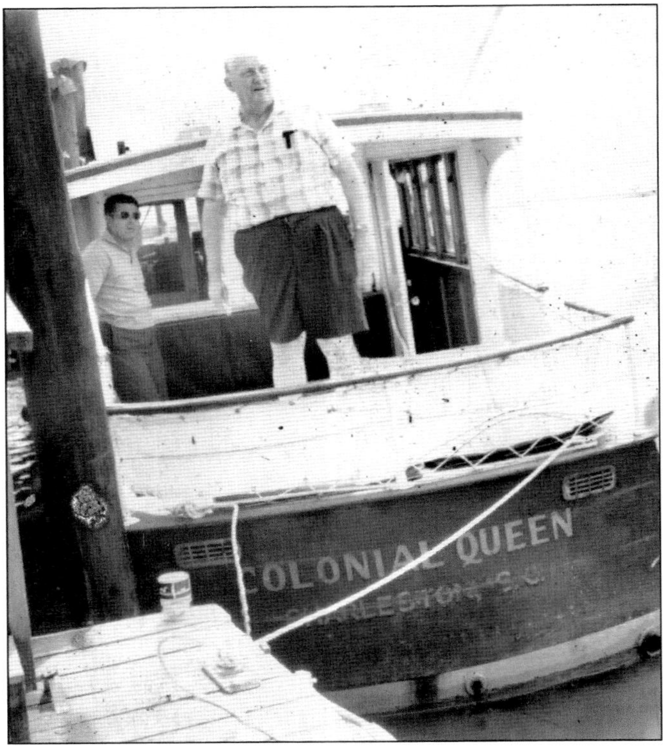

Raymon Finch Sr. stands proudly at the stern of his boat, the *Colonial Queen*. The boat was tied up to the Esso dock at Breach Inlet to fuel up for a relaxing day of cruising.

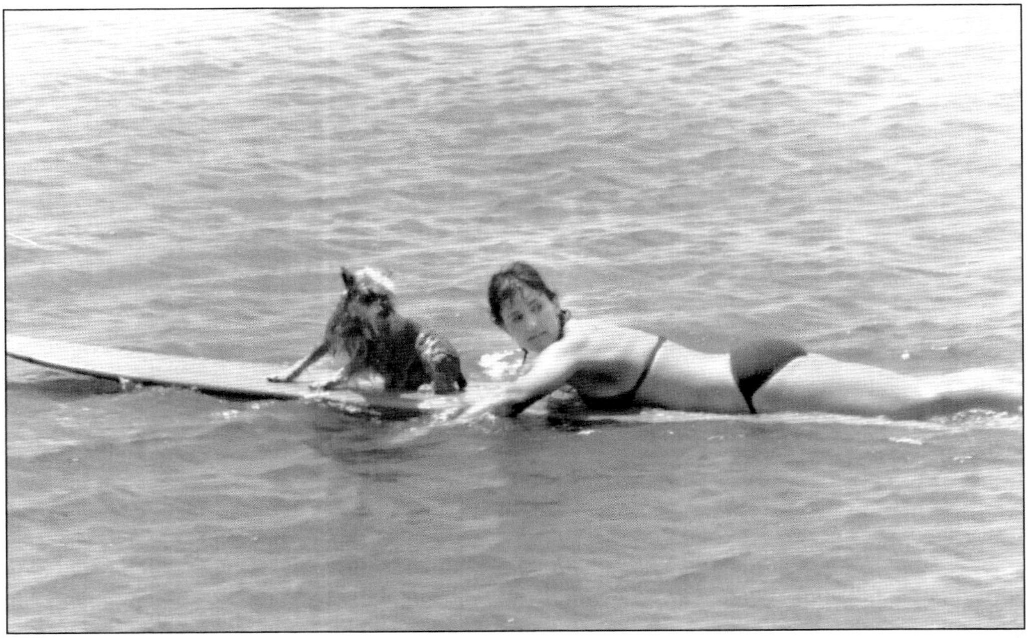

Surfing on Isle of Palms did not gain its due respect until the 1980s. Terrye Campsen (Seckinger) hangs 10 while her canine friend looks for the right wave. In the early 1900s, surfing was referred to as "plank bathing." Bathers would carry out a light plank beyond the breakers, mount it, and ride it through the surf, affording great sport.

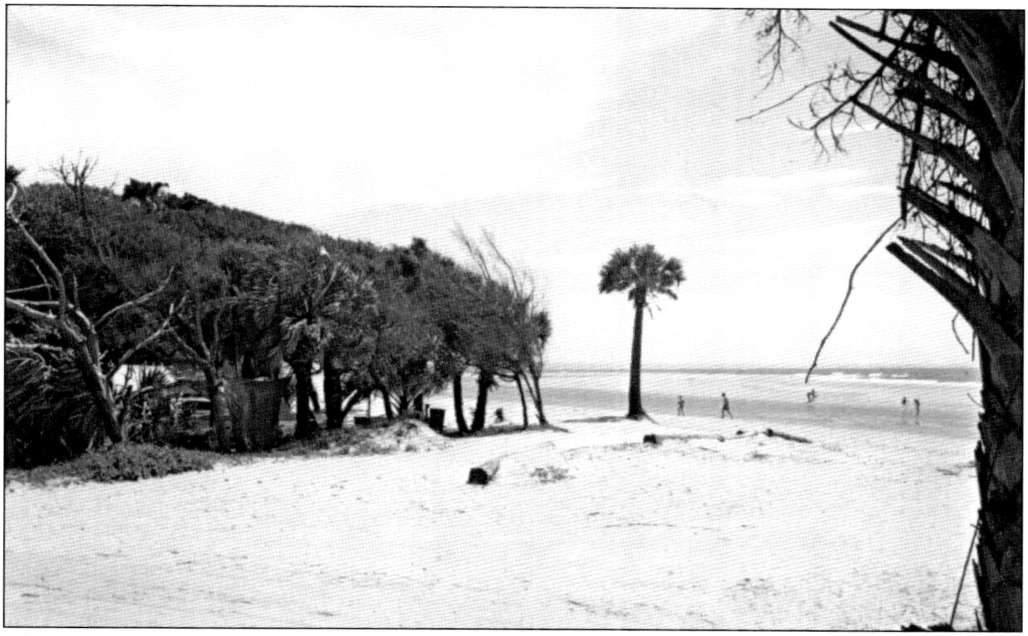

The Sand Dollar Campground was located at the north end of the island. Campers enjoyed the vast expanse of the beach and the natural canopy of pines, oaks, and palmettos. The facility offered 100 campsites with access to restrooms, power, and city water. It was open from March through November.

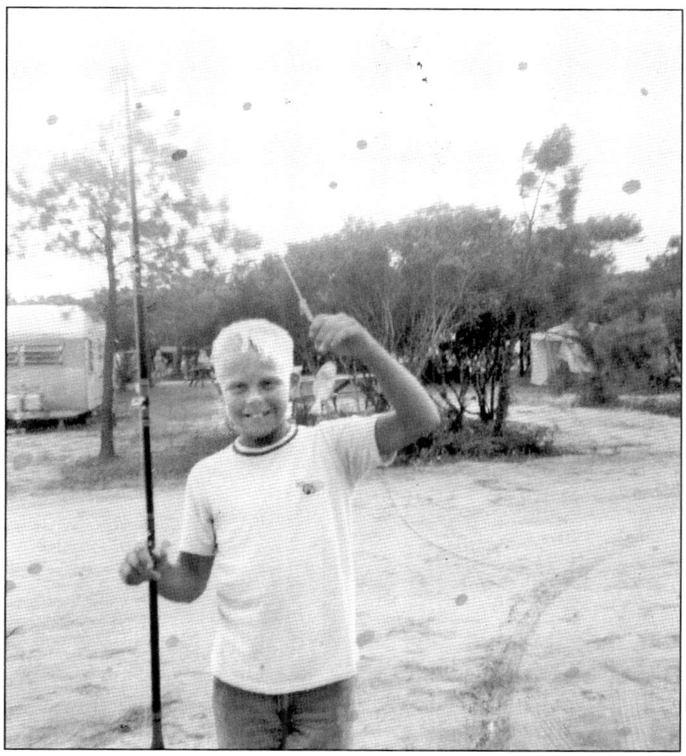

Lance Nilsen holds what is hopefully his bait and not his catch at the Sand Dollar Campground in 1966.

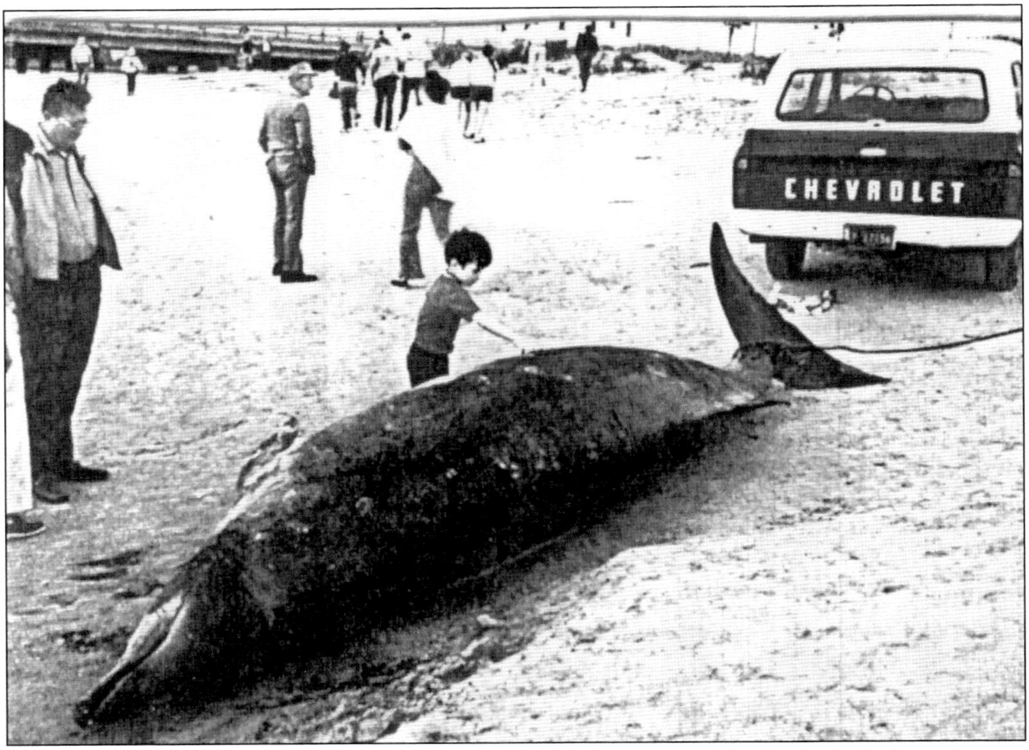

The beaked whale is the deepest and longest diving of all cetaceans. Because they communicate and navigate almost entirely using sound, they are very sensitive to acoustic pollution. This whale could have washed up at Breach Inlet due to all the shipping noise in Charleston Harbor. It is possible that sonar used by the ships from the Charleston Navy Base disoriented the whale. Since the time this picture was taken, the U.S. Navy has factored the welfare of sound-sensitive marine life into sonar development.

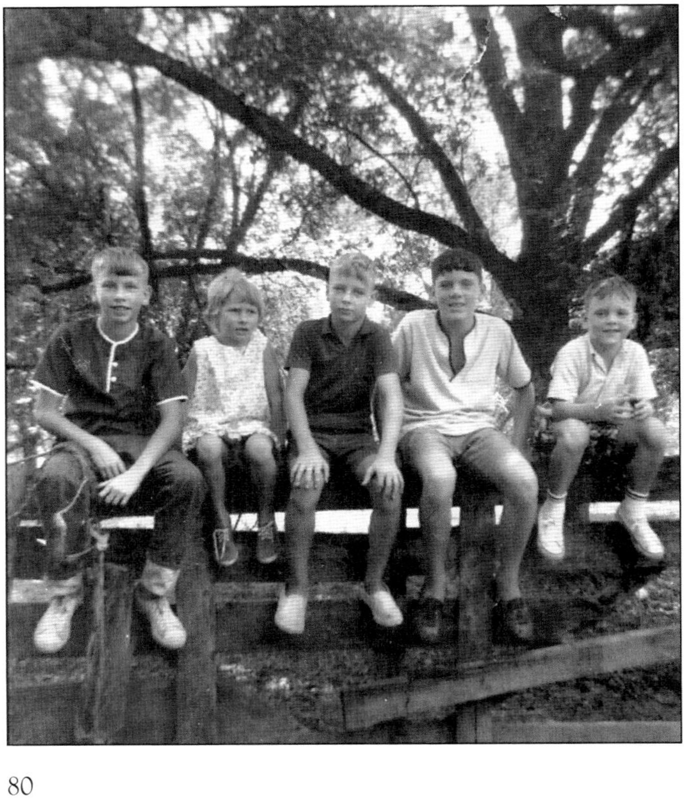

Skipper Shaffer, Susan Shaffer, Scott Breland, Lon Ferguson, and Joey Ferguson take a break from the beach and relax on an oyster table.

This trio, known to many as Snap, Crackle and Pop, are friends of 45 years. All long-time Isle of Palms residents, they are Snap Campsen (left), Phyllis Shaffer (center), and June Schirmer (right).

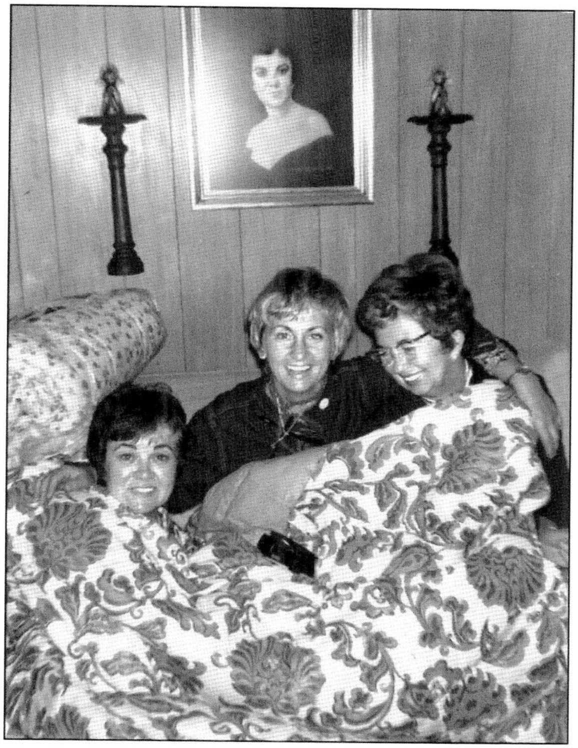

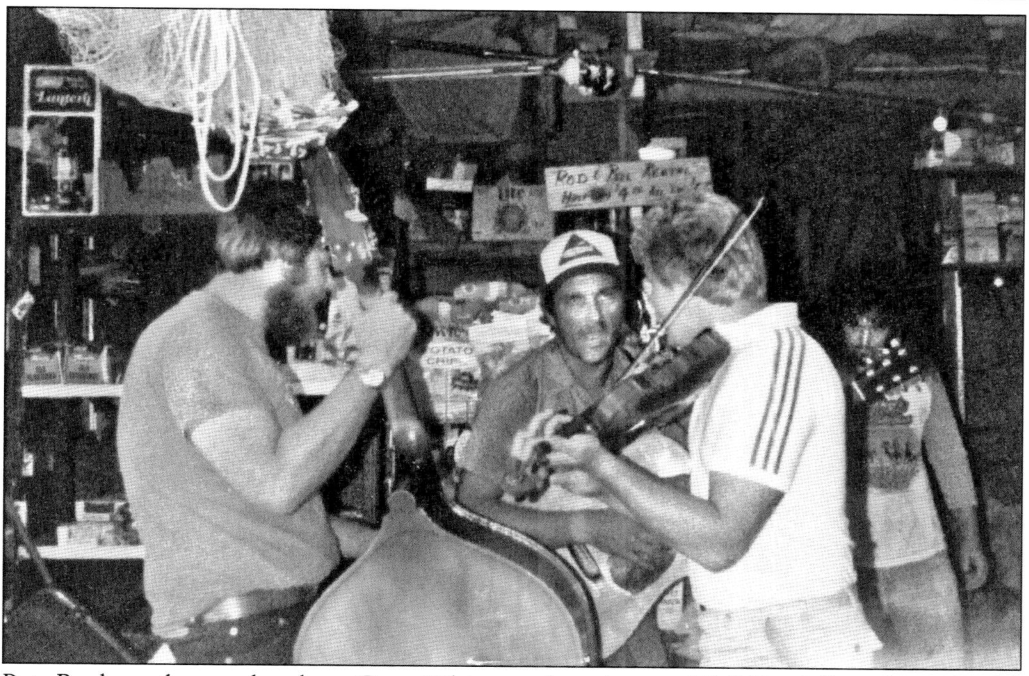

Pete Rock on the stand up bass, Gene White on the guitar, and Bill Kendall on the violin fill the old Texaco Marina with the sweet melody of bluegrass music. The trio played with the Homeboys, a local band popular with island residents.

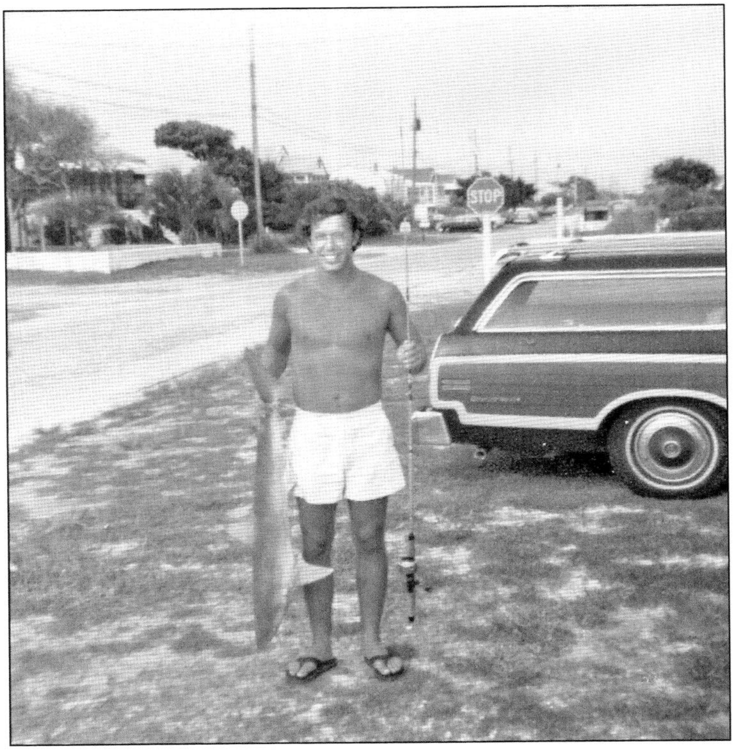

It is nice to know that fishermen like Hammond Bamberg curtail the shark population in an ocean so inviting to swimmers.

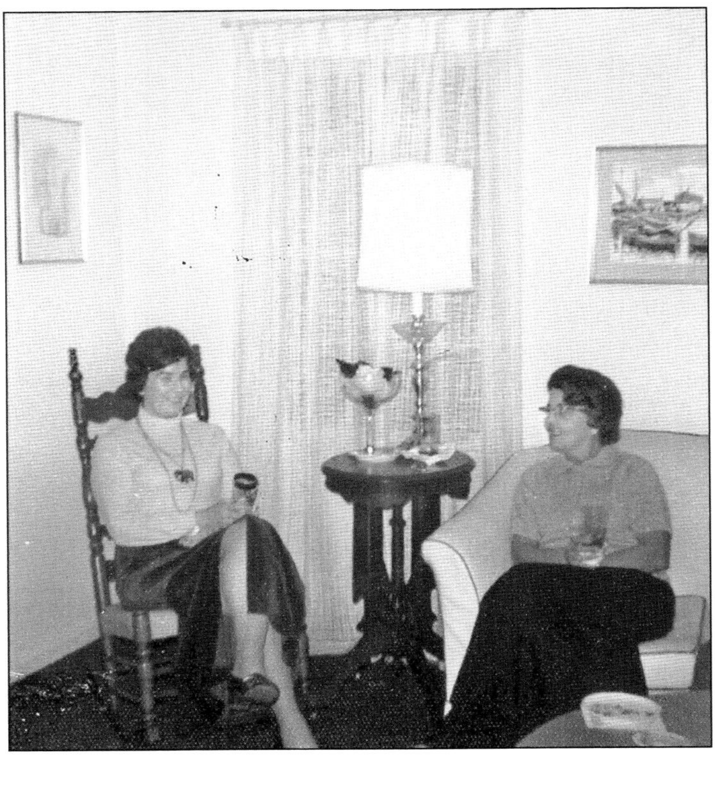

Mary Fletcher and Mariana Blair were fixtures on Isle of Palms. This photo was taken at James and Marge Sexton's 25th anniversary party in 1972.

Will Hegler dabbles his toes in the surf. Hegler, now a local artist, uses his Lowcountry roots as inspiration to create unique paintings in oil. His work is available through his Mount Pleasant studio and website, *www.heglerart.com*.

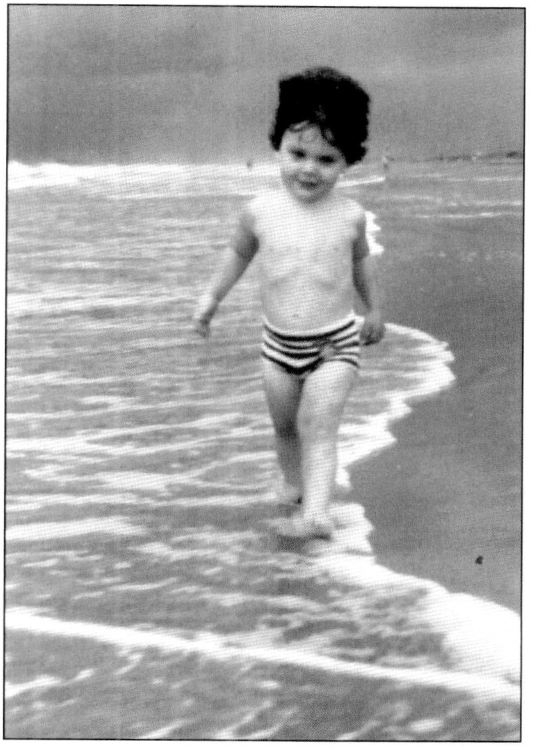

These youngsters enjoy the day at the Exchange Club's Junior Fishing Rodeo, held at the Isle of Palms fishing pier. Participants of the event included Timmy Dangerfield, Herman Lamkin, Carl McCants, Puggie Dudley, Bill Chamness, John Masnick, Roy Wilson, Charlie Turner, Jimmy Wear, and Fred Eschweiler.

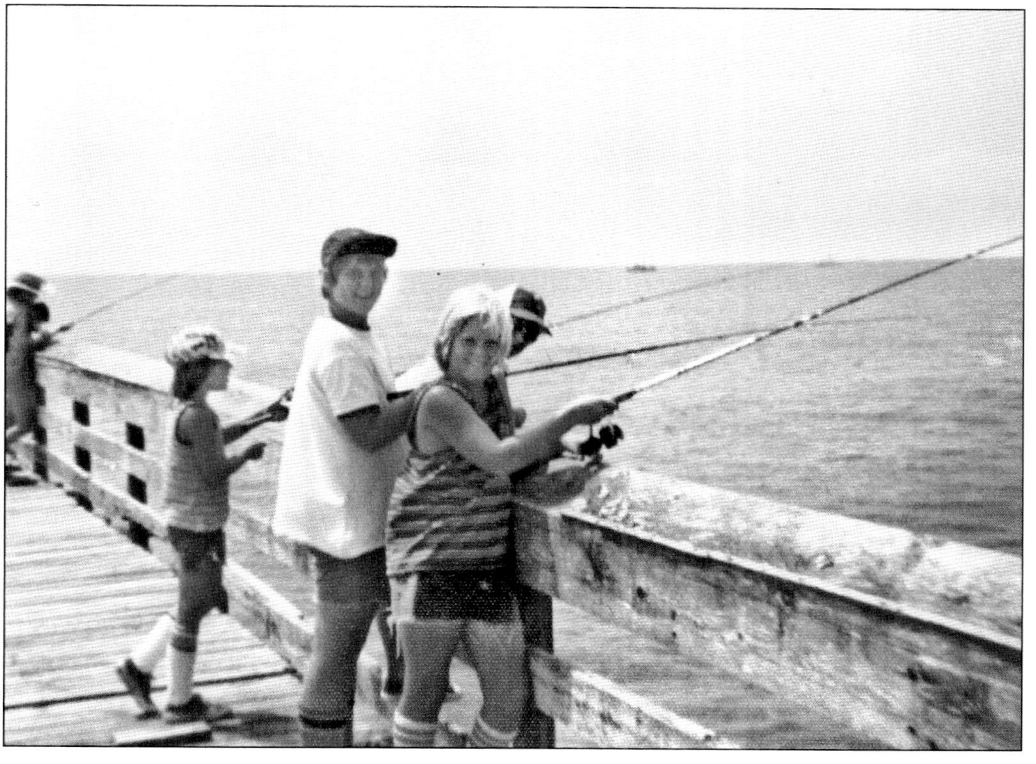

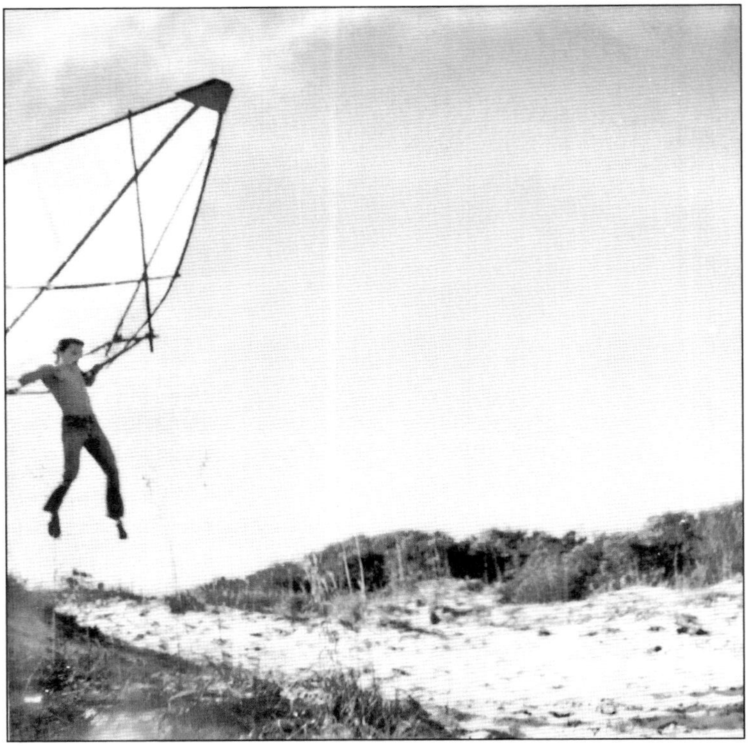

The recreation possibilities on the island are endless. Lang Shaffer lands his hang glider on the white sand beach.

Wendy Nilsen (Pollitzer) shows off her Windjammer Beach Bash of 1977 T-shirt. Although too young to attend herself, surely Wendy's parents had themselves a "jam good time!"

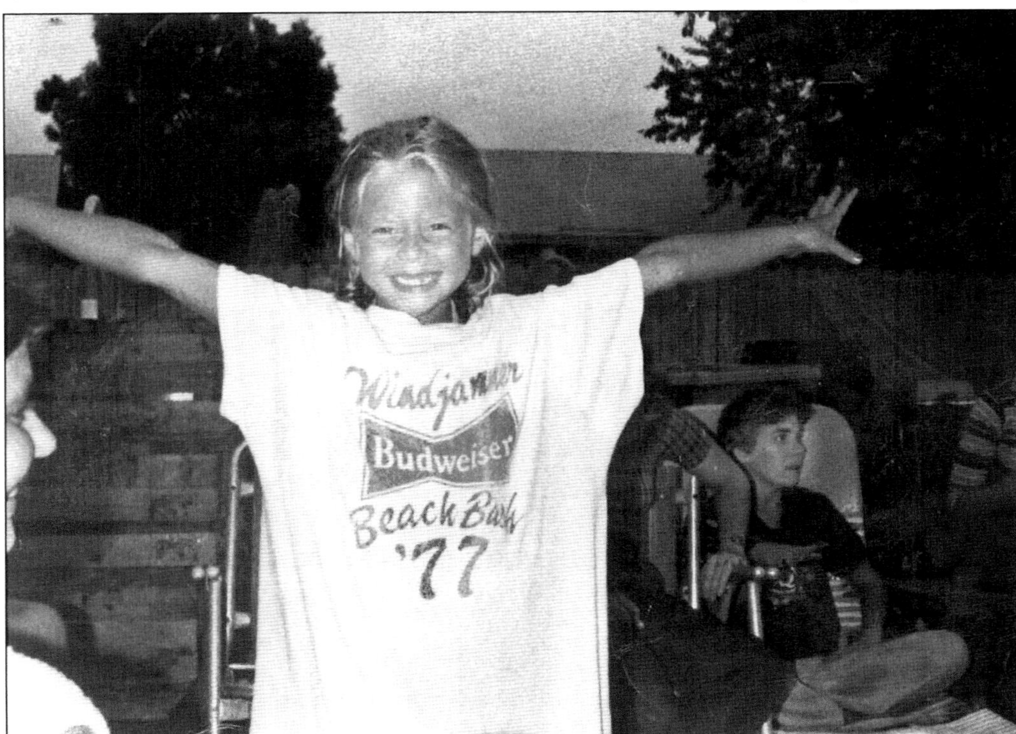

Jim Sexton Sr. returns a volley at Isle of Palms Beach and Racquet Club in 1978. The mobile unit in the rear served as the club's office in the early years.

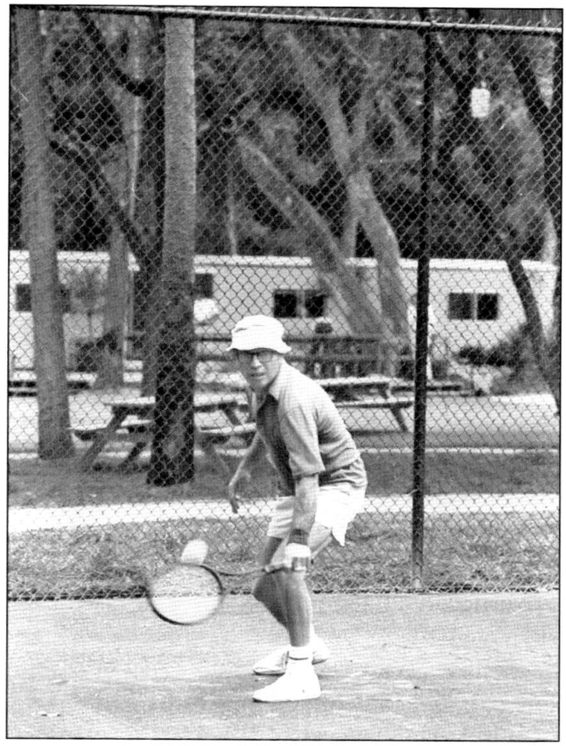

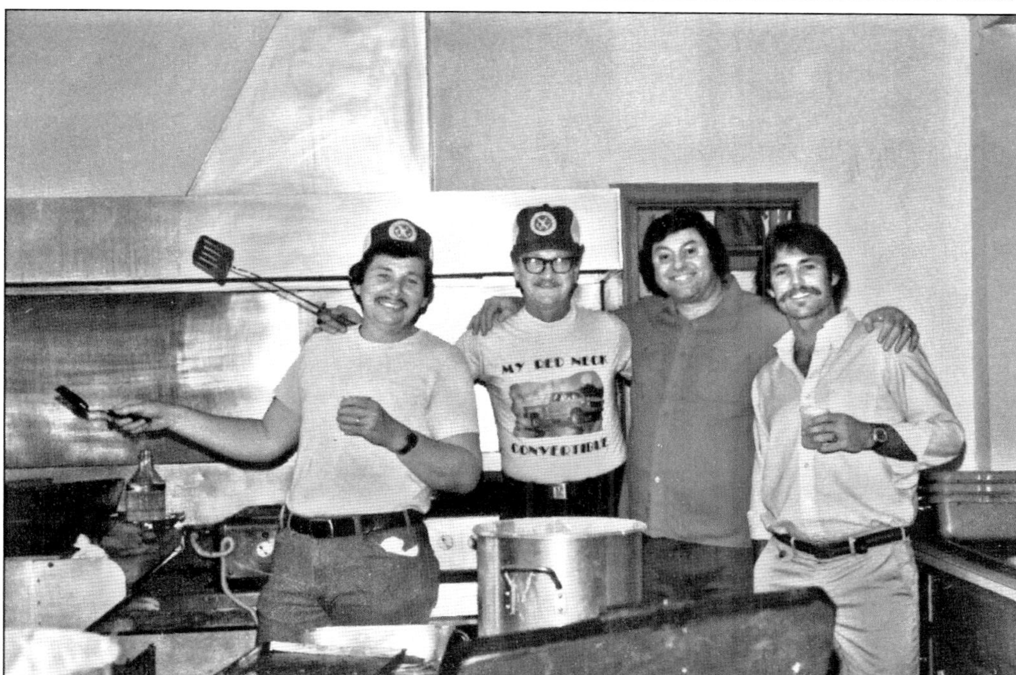

Cooks Buddy Campbell, John Masnick, Nat Joyner, and Jim Carroll take a break from flipping flapjacks at the Exchange Club's annual Easter pancake breakfast.

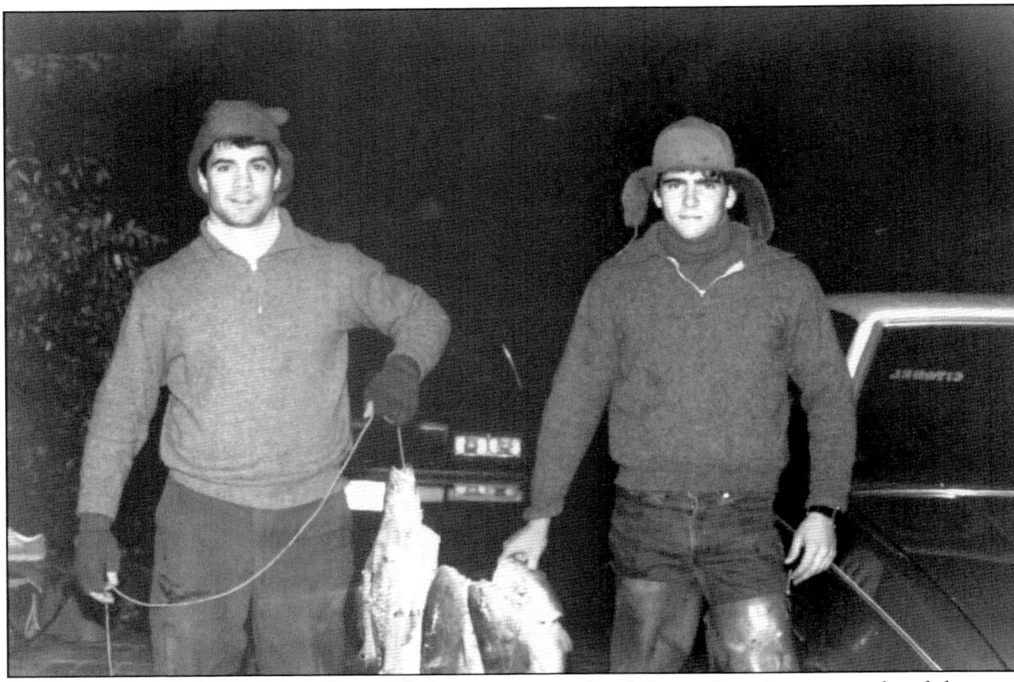

Chip and Richard Campsen show off their stringer of red drum. In winter months, fishermen enjoyed gigging for spottails rather than casting for them. The fish are slower than normal, making them easier to spear.

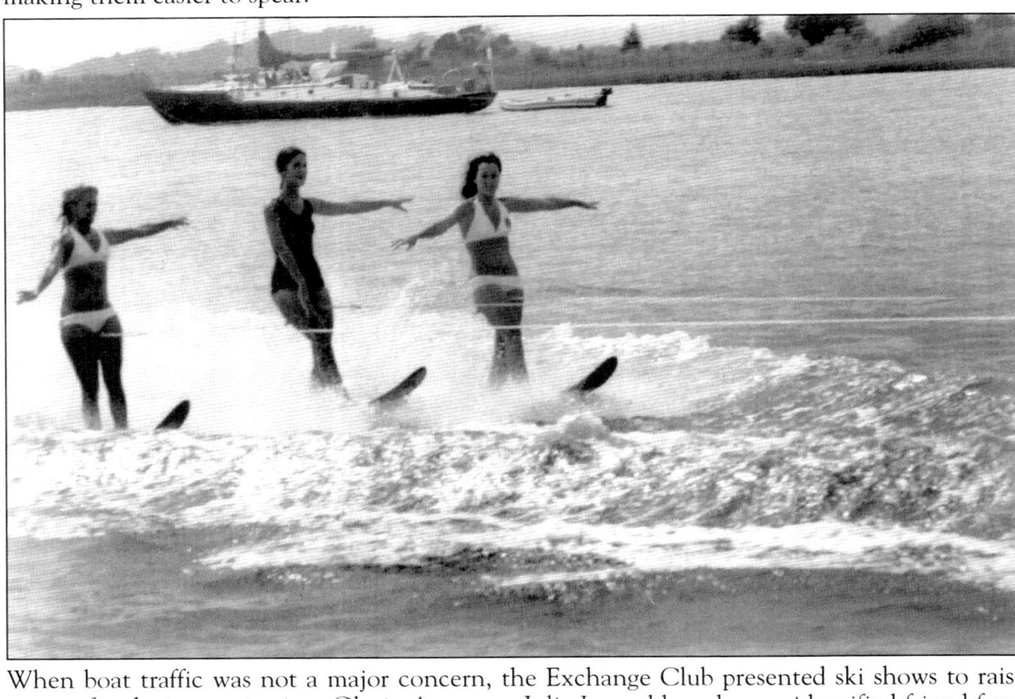

When boat traffic was not a major concern, the Exchange Club presented ski shows to raise money for their organization. Gloria Amerson, Julie Leopold, and an unidentified friend from Charleston slalom gracefully on top of the glass-like water.

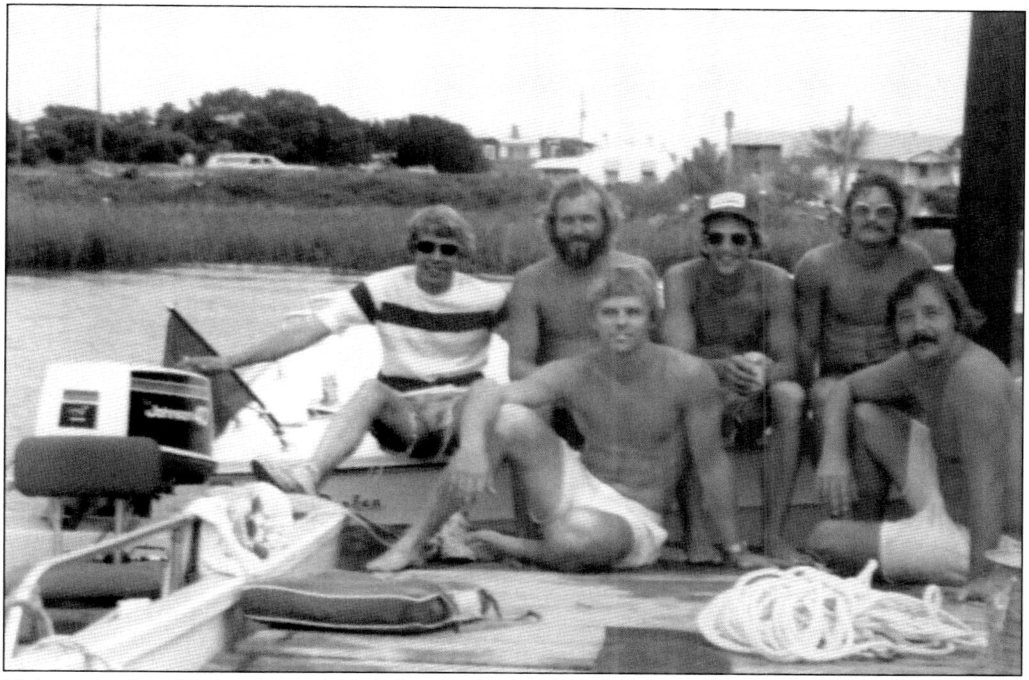

Volunteers for the ski show, from left to right, included (front row) an unidentified volunteer and Roy Leopold; (back row) Mike Rumph, Gene White, Thomas Siegler, and Gary Hazelton. Is there a better way to raise money than to spend an afternoon on the boat?

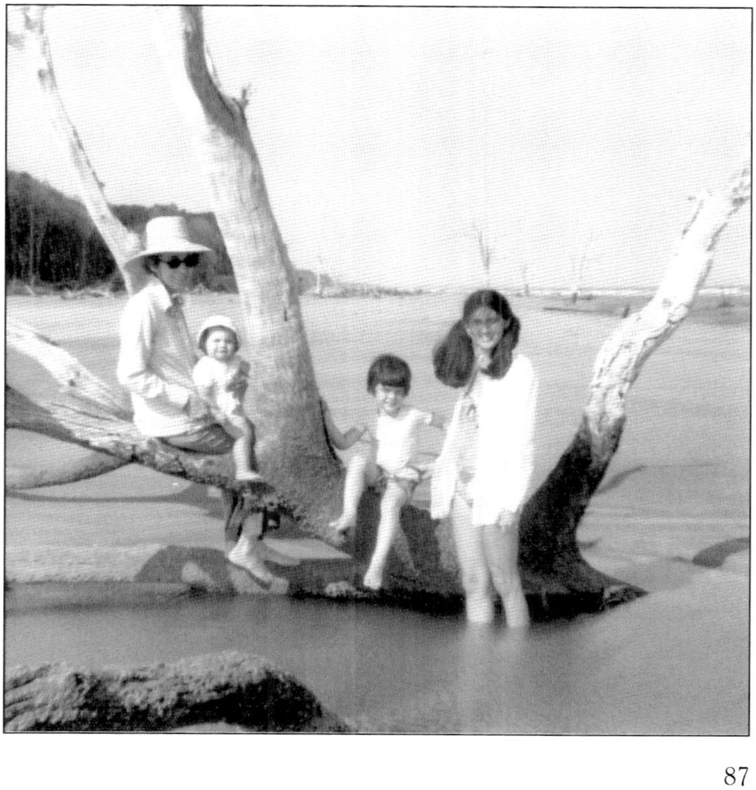

Mary, Ginny, Will, and Dale Hegler pose on a large piece of driftwood in the "boneyard" on Capers Island, another barrier island just north of Isle of Palms. Capers is a heritage preserve maintained by the South Carolina Department of Natural Resources (SCDNR). The island is open to the public year round, and primitive camping is allowed.

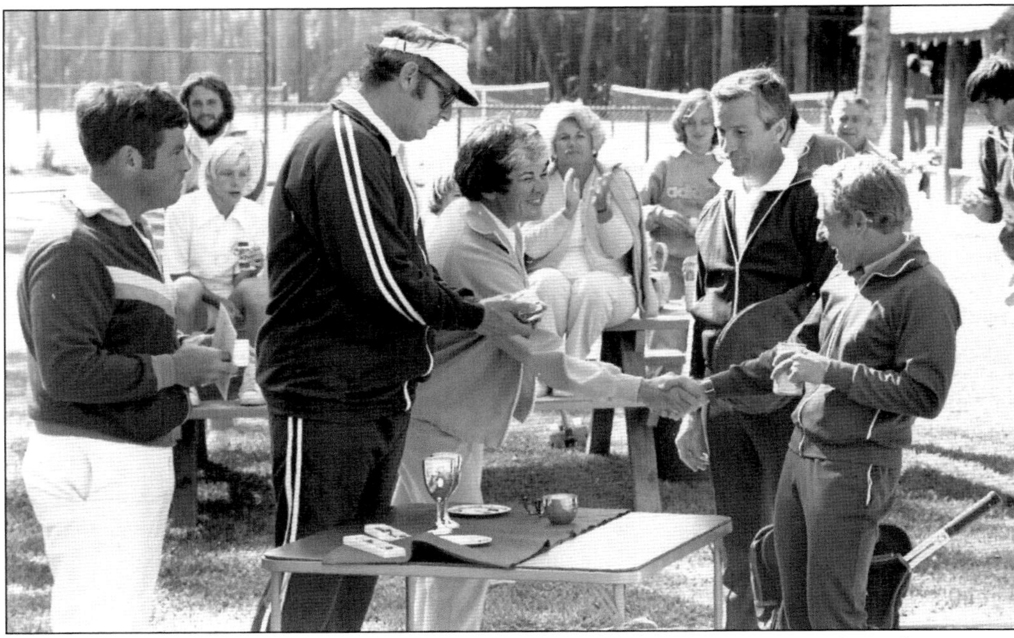

Billy Silcox looks on while Henry Finch and Snap Campsen present awards to the winners of the first Men's Doubles Tournament at the Isle of Palms Beach and Racquet Club in 1977. Accepting the prize are Dr. Peter Hairston and Dr. Bart Antine.

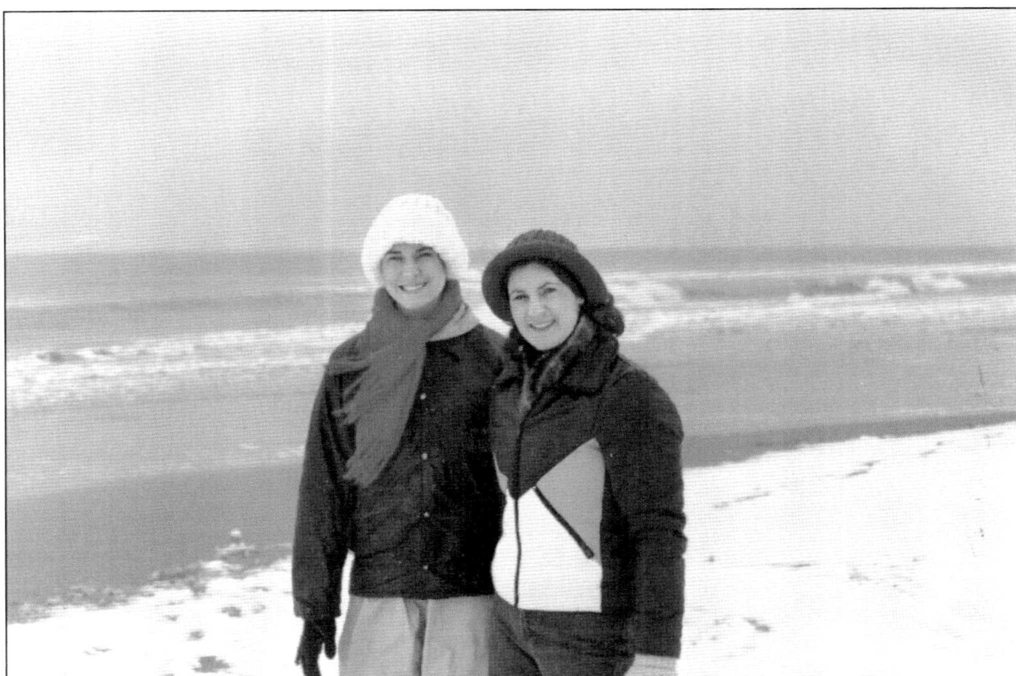

Cyndi Campsen (Mosteller) and Terrye Campsen (Seckinger) pose on the snow-covered beach, an oh-so-rare sight on Isle of Palms.

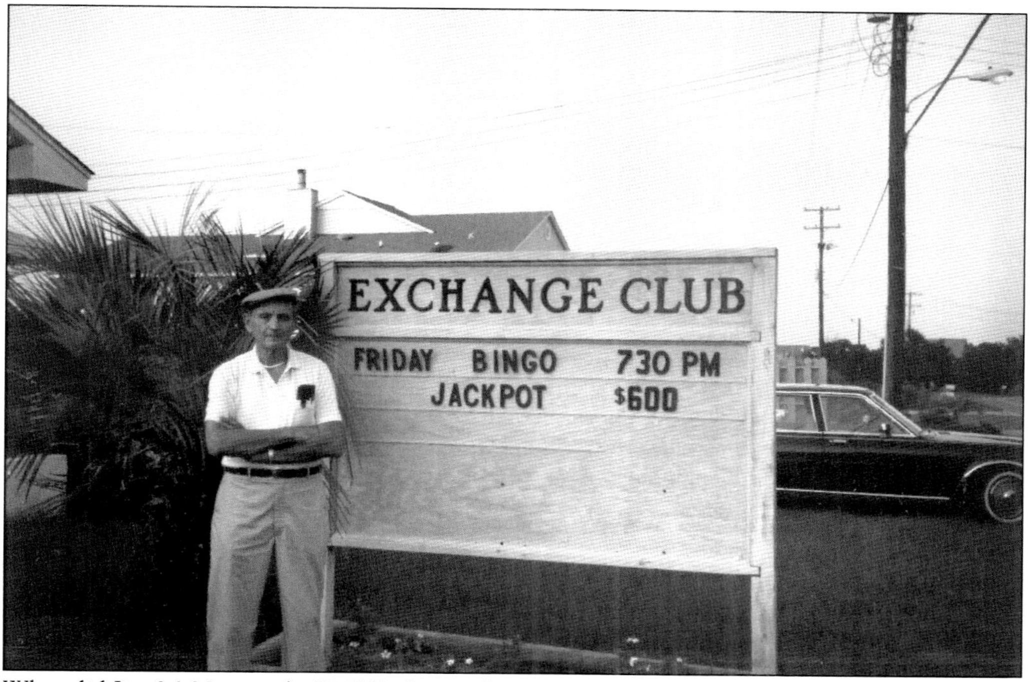

What did Jim McNamee do "B4" Friday Night Bingo? The "King of Bingo" earned his title by serving as the chief caller for 500 nights.

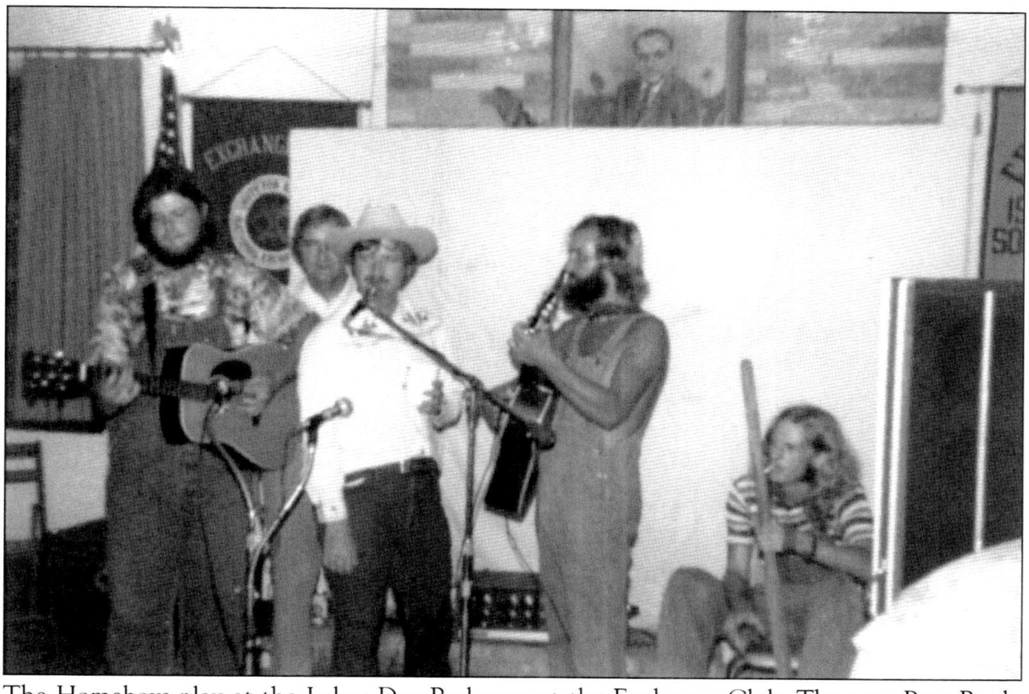
The Homeboys play at the Labor Day Barbeque at the Exchange Club. They are Pete Rock, Gary Irvine, Ernie Passailaigue, Gene White, and Ricky Morris. Members of the band not pictured are Bill Kendall and Doug Rock.

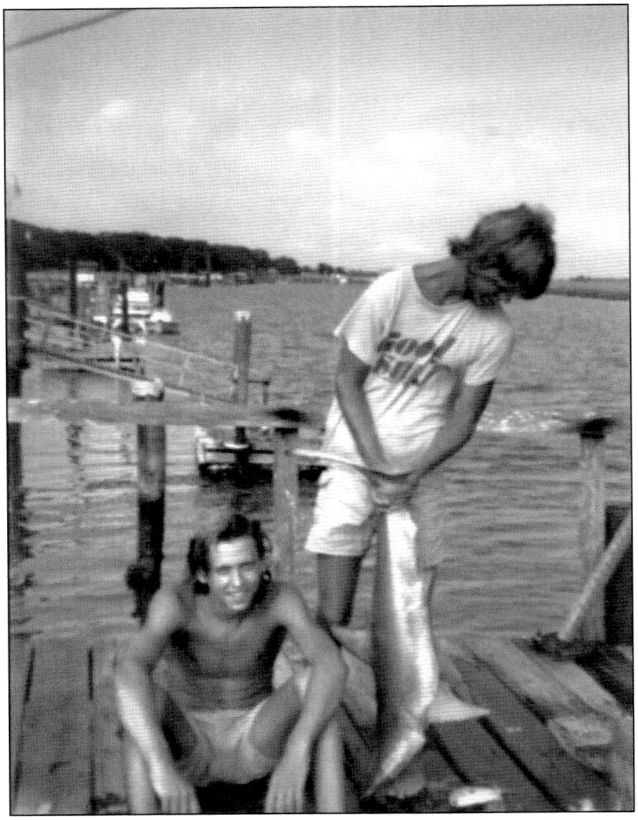

On a dock in Hamlin Creek, Lang Shaffer and Tommy Smith catch a small shark. Bathers and skiers beware!

McKevlin's Surf Shop, the oldest surf shop in South Carolina, opened on Isle of Palms in 1968. The cinder-block building stood where the Pavilion Shops stand today. Pictured are, from left to right, (front row) Donald Moody, Chris Casias, Kristina Falkehag, and Susan Prine; (back row) Francie McNeil (Varn), Lenny Spears, Mark Somersett, Steve Pugh, John Matthews, Jimmy Cole, Bob Fetter, Jerry Issac, Dolph Farmer, Phil Waselchalk (Lein), Ronnie Edwards, an unidentified young man, Greg Butler, and another unidentified passerby.

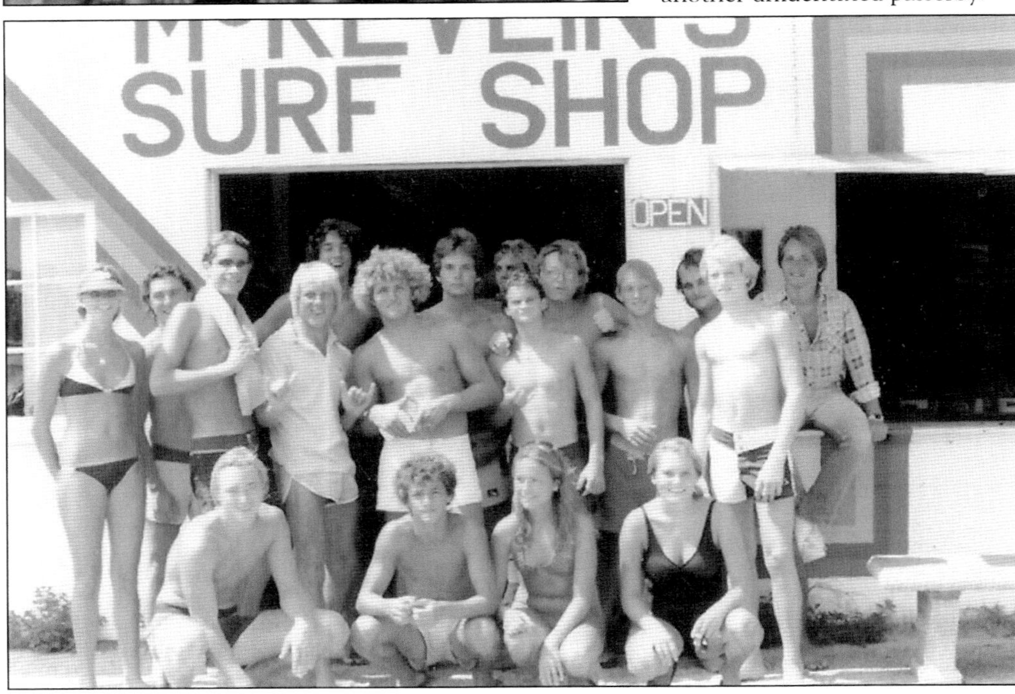

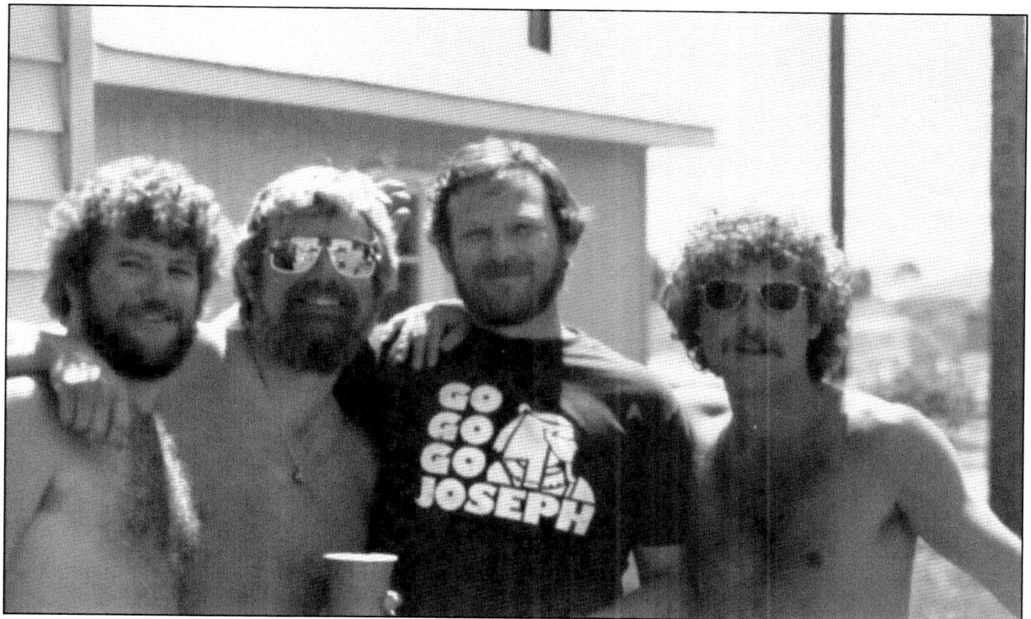

Allan Garner, Malcolm Burgis, Chuck Wheatley, and Bobby Ross enjoy a beautiful afternoon on the island. Malcolm's backyard hosted many a get-together for close friends.

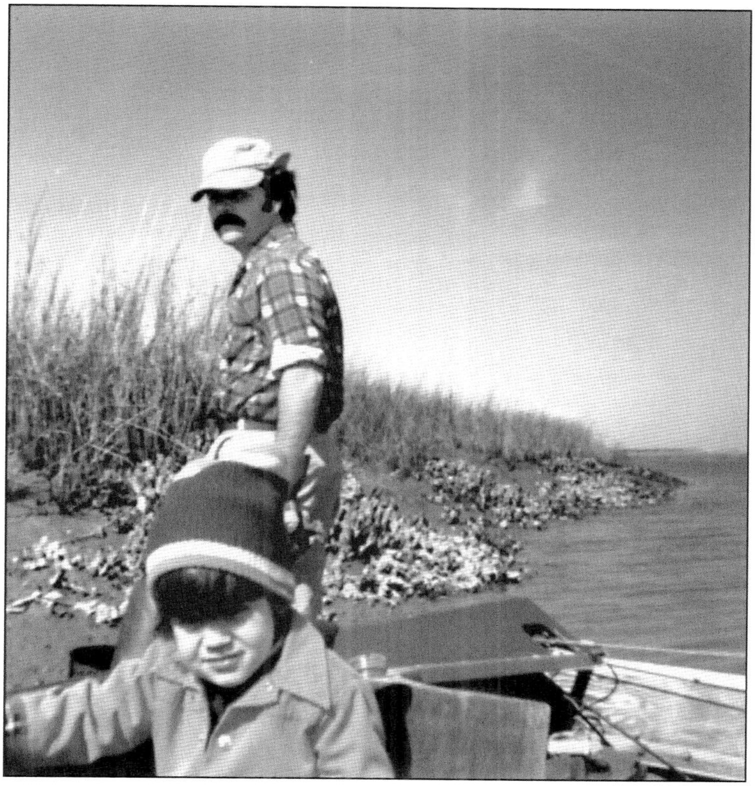

Theron and Will Hegler navigate their boat alongside oyster banks in Morgan Creek in search of a plentiful bed from which to harvest the saltwater mollusks. Shucking the steamed delicacies at the end of the day with the same callused hands that gathered them is quite a satisfying reward for the arduous task of oystering.

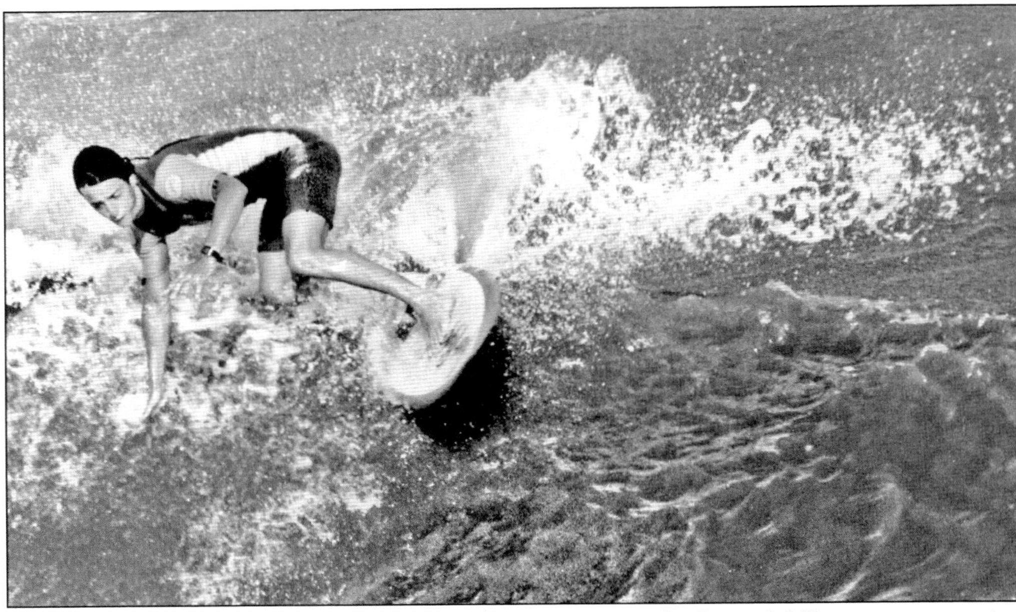

Dedicated surfers ride the waves year round. Mastering cut-backs and 360s requires practice, even in the winter months. Former Isle of Palms resident and surfing veteran Chris Casias maneuvers his board in the breaking wave. Now a real-estate agent with The Beach Company, Chris has traveled to Hawaii, Costa Rica, Cape Hatteras, and various spots in Florida to pursue his passion for surfing.

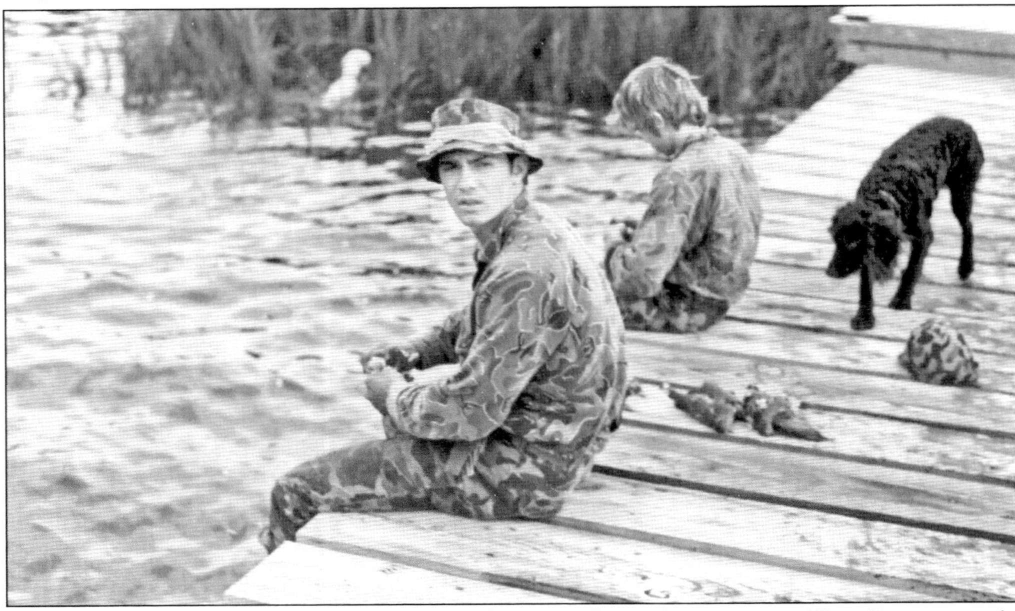

Chip and Richard Campsen and their dog Duka return from a hunting trip. Chip Campsen is the current state senator representing District 43. An honorable statesman, Mr. Campsen's awards include the Order of the Palmetto, given by Gov. Mark Sanford, and Conservationist of the Year, given by the South Carolina Wildlife Federation. A strong advocate of land conservation, Chip credits his love for nature to his active childhood on Isle of Palms.

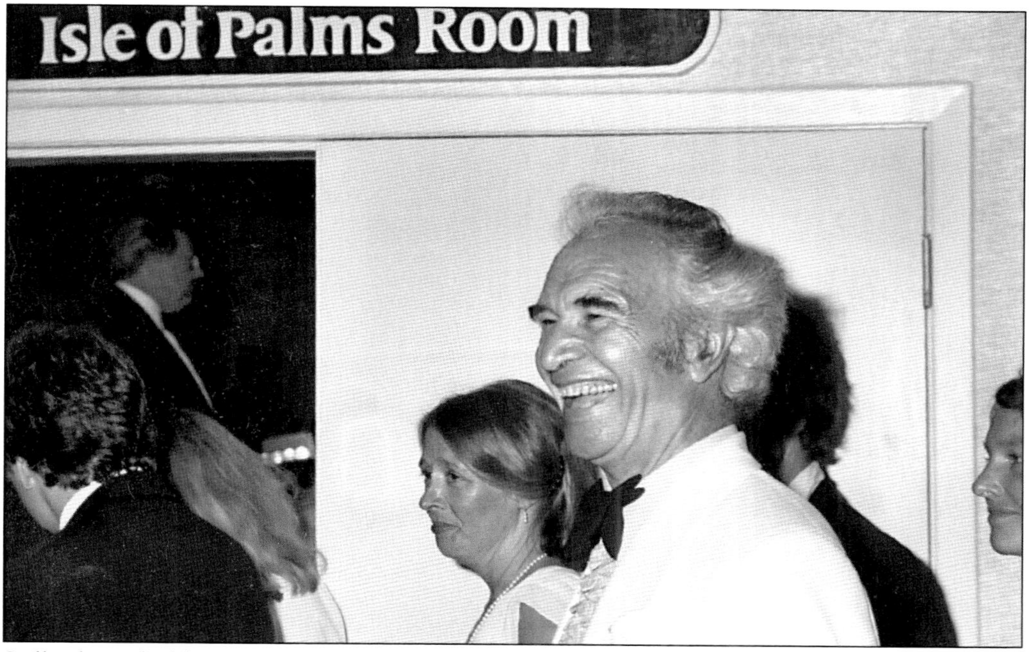

Still a household name in modern jazz, Dave Brubeck is a legendary pianist who, along with icons like Miles Davis and John Coltrane, popularized jazz for the masses. The Dave Brubeck Quartet, featuring saxophonist Paul Desmond, was a central attraction at almost all major international jazz festivals. He is seen here after performing at a Spoleto event outside of the Isle of Palms Room at Wild Dunes.

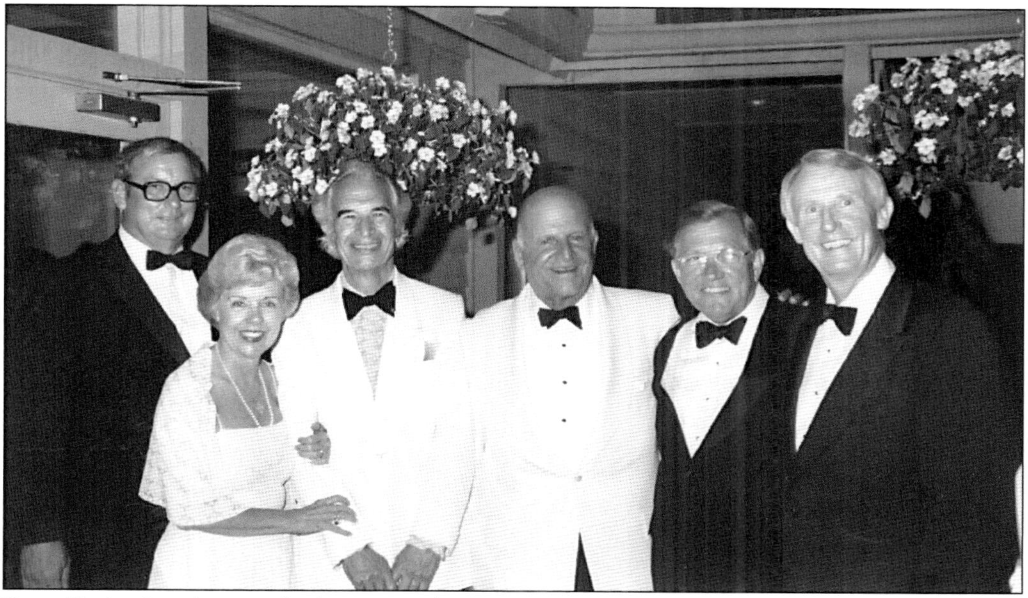

Dave Brubeck is known for his unusual time signatures and mismatched key signatures. His credits include "Take Five" and "Blue Rondo a la Turk." Henry Finch, First Lady of South Carolina Ann Edwards, Brubeck, Ted Stern, Gov. James B. Edwards, and Raymon Finch Jr. mingle after the sensational performance.

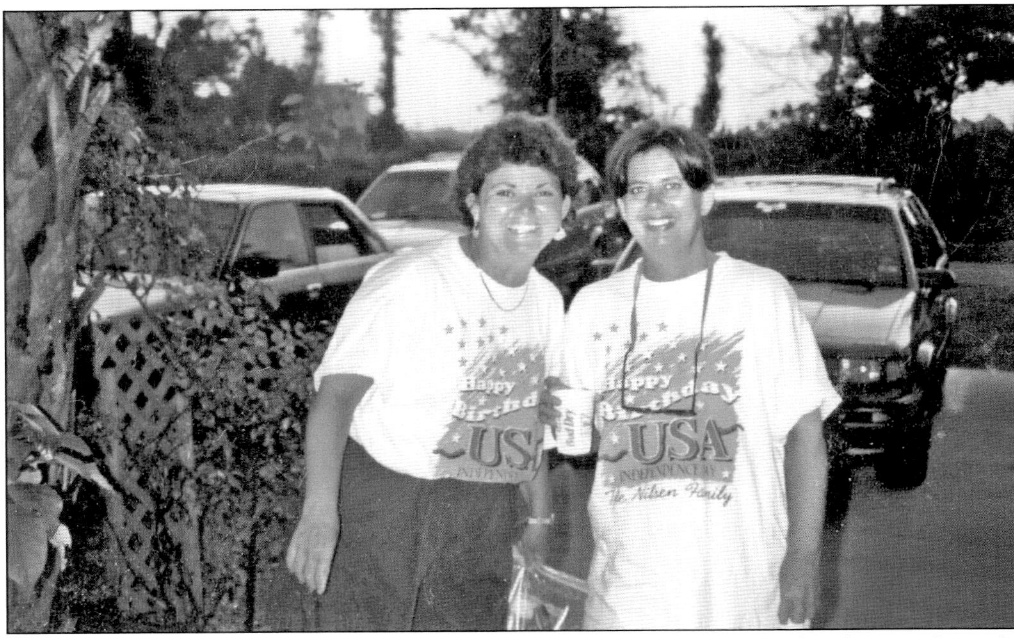

Dale and Shirley Nilsen celebrate Independence Day on Isle of Palms with t-shirts wishing the United States a happy birthday. The Fourth of July has been a favorite holiday for families on the island for years. Although fireworks are banned for personal use, the City of Isle of Palms, Wild Dunes, and island businesses put on a spectacular fireworks show free of charge.

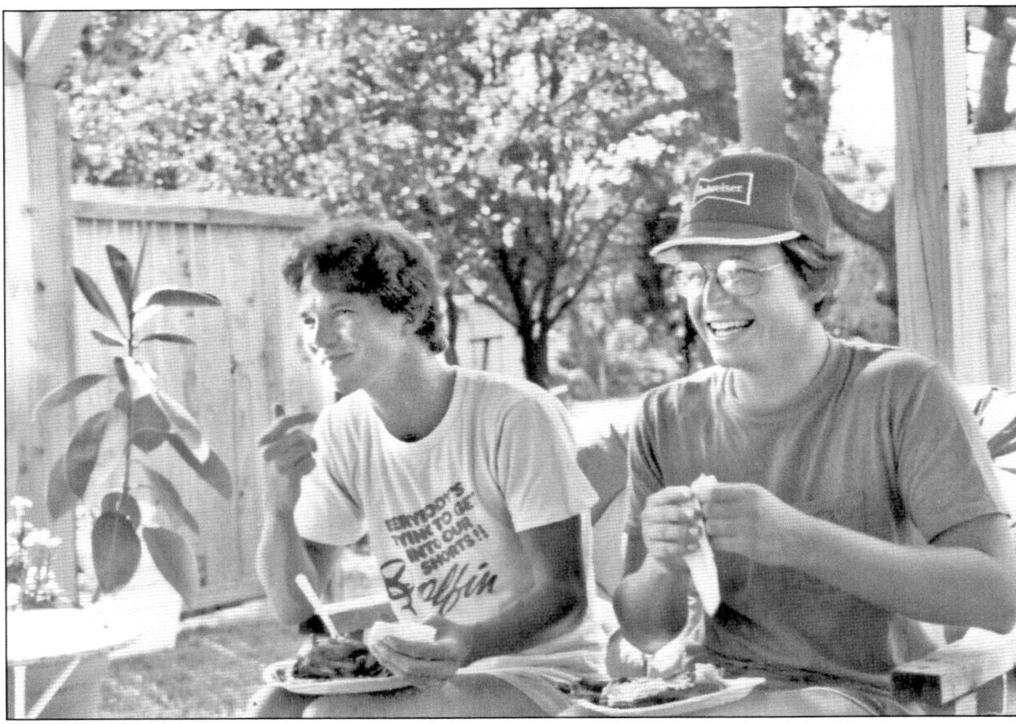

Island pals Timi Kennedy, left, and Phil Waselchalk (Lein) enjoy a backyard barbeque.

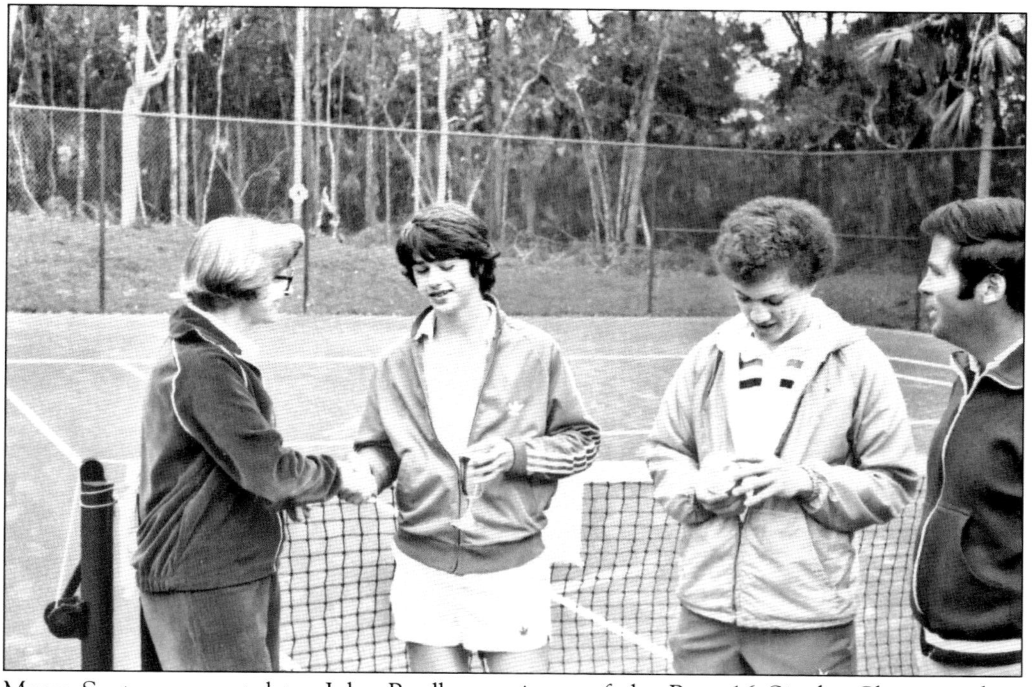

Marge Sexton congratulates John Bradham, winner of the Boys 16 Singles Championship. Standing beside John are runner-up Fred McKay and Billy Silcox.

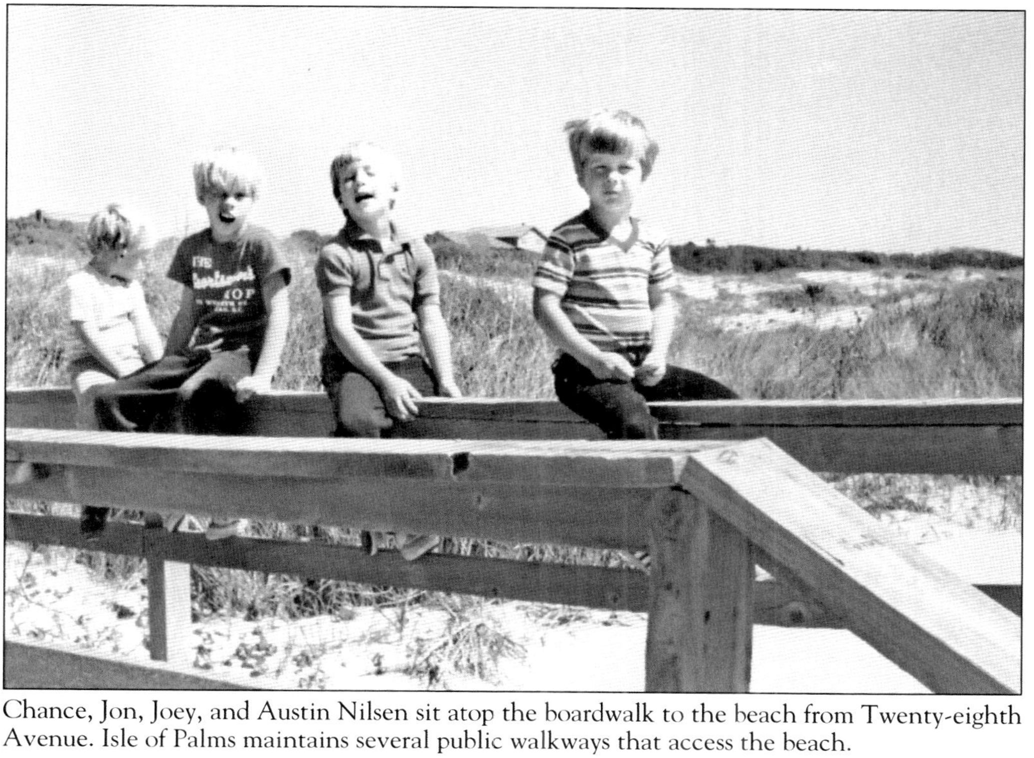

Chance, Jon, Joey, and Austin Nilsen sit atop the boardwalk to the beach from Twenty-eighth Avenue. Isle of Palms maintains several public walkways that access the beach.

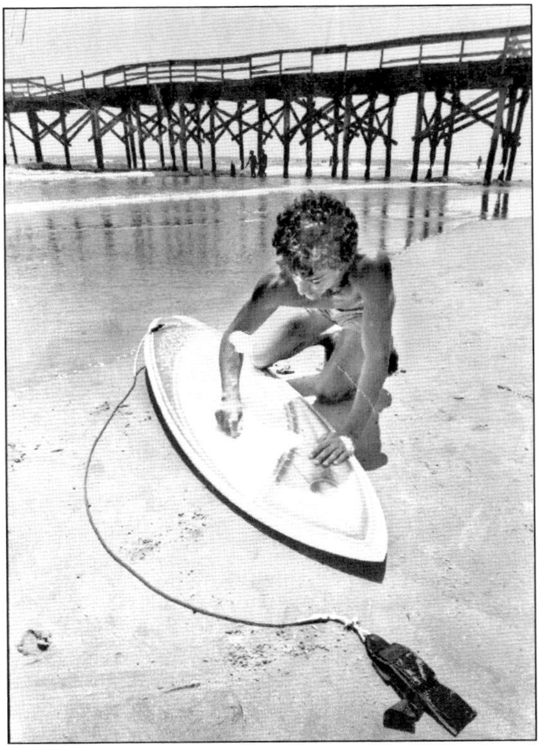

Chris Casias waxes his twin-fin board on the beach in front of the collapsing fishing pier. A popular surfing spot in 1981, the pier attracted athletes from all over the Lowcountry. Summer months are still the best for fine surfing on Isle of Palms, especially when low-pressure systems stall off the coast.

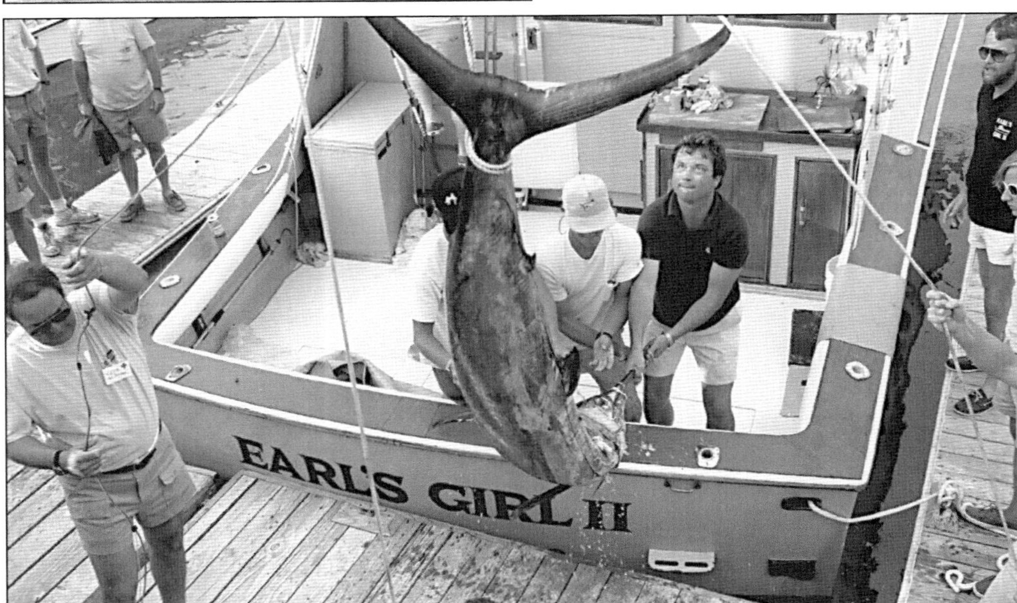

Angler Bo Stallings landed this 206-pound blue marlin caught on *Earl's Girl II* in May 1987. These fish make trans-Atlantic migrations, moving toward the equator in winter and away from it in the summer. Blue marlin are more scattered off the Carolina coast in the summer since temperatures do not restrict them to the Gulf Stream. They are most abundant in 300 to 1,200 feet of water.

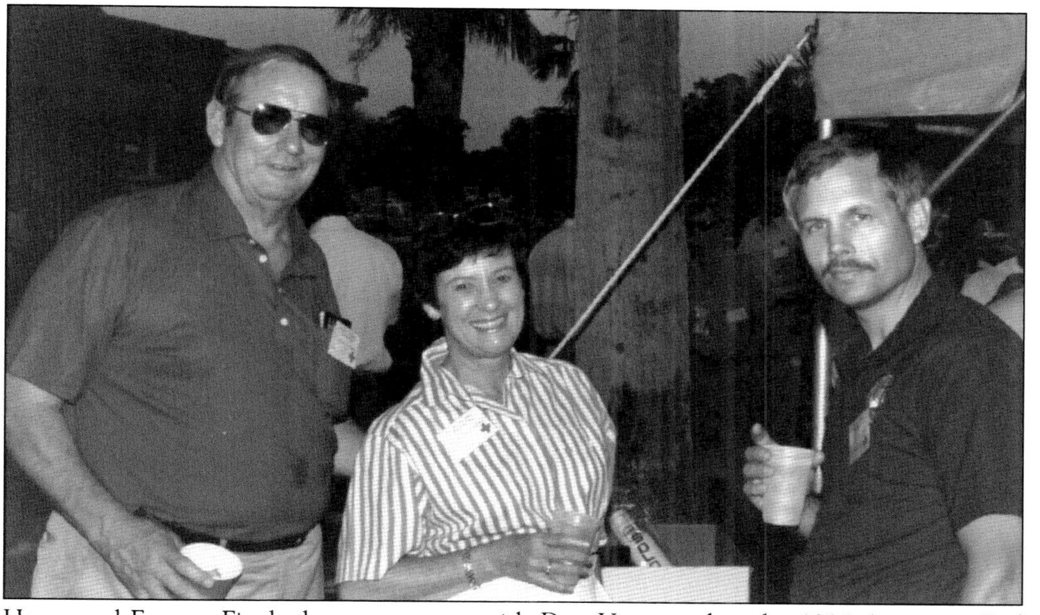

Henry and Frances Finch share a moment with Don Hammond at the 1988 American Red Cross Fishing Tournament at Wild Dunes Yacht Harbor (now Isle of Palms Marina). Mr. Hammond is the Governor's Cup Billfishing Series director for SCDNR. The series encourages the tagging and release of tournament billfish and awards points to anglers who participate in the very successful program.

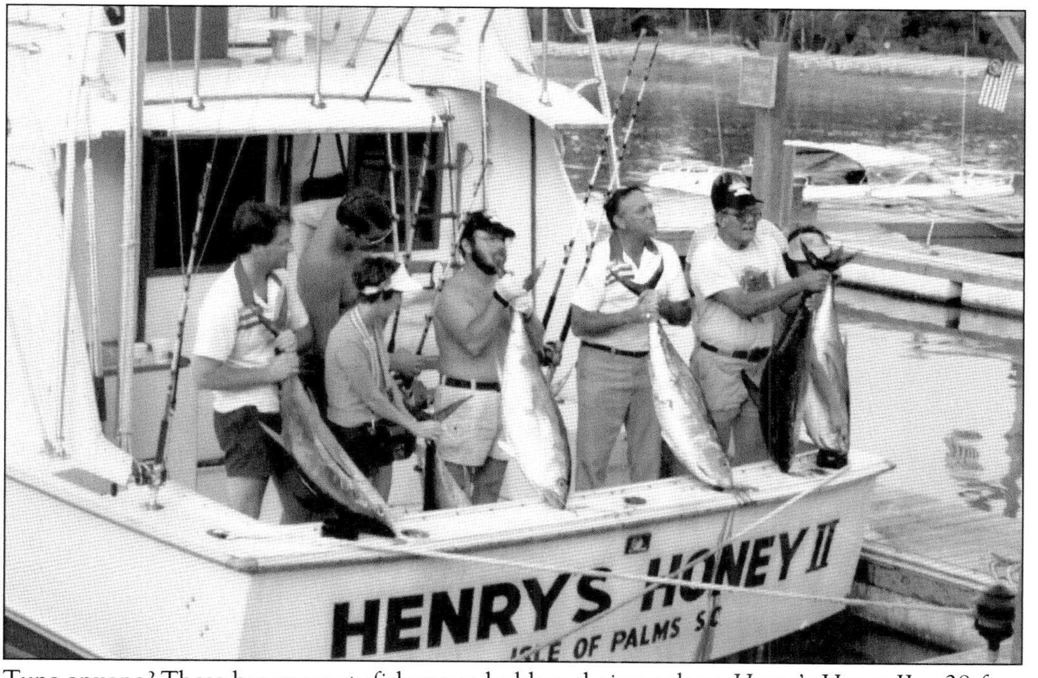

Tuna anyone? These happy sports fishermen hold up their catch on *Henry's Honey II*, a 38-foot Hatteras from the Isle of Palms. Hatteras boats were the first in the industry to use solid fiberglass hulls, allowing for calmer rides on rough seas.

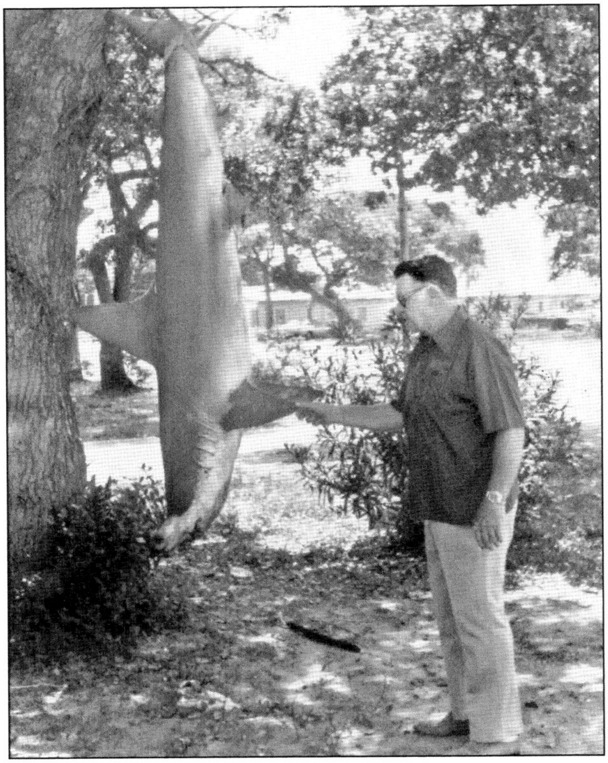

Stanley "Swede" Nilsen checks the fin on this large hammerhead shark caught off the beach. Danger lurks beneath the deep blue sea—or, in this case, beneath a tall oak tree!

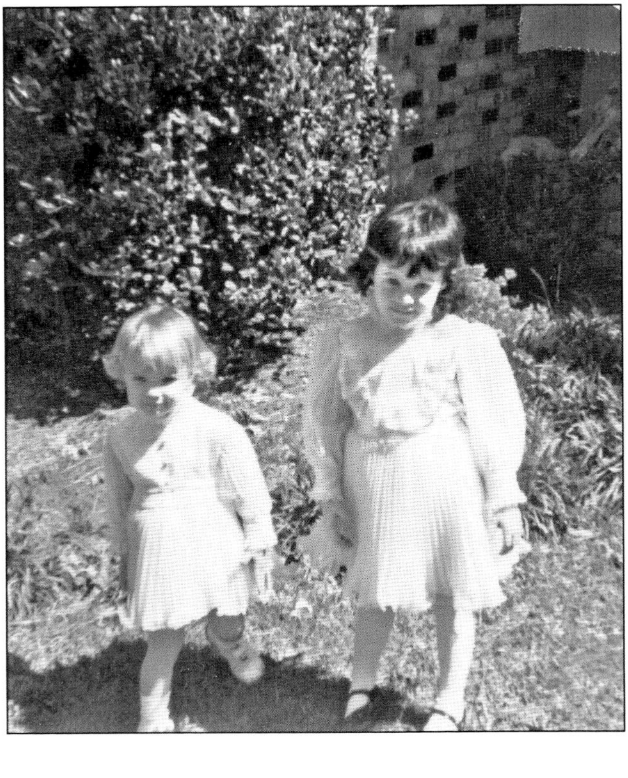

Robin Potter (Price) and Wendi Potter (Lynn) show off their Easter outfits before heading to Sunday school at Isle of Palms Baptist Church. On a nice day, the girls could walk from their house on Twenty-first Avenue to the church on Twenty-fourth.

Randy Webb dangles a red drum from his Boca Grip, a measuring handle used to weigh the trophy fish prior to releasing it. Randy's apparel is evidence enough that red drum remain abundant in tidal creeks and estuaries throughout the year.

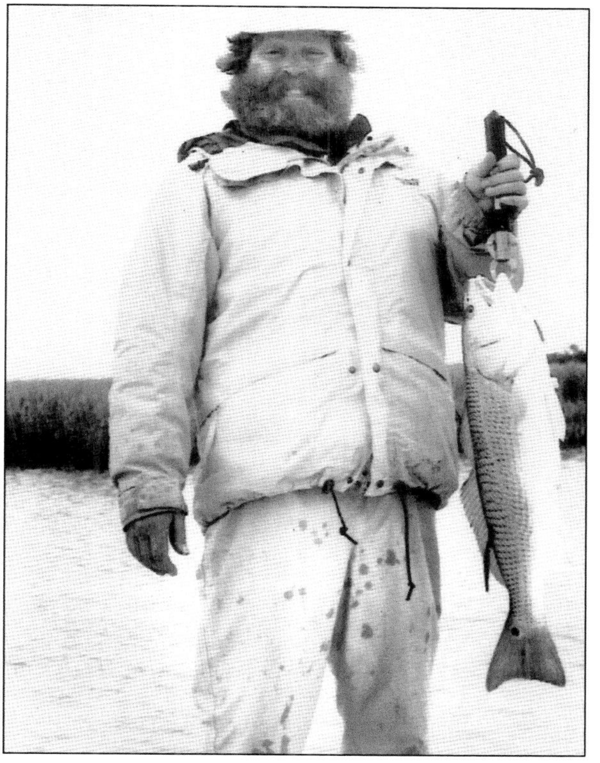

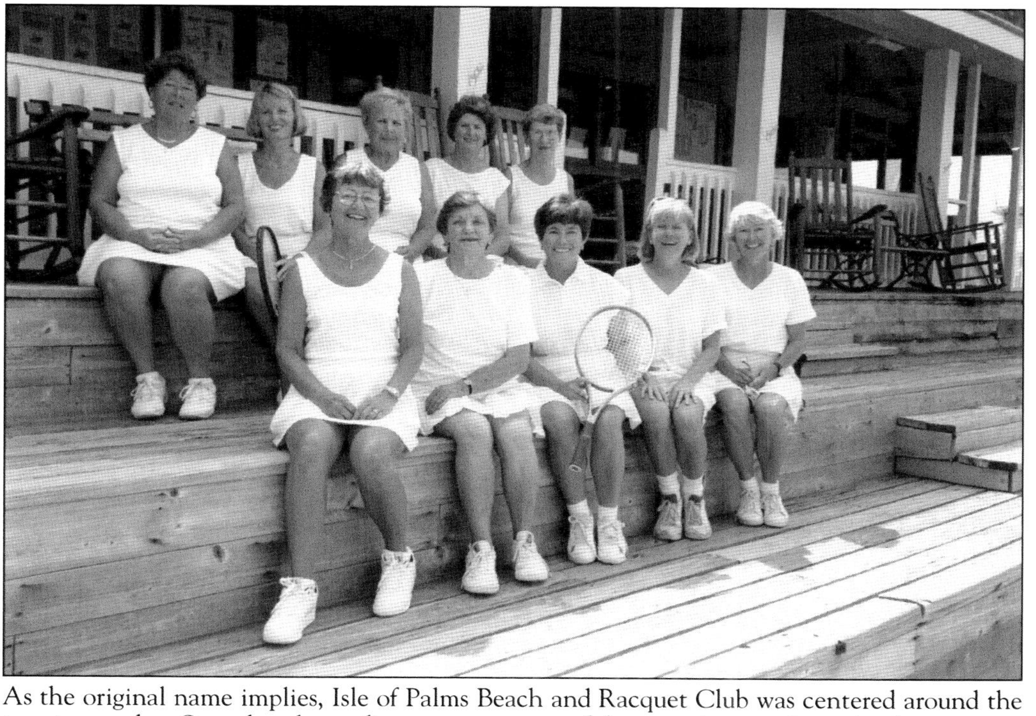

As the original name implies, Isle of Palms Beach and Racquet Club was centered around the tennis complex. Seated at the stadium court are one of the resort's state championship teams.

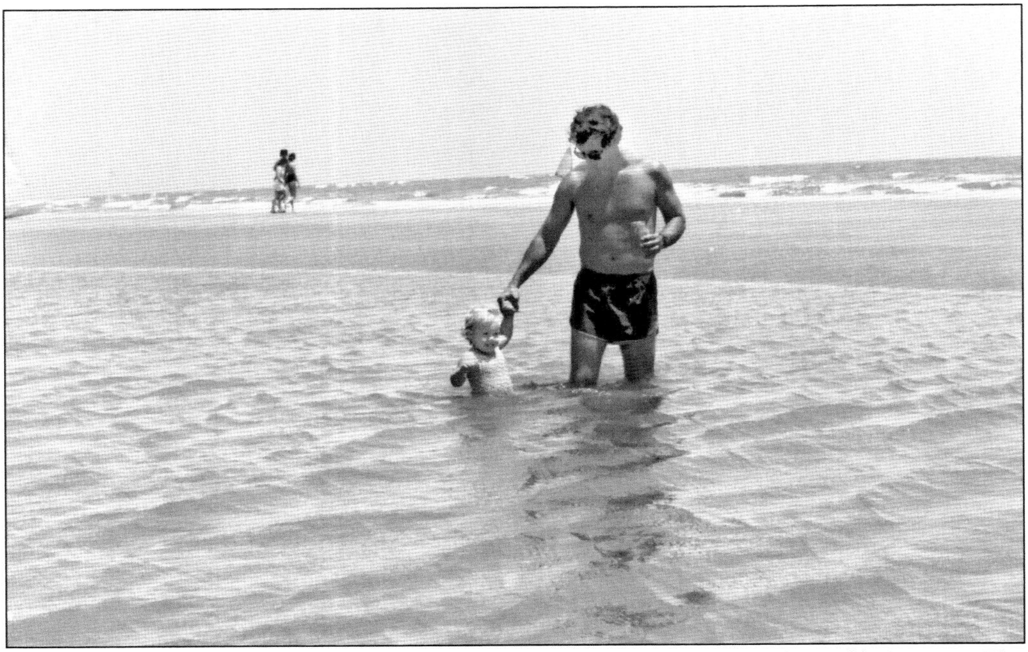

Hammond Bamberg and his daughter, Shay, wade through the tidal pool at Fifth Avenue. The huge gully appears at low tide every day between Third and Tenth Avenues. The warm water and lack of waves makes it an ideal spot for small children.

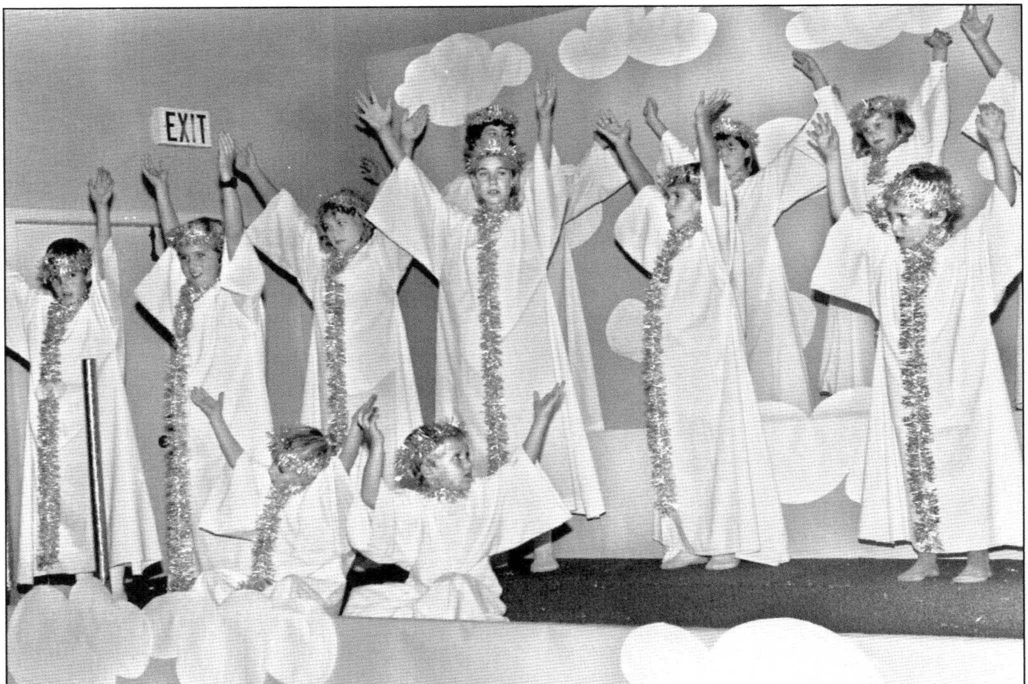

These young performers sing "Hark, the Herald Angels Sing" at the children's Christmas program at Wild Dunes on December 4, 1983.

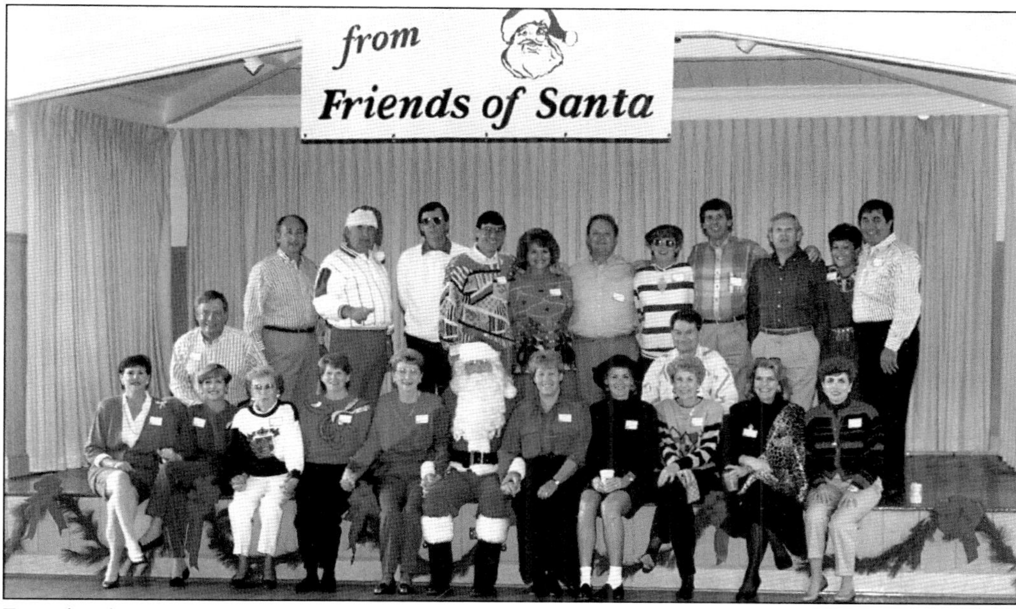

Friends of Santa is a special group dedicated to helping the less fortunate during Christmas. Proceeds help feed, clothe, and bring gifts to needy residents East of the Cooper. Pictured are, from left to right, (front row) Diane Finklestein, Nancy Rotteger, Bill Rotteger, Rita Tener, Chris Williams, Anne Shaffer, Santa (Henry Shaffer), Joyce Baxter, Janice Fetter, Bill Lee, Tootie Lee, Louise Webb, and Beth Murph; (back row) Stuart Fetter, Bill Tener, Jim Williams, Ted van Thullenar, Barbara van Thullenar, Bobby Bryant, Jackie Wear, Tom Murph, Lester Finklestein, Linda Weed, and Jimmy Wear.

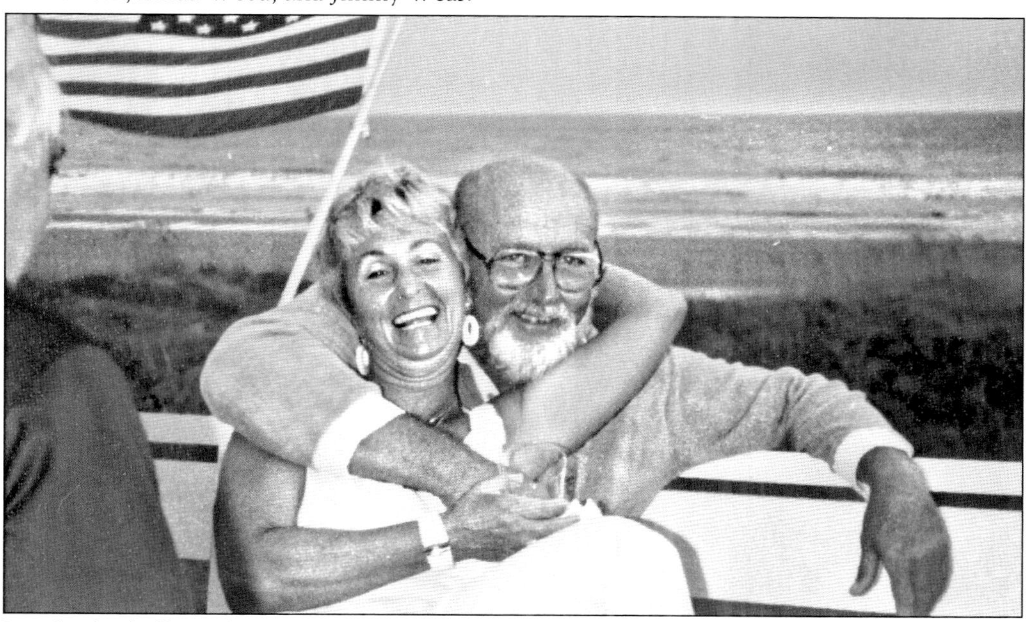

Lovebirds Phyllis and Wally Shaffer Jr. share a hug on a beautiful evening in July. The two wed in 1952 and spent all of their married years on Isle of Palms. Behind them, the American flag waves and the sea oats dance to the summer breeze coming off the magnificent Atlantic.

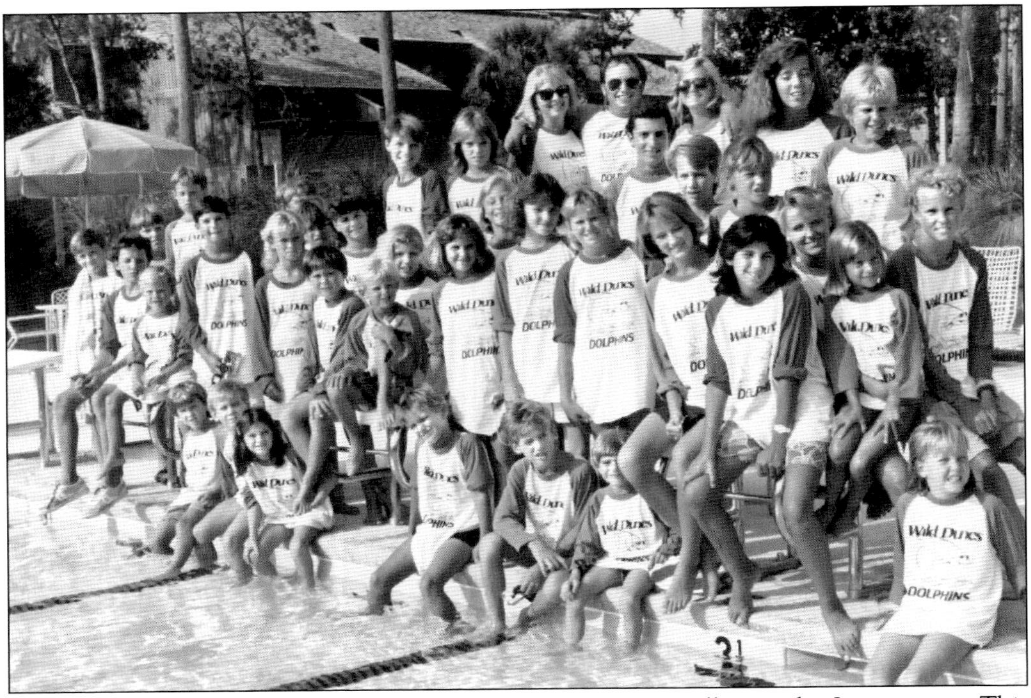

The 1986 Wild Dunes Dolphins competed with swim teams all over the Lowcountry. This group shot was taken right before a meet.

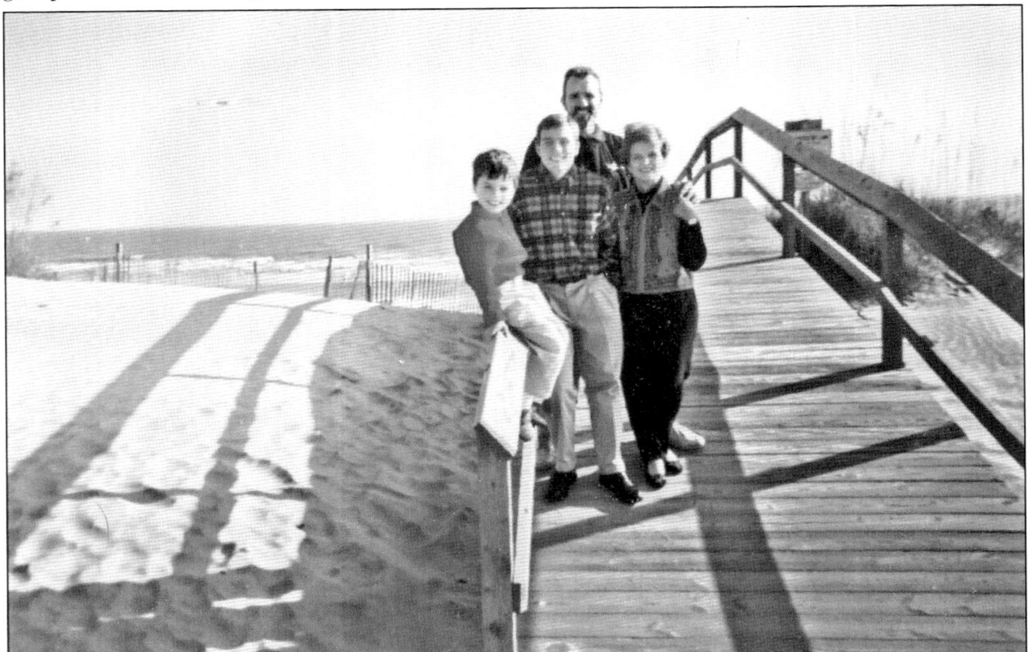

Bill, Norma, Will, and Josh Kulseth gather on the boardwalk for a family photo. Bill, co-owner of the Windjammer, and Norma, a schoolteacher at Laing Middle School, settled on Isle of Palms because it is such a wonderful place to raise children.

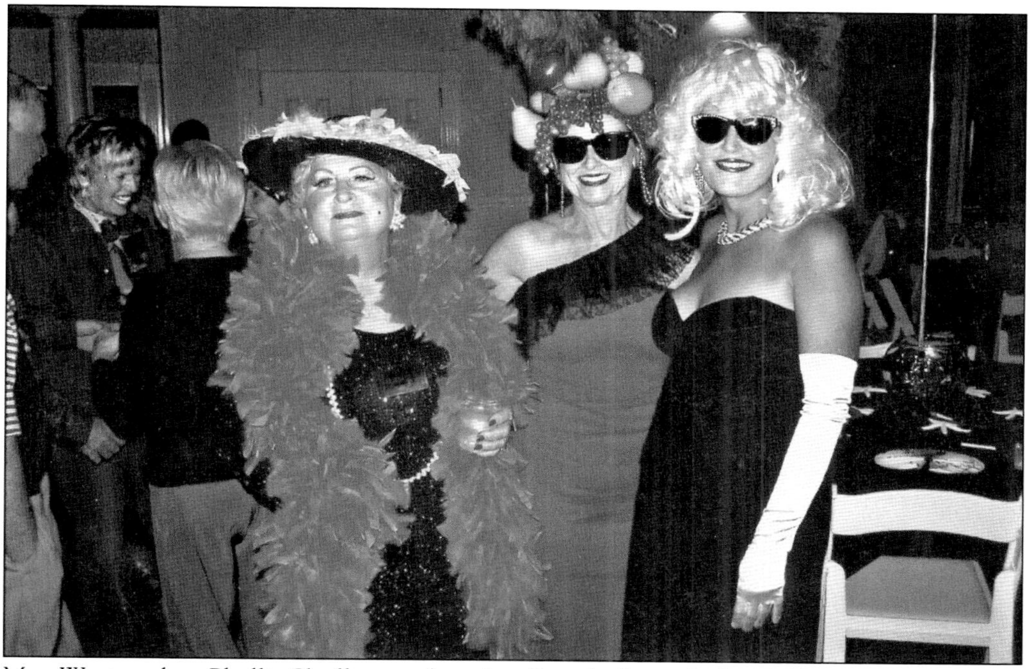

Mae West—a.k.a. Phyllis Shaffer—and starlets Brenda Rosenthal and Sharron Martin share a photo opportunity at an annual bash given by Isle of Palms resident Vicki Hollingsworth (not pictured).

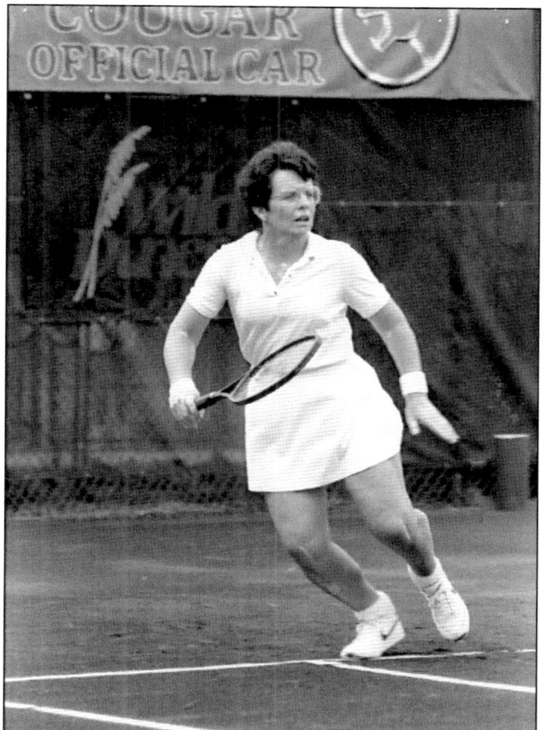

Billie Jean King played at Wild Dunes in 1985 at the Lincoln-Mercury Tennis Classics Tournament. King was a crusader for women and their right to earn comparable money in tennis and other sports.

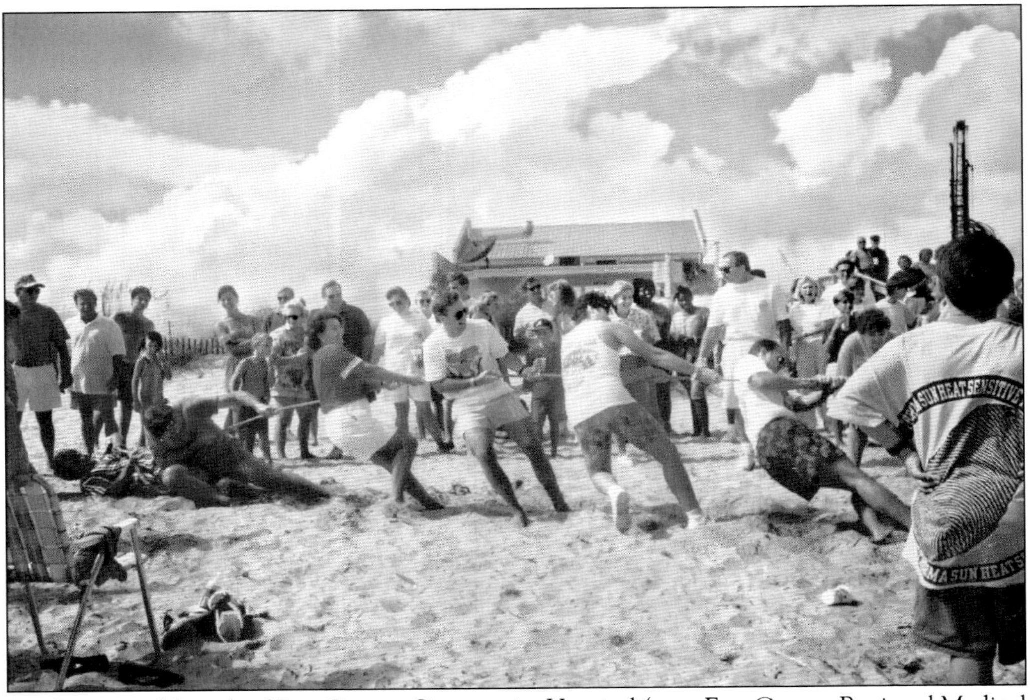

Employees and friends of East Cooper Community Hospital (now East Cooper Regional Medical Center) participate in a tug-of-war contest on the beach in front of the new Windjammer. The facility, the closest hospital for Isle of Palms residents, is located in Mount Pleasant.

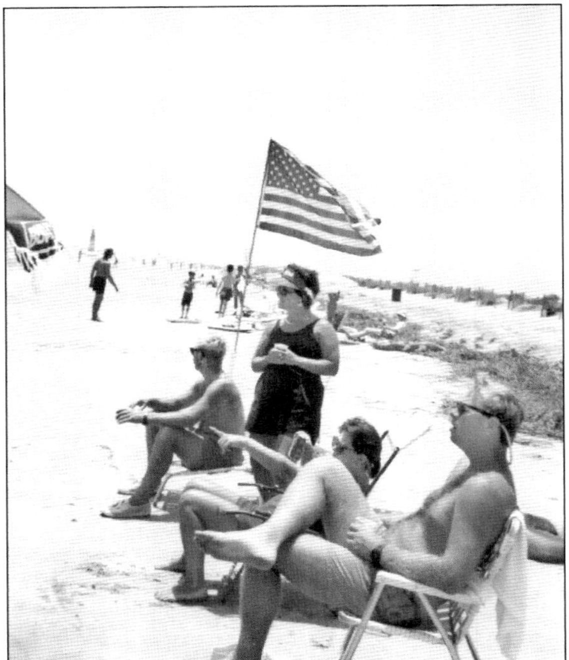

Lance, Dale, Shirley, and Stewart Nilsen enjoy this July afternoon as the Stars and Stripes waves behind them.

Capt. Wally Shaffer Jr. looks confident about his catch for the day. Captain Wally was a commercial shrimper for 37 years and former executive director of the South Carolina Shrimpers Association, as well as president of the Gulf and South Atlantic Fisheries Development Foundation.

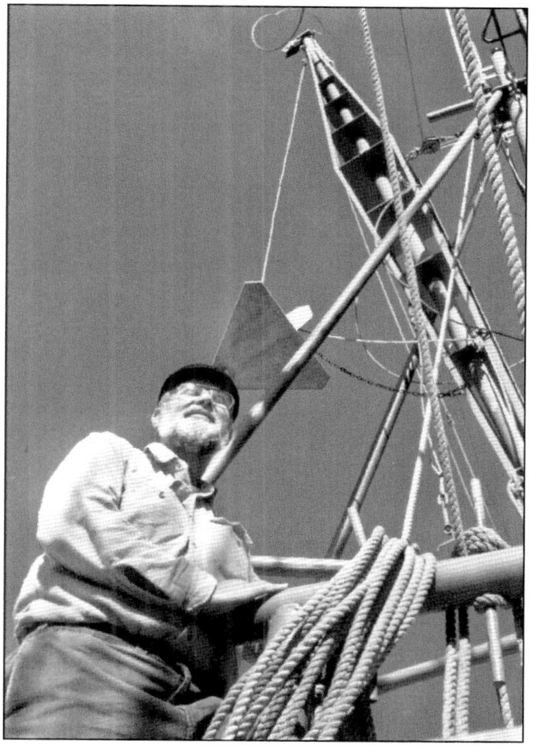

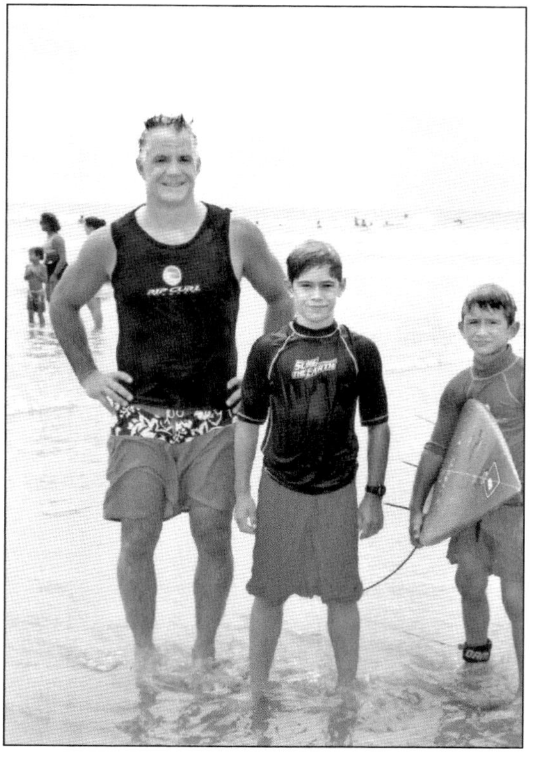

Chip, George, and Boyce Campsen take a break from the waves. The Campsen men are surfing aficionados, taking every opportunity to find the perfect wave. If they are not surfing, you can find them fishing or hunting. It is rare that you'll find them indoors!

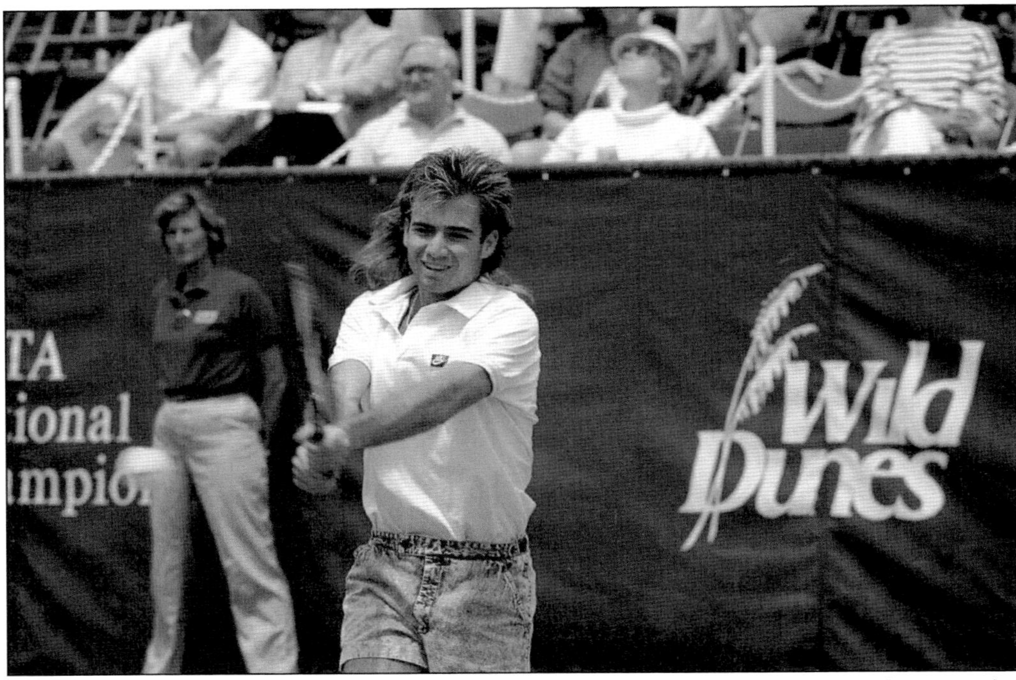

Tennis superstar Andre Agassi returns a ball at the U.S. Men's Clay Court Championship in 1989 at Wild Dunes. Extra bleachers and risers transformed center court into a grandiose stadium to accommodate all the spectators.

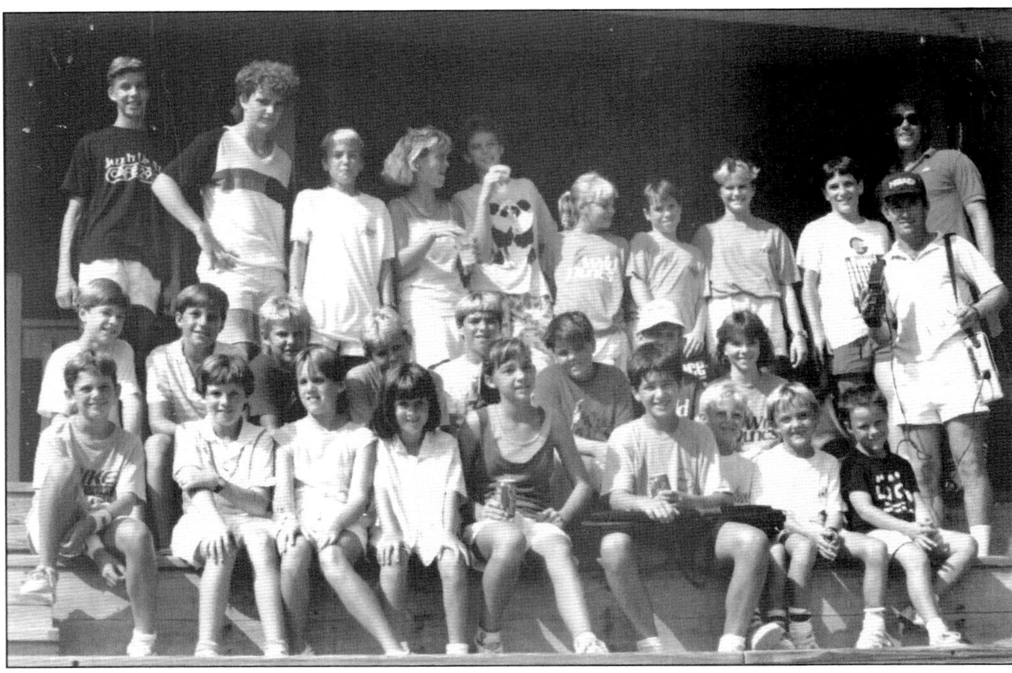

When the U.S. Men's Clay Court Championship came to Wild Dunes in 1989, this group of youngsters served as ball girls and boys.

One fish, two fish, red fish, blue fish . . . Stewart Small, Grace Peterson, and Davis Peterson line up their catch on nearby Goat Island.

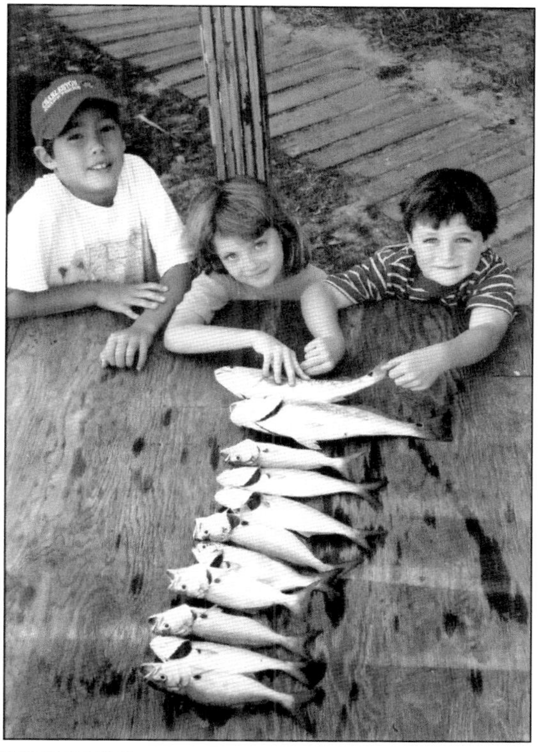

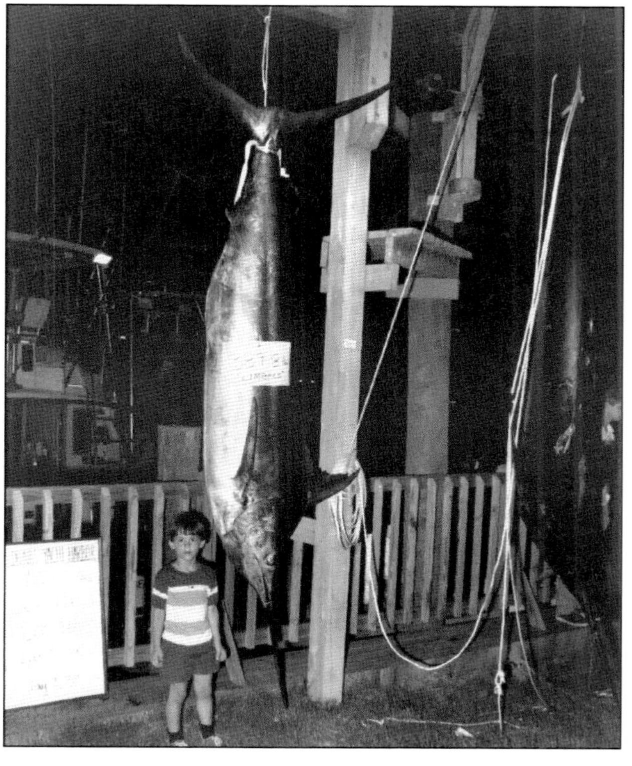

Justin Finch pales in comparison to this marlin almost four times as big as him. Can you figure out which one weighs 389 pounds?

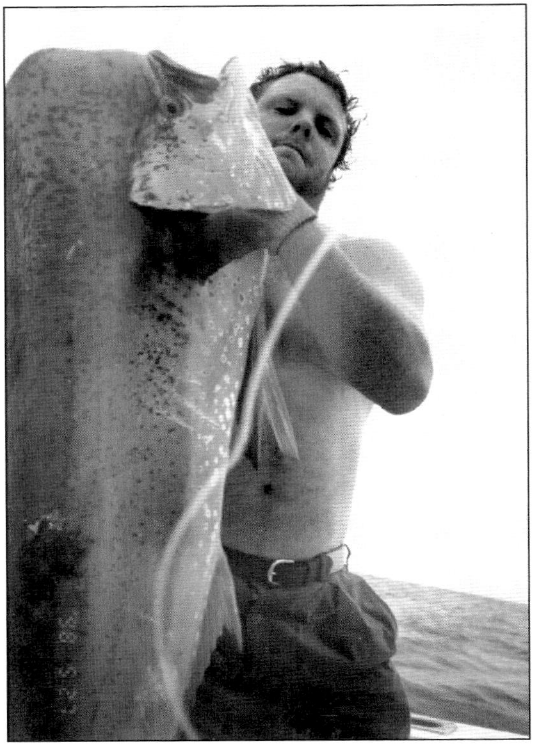

Tuck Altman holds up this monster dolphin, one of the most prized gamefish in the ocean. The dolphin is revered among anglers for its aggressive strikes, long, fast runs, stunning aerial acrobatics, and vibrant neon colors.

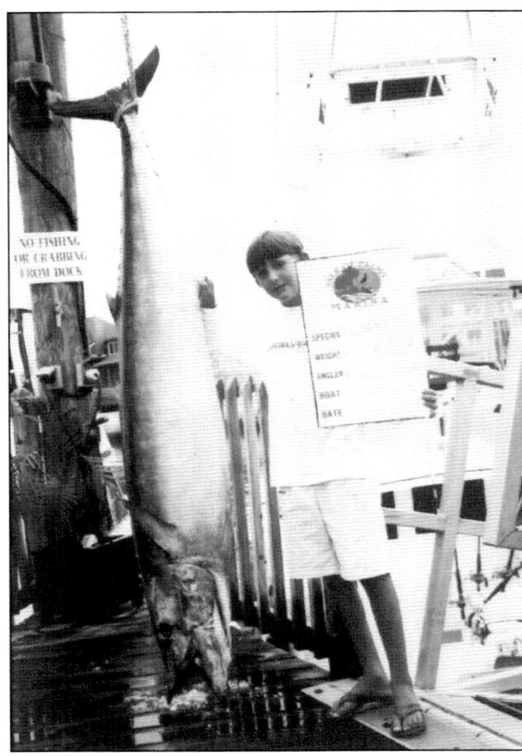

The wahoo seen here, caught by 13-year-old Royall Shore, weighed 113.6 pounds. The fish was caught on the *Chasin'* at the 2001 Governor's Cup Series at the Isle of Palms Marina. The state record was 130.5 pounds, and the previous record was 109 pounds; therefore, this wahoo is unofficially the second largest in the state.

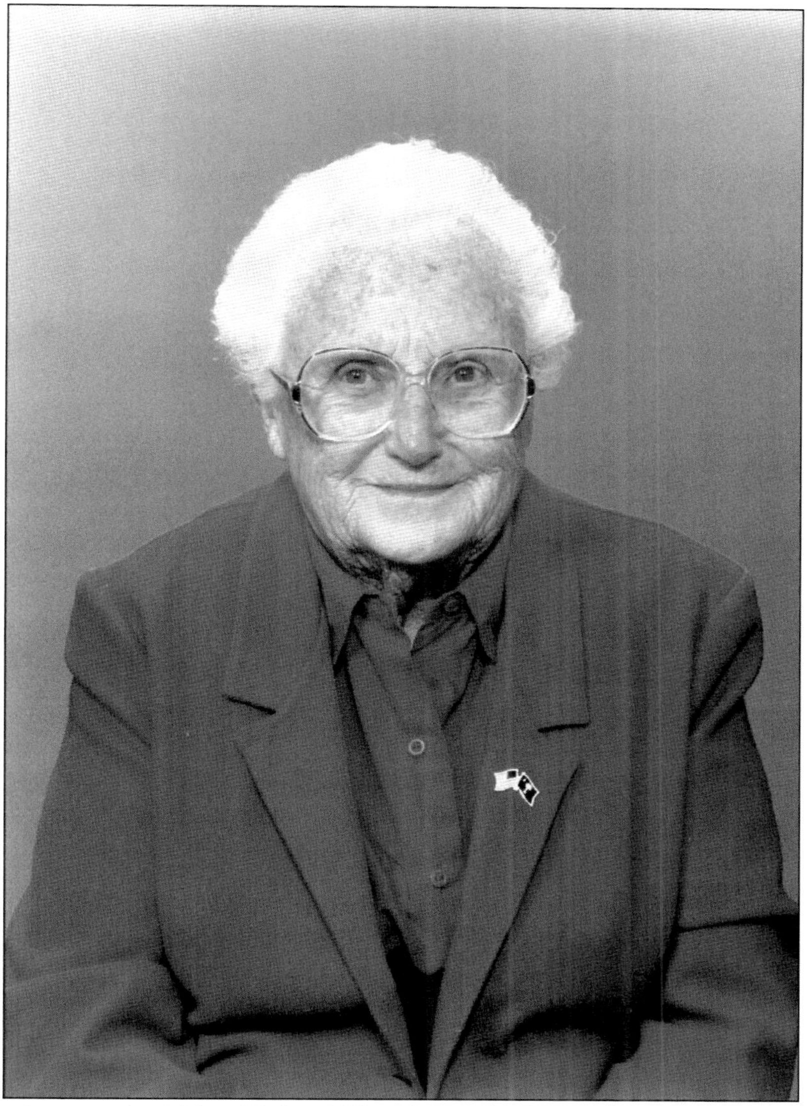

The beloved matriarch of Isle of Palms, Helen Carter Clarkin, volunteered for any committee she thought would benefit the island. Whenever something needed to be done at St. Mark's Lutheran Church or the Isle of Palms Garden Club, Mrs. Clarkin was ready to take it on. A member of VFW Post 3137, Mrs. Clarkin served in the U.S. Navy as a naval intelligence officer, often accompanying Eleanor Roosevelt on speaking tours. The "lady in red" was also very involved in politics. She was a charter member and former president of the Charleston County Democratic Women's Club, chair of the Isle of Palms Election Commission, and election poll manager for 50 years. In addition, she served as commissioner of the Isle of Palms Recreation Department and as a member of the Legislative and Governmental Affairs Committee. She owned Helen Clarkin Realty and directed the Charleston Trident Association of Realtors. Helen Clarkin remained active in real estate as a broker associate with Carroll Realty on Isle of Palms until her death in 2003. She loved Isle of Palms and thought using the acronym IOP was disrespectful. In honor of all her work on Isle of Palms and out of tremendous respect for a great lady, this book is IOP free!

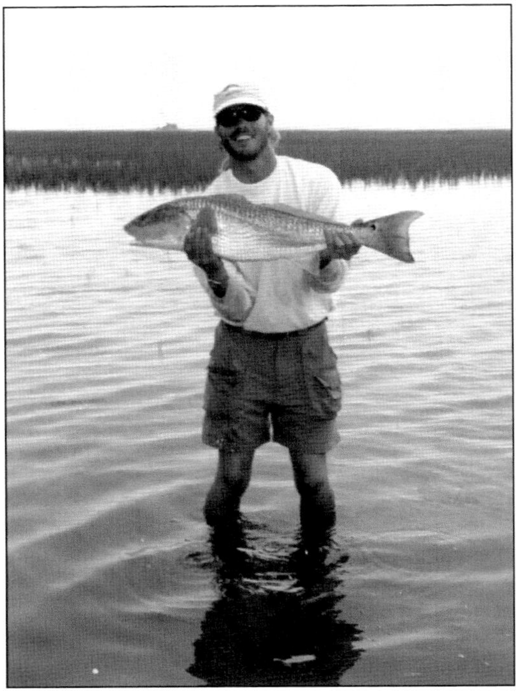

The red drum—or spottail bass, as it is often called—is by far the most popular inshore marine game fish in South Carolina. Capt. Chad Ferris holds a red drum on a mud flat near Isle of Palms. With the help of anglers like Chad, close to 45,000 red drum have been tagged since 1989 in the SCDNR's Tag and Release program. Biologists are provided valuable information on movement, seasonality trends, growth rates, and general population dynamics of gamefish through the cooperation of participants.

George Campsen lifts this large red drum out of the surf. Regulations determined by SCDNR now restrict the limit to two red drums between 15 and 24 inches long per angler per day in state waters. The size limit allows juveniles to grow and larger fish to produce more eggs for a more substantial population.

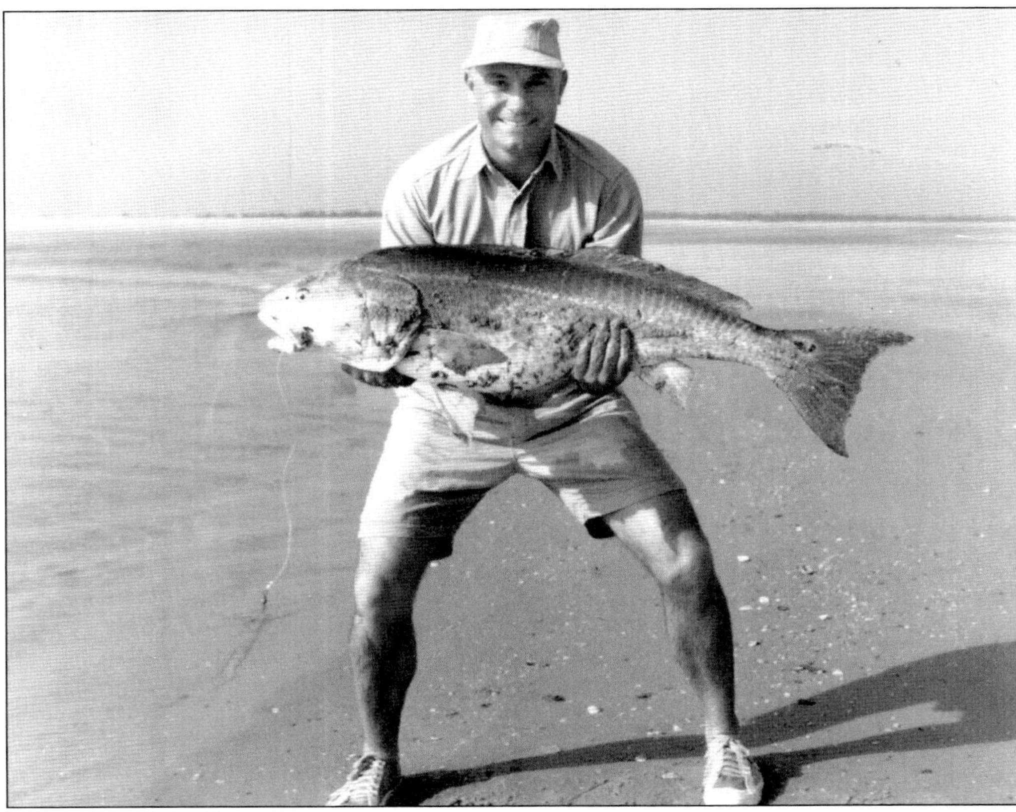

Ty Venable, Richard Pollitzer, Sally Pearson, Carol Nilsen, Lance Nilsen, Frank Pearson, Stanley Pearson, Wendy Nilsen (Pollitzer), Stewart Nilsen, Shirley Nilsen, Sally Altman, Dale Nilsen, Austin Nilsen, Joey Nilsen, and Tommy Litwin gather on the stairs inside the new Windjammer for Shirley Nilsen's 50th birthday party.

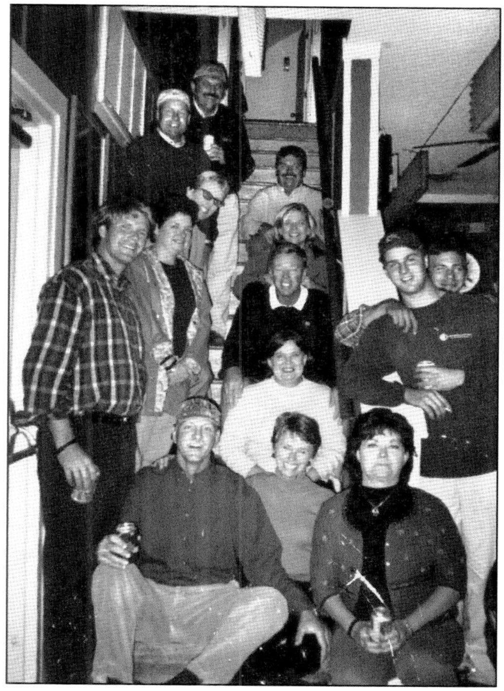

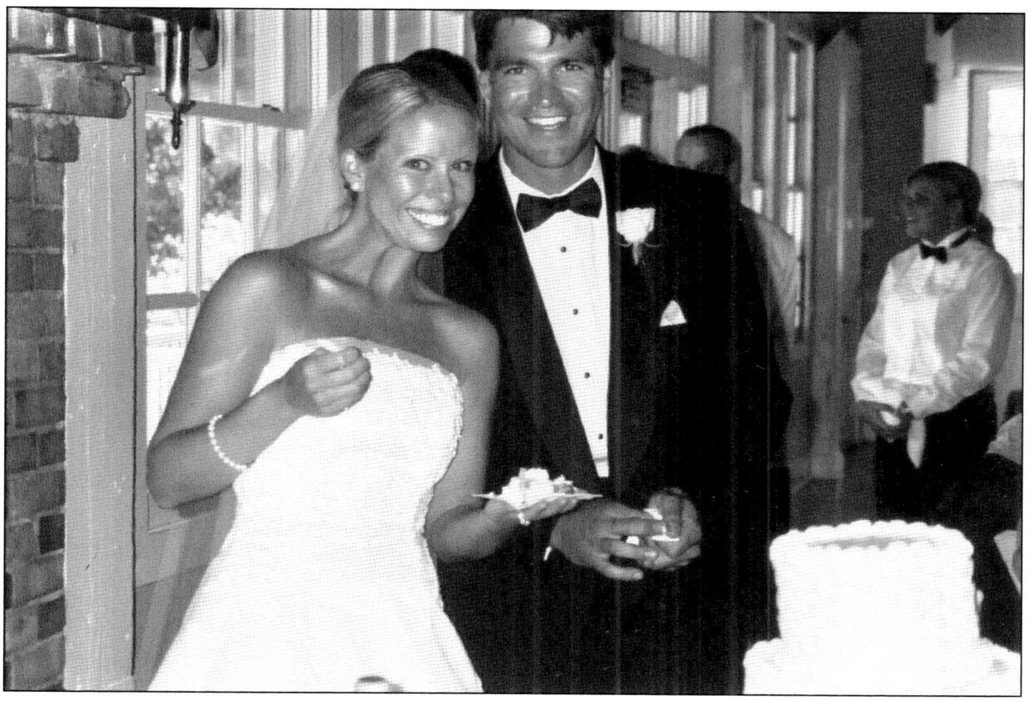

Amy and Tommy Litwin celebrate their marriage. Both former residents of Isle of Palms, the two wed in 2003. Receptions are often held at various venues on the island. Wild Dunes has a number of facilities to host special events, as does the Citadel Beach Club. Weddings sometimes even take place on the beach, where romance fills the Atlantic air.

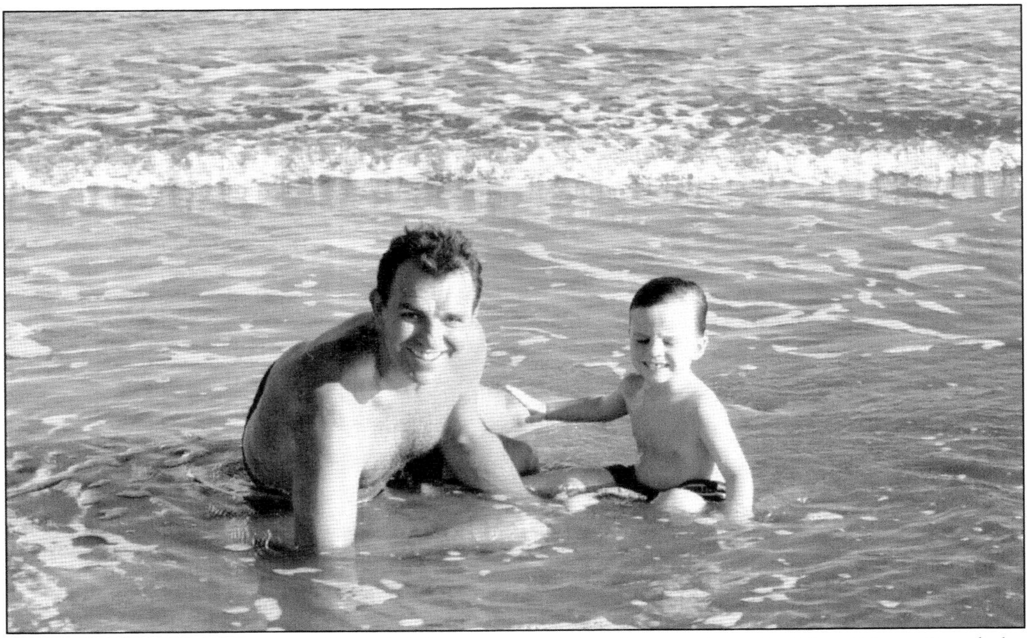

In May of 2002, the City of Isle of Palms received the designation of a Blue Wave Beach by the Clean Beaches Council, America's first environmental certification program for beaches. Isle of Palms is the only Blue Wave beach in South Carolina, signifying a clean and safe destination managed with consideration for the environment. Bill and Josh Kulseth relax in the Atlantic blue.

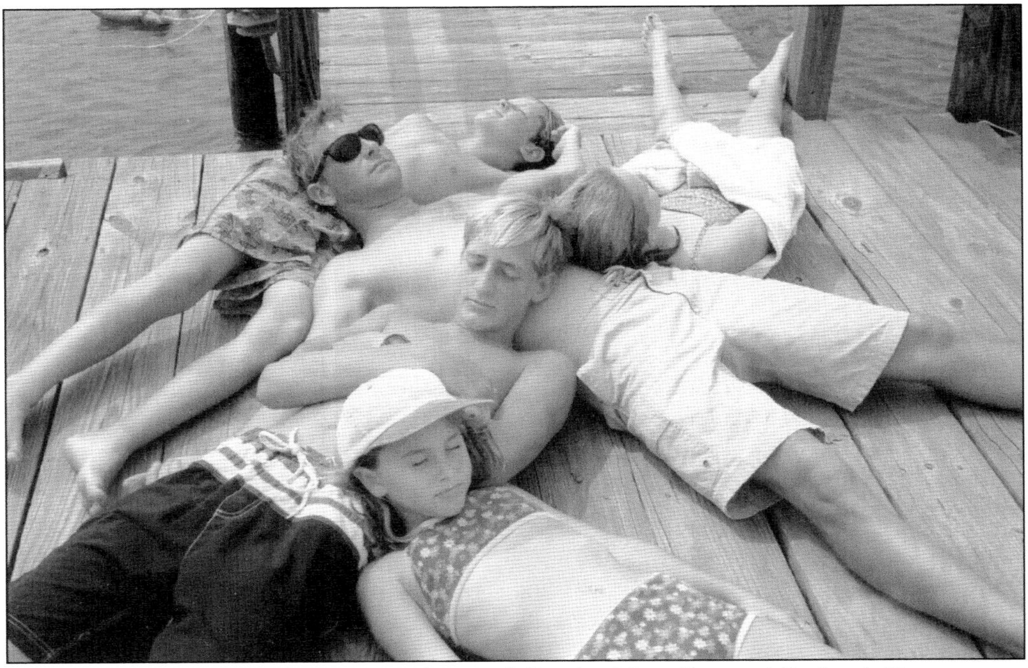

Trenton and Trevor Seckinger, Caroline and Brooke Mosteller, and Richard Campsen are wiped out on the Campsen family dock on Hamlin Creek.

Four

Before and After Hugo

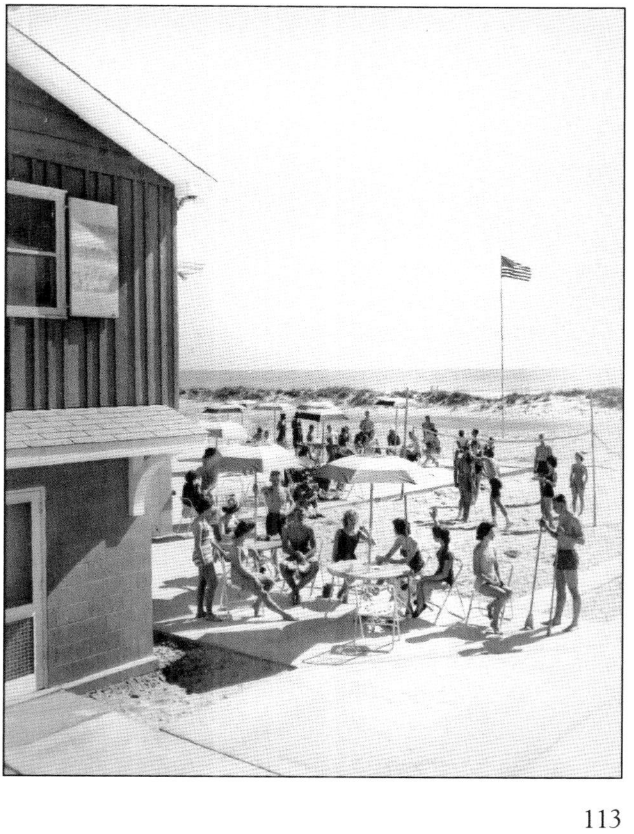

The Citadel Beach Club sat on a five-acre tract with a volleyball court, shuffleboard pads, and a sheltered picnic area. The two-story clubhouse accommodated activities like oyster roasts, barbecues, and dances. Cadets also used the facility on summer weekends and took advantage of the rest and relaxation at the beach. The club housed a ballroom, bathhouse, kitchen, and screened porch for all types of parties. Hurricane Hugo demolished the original building in 1989. A few years later, the more luxurious Citadel Beach House opened with all the amenities as the first club and more. (Photo courtesy of The Citadel Archives and Museum.)

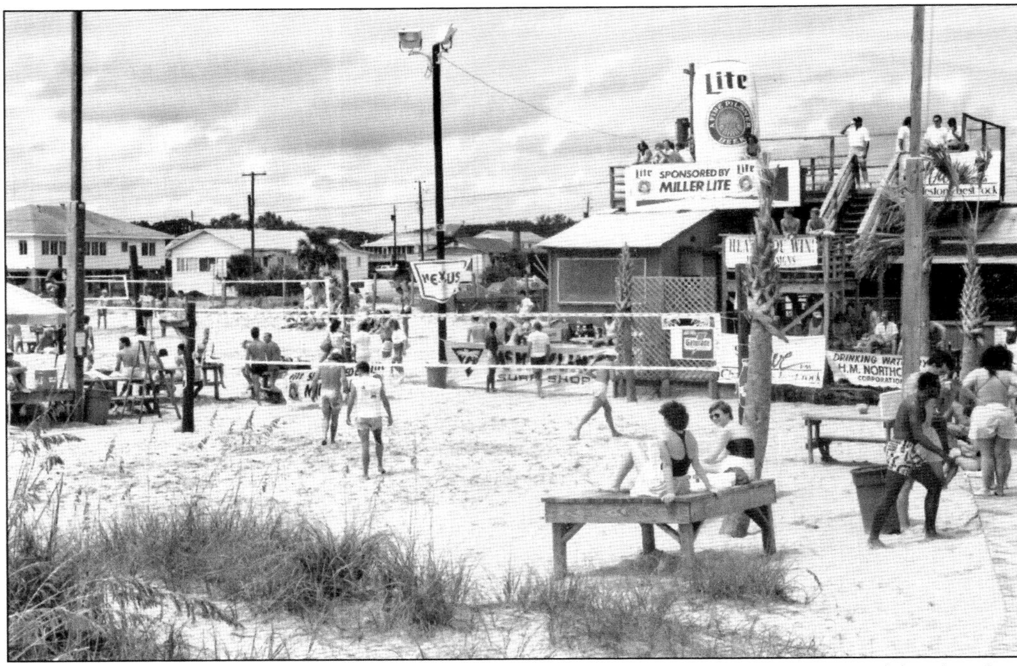

A typical Saturday at the Windjammer was always packed! Malcolm Burgis and his brother, James, opened the legendary watering hole in April 1972. In 1974, James sold his share to Bill Kulseth. Partners for over 30 years, Malcolm and Bill ran one of the most successful businesses in the Lowcountry. The Windjammer is still a favorite venue for local and regional bands, as well as a gathering spot for many thirsty patrons. Oh yeah . . . they serve the best cheeseburger on the island!

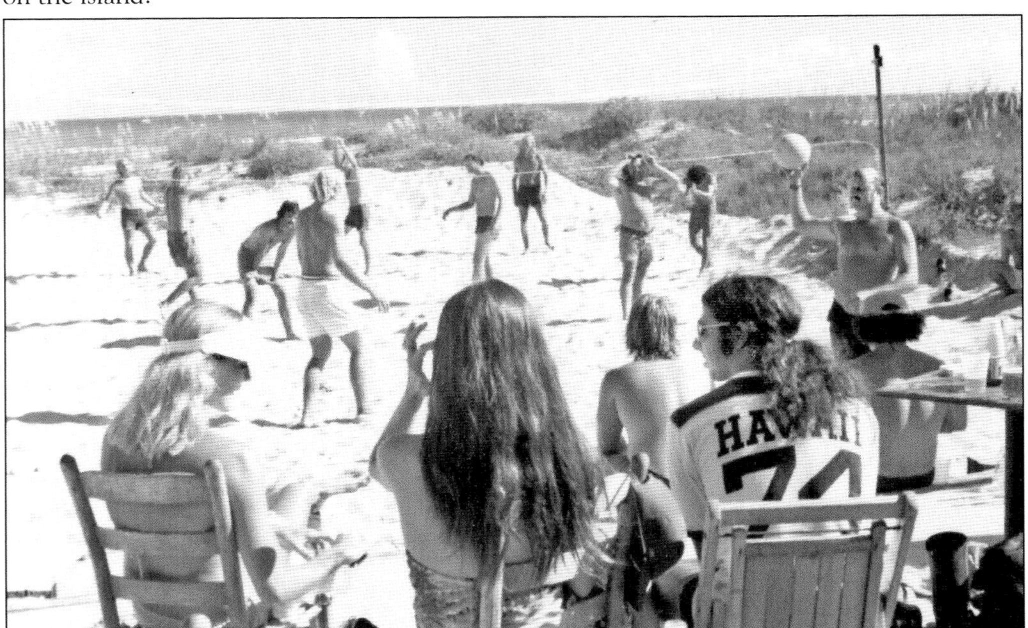

The Windjammer had beach volleyball before it was even cool!

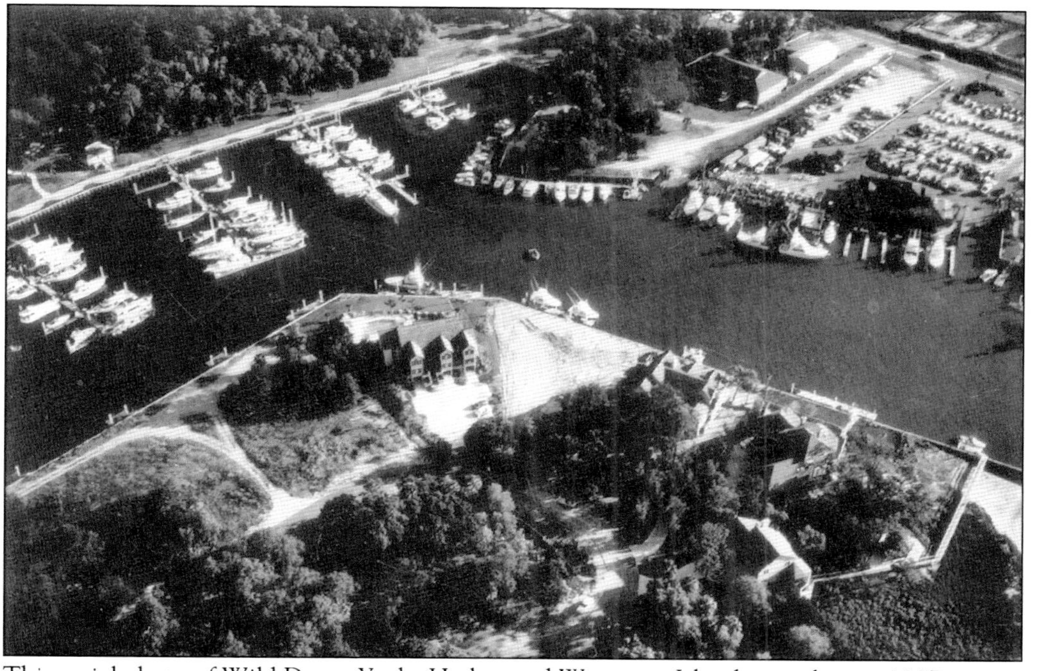

This aerial photo of Wild Dunes Yacht Harbor and Waterway Island was taken in 1987.

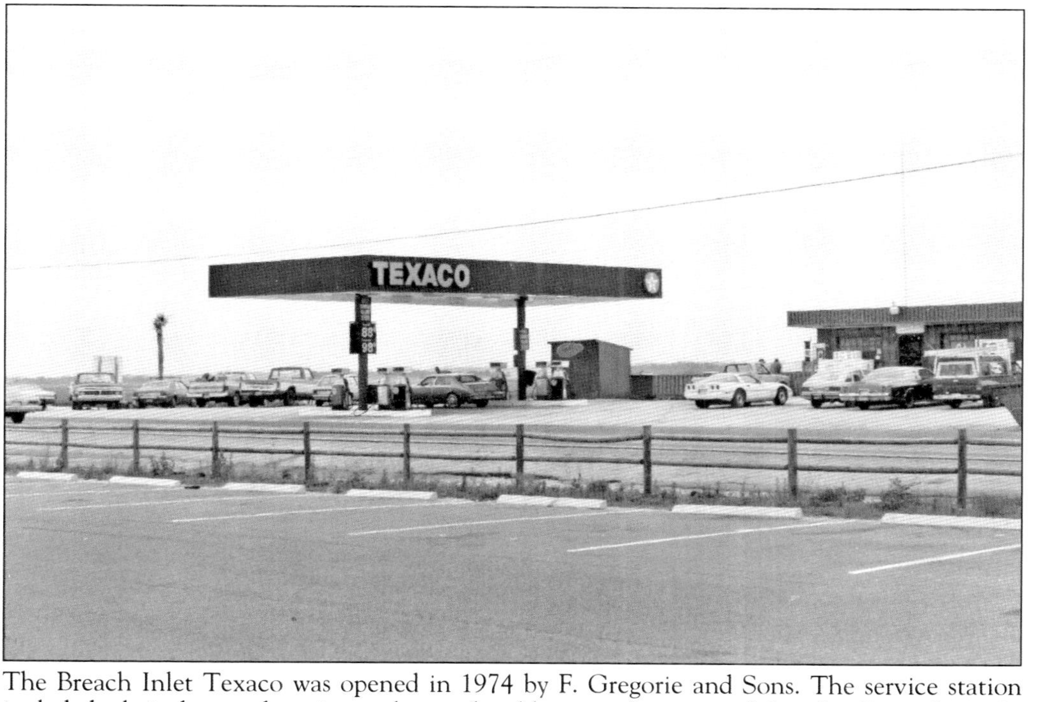

The Breach Inlet Texaco was opened in 1974 by F. Gregorie and Sons. The service station included a bait shop and marina and was a local hangout for many of the island's residents. In 1996, the waterfront building was converted into the Boathouse Restaurant.

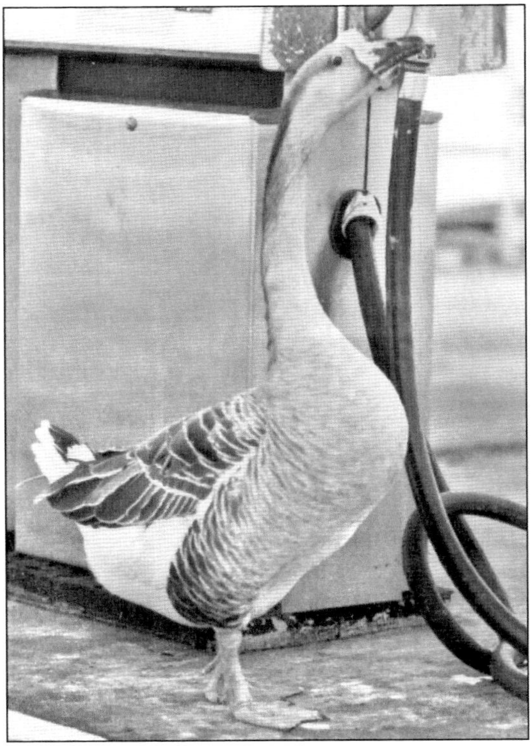

Huey, the infamous goose who lived at the Breach Inlet Texaco, made quite a few friends of the female variety on the island. Huey was not a fan of men but was extremely fond of the women who pumped their gas at his self-service station. However, if any woman pulled up with the color red on, Huey attacked! He would lift his wings and charge the woman, ready to strike. Gene White had to calm Huey down after encounters with ladies in red.

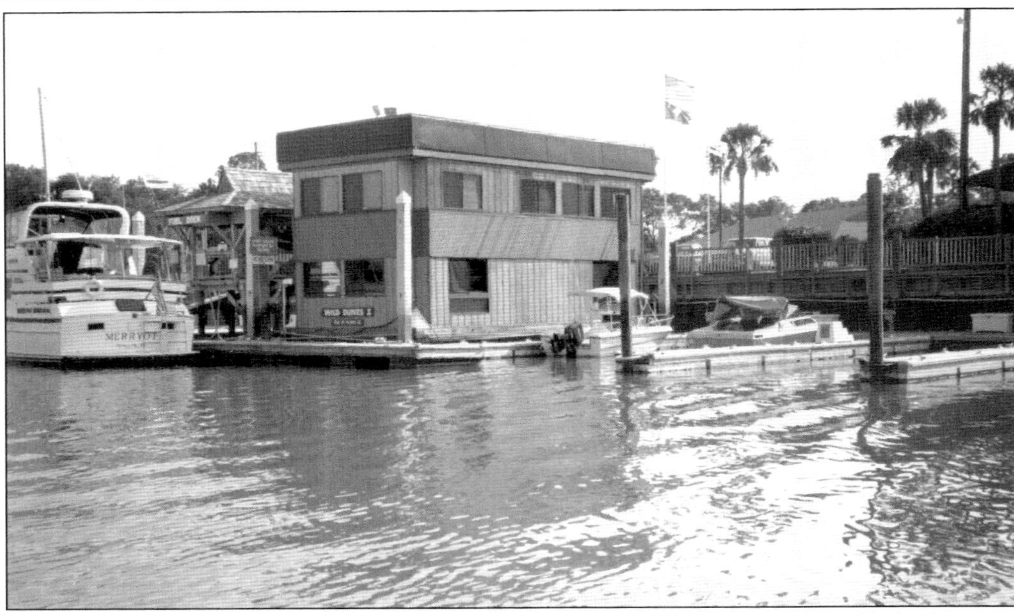

The old marina offices and fuel dock at Wild Dunes Yacht Harbor were literally built on the water. Henry Finch bought the marina from Wild Dunes in 1984 and gave half of his share to his five children, Henry J. Finch, Mac Finch, Bill Finch, Susie Finch (Stevens), and Nancy Finch (Moore). The siblings eventually bought their father out and successfully converted the commercial property into dockominiums with over 100 slips for individuals to purchase.

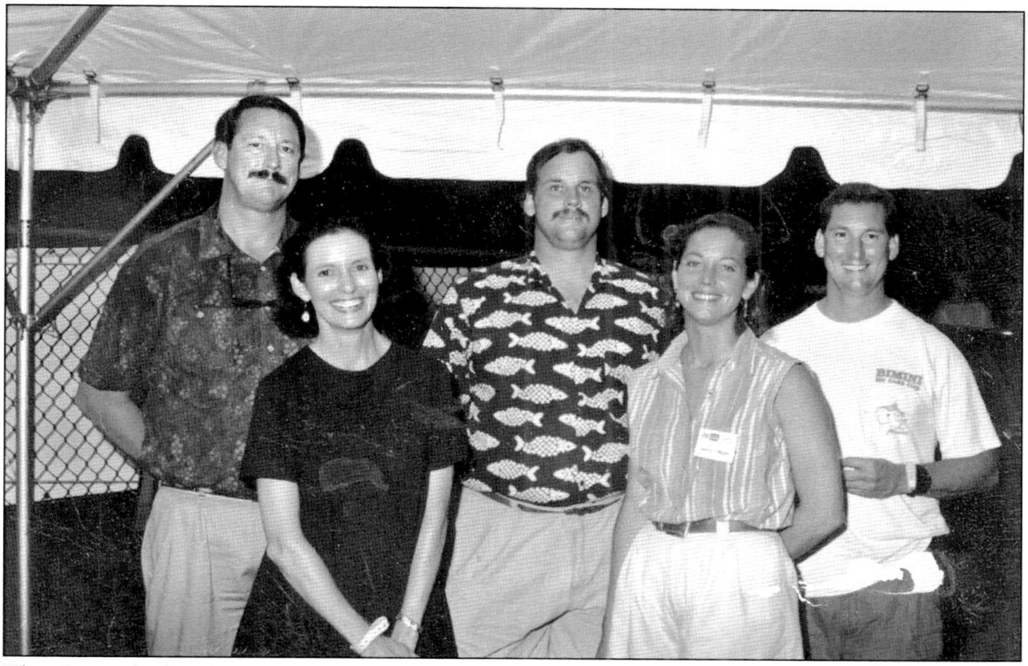

The City of Isle of Palms bought the marina in 2000 from Henry J. Finch, Mac Finch, Bill Finch, Susie Finch (Stevens), and Nancy Finch (Moore).

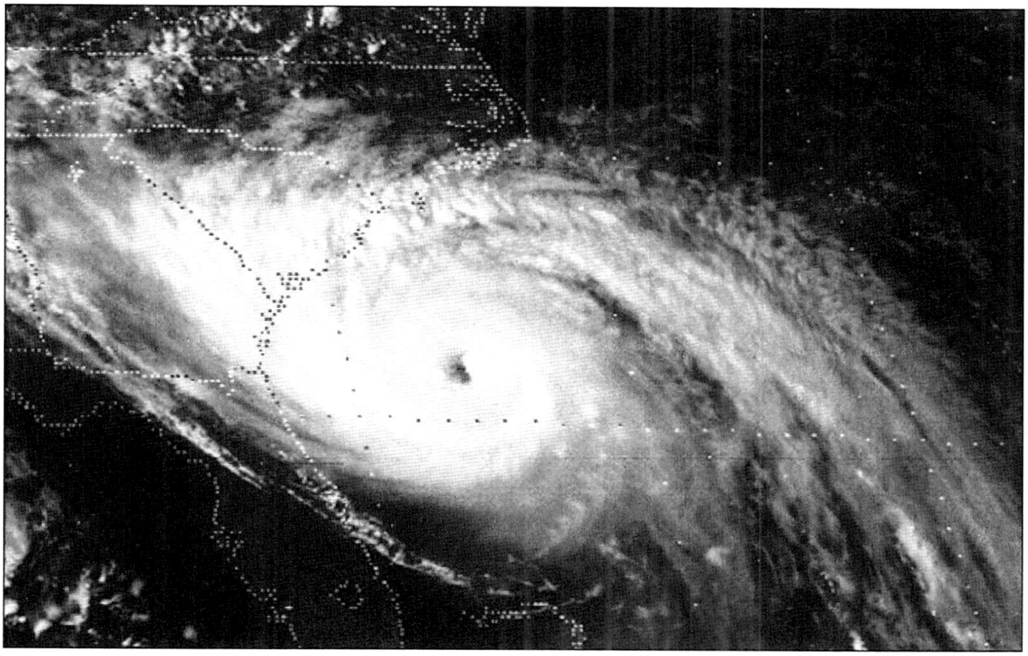

At 12:01 a.m. on September 22, the eye of Hurricane Hugo passed directly over Isle of Palms. The storm was one of the greatest national disasters to ever hit the United States, causing $7 billion in damage and claiming 35 lives nationwide. From that point on, everything measured by time in the area would be referred to as before and after Hugo.

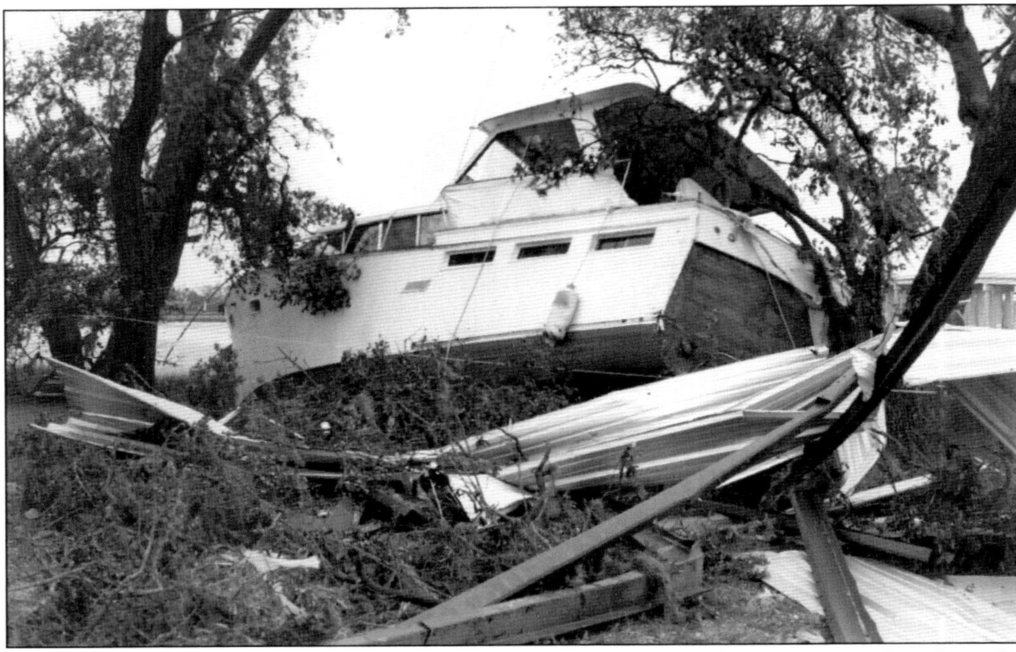

Boats were tossed off their moorings all over the island. When the surge poured in from the Atlantic, these vessels floated wherever the tide took them. After the ocean waters receded, the boats were stranded in places previously unimaginable.

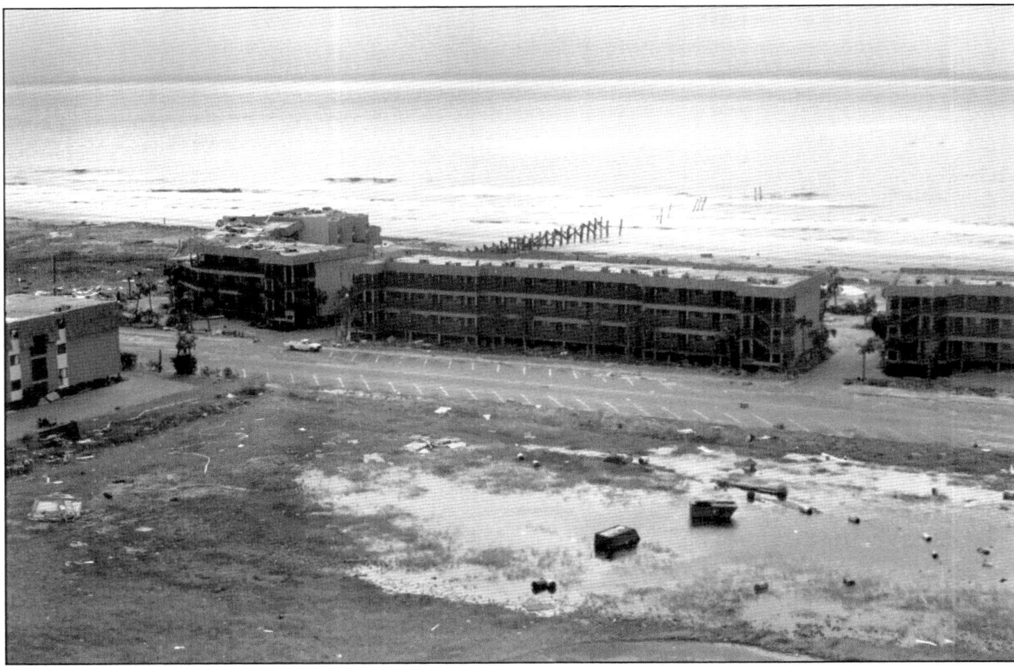

The fishing pier was totally destroyed, while heavy winds ripped off the roof of the Sea Cabins.

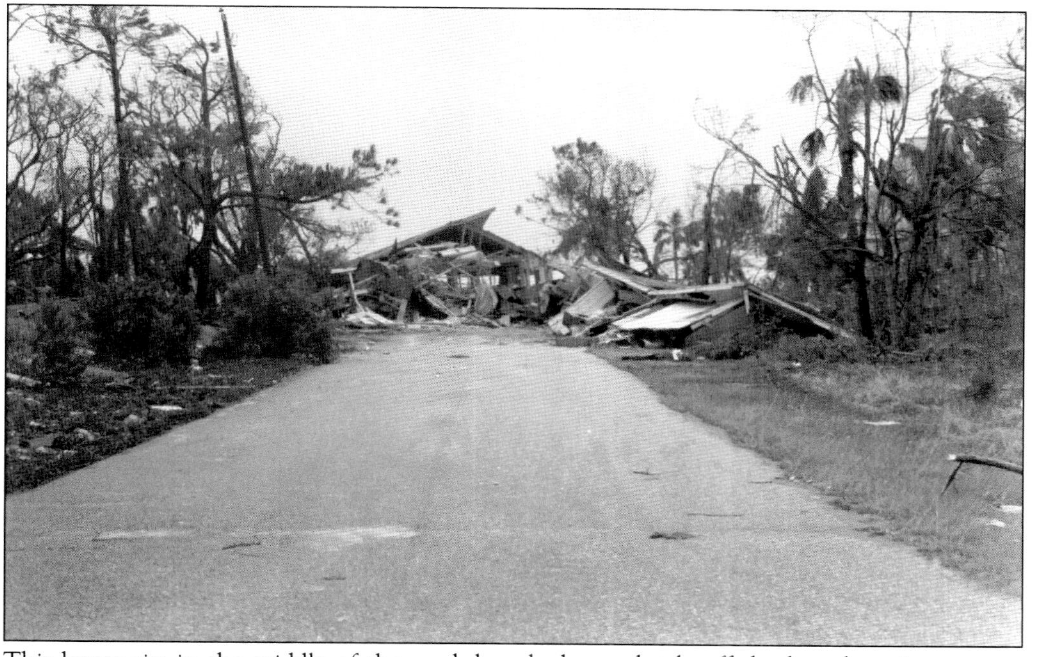

This house sits in the middle of the road, knocked completely off the lot where it once sat. Sustained winds were measured between 105 and 135 miles per hour. Gusts reached 175 miles per hour.

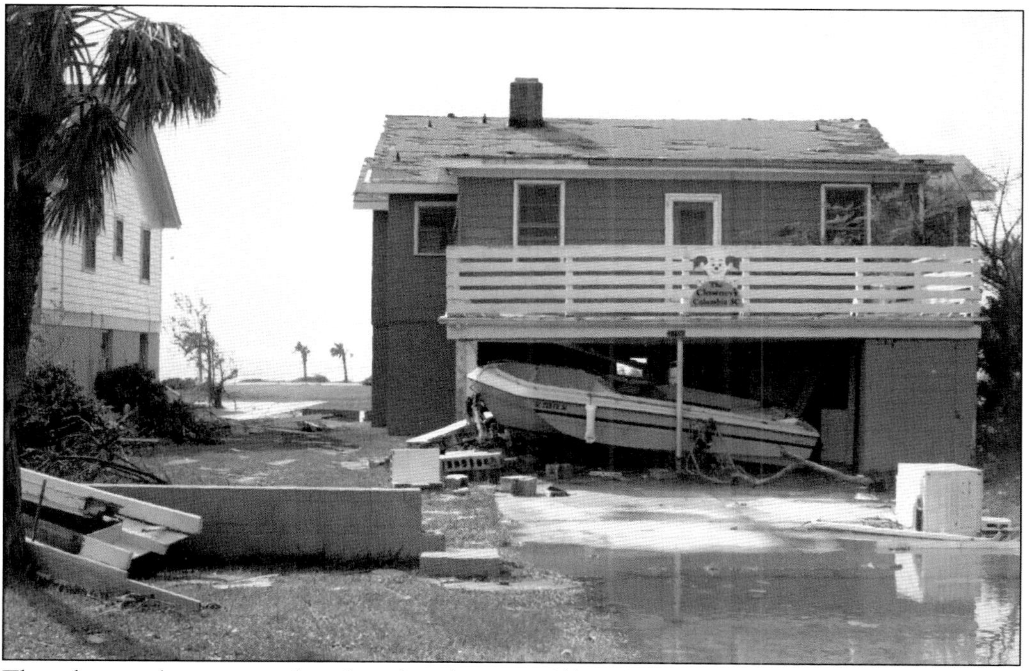

Those houses that remained on their foundations still lost shingles from their roofs and sustained disastrous flood damage from the storm's 20-foot surge. It was not unusual to find neighbor's belongings, like cars and boats, in your front yard.

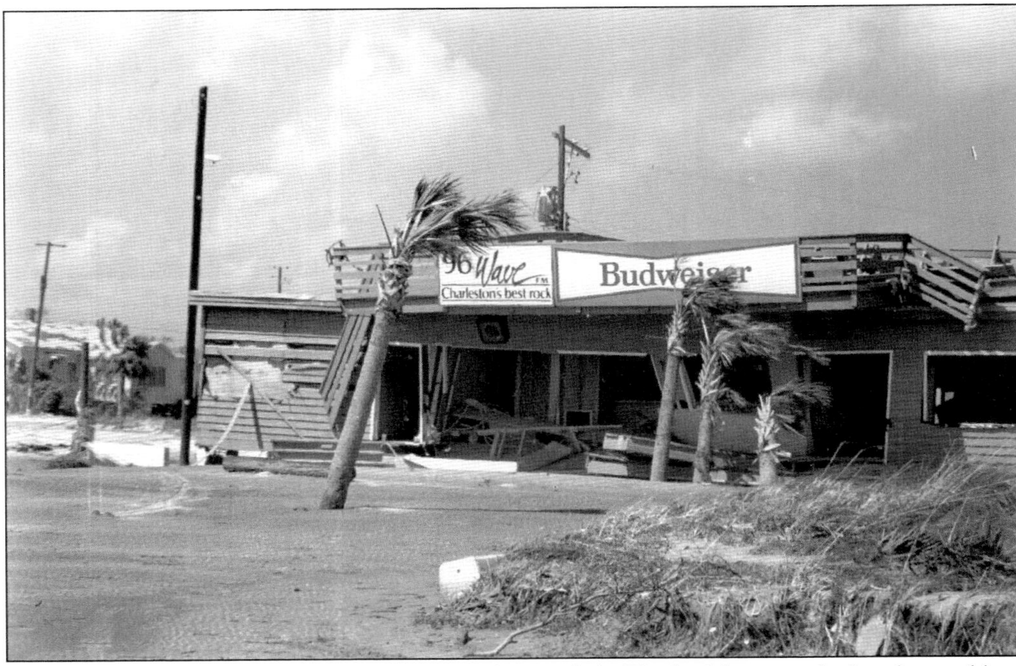

The old Windjammer is long gone, but its soul never left! The building was declared a total loss, but its owners, Malcolm Burgis and Bill Kulseth, rebuilt the island landmark bigger and better than ever before.

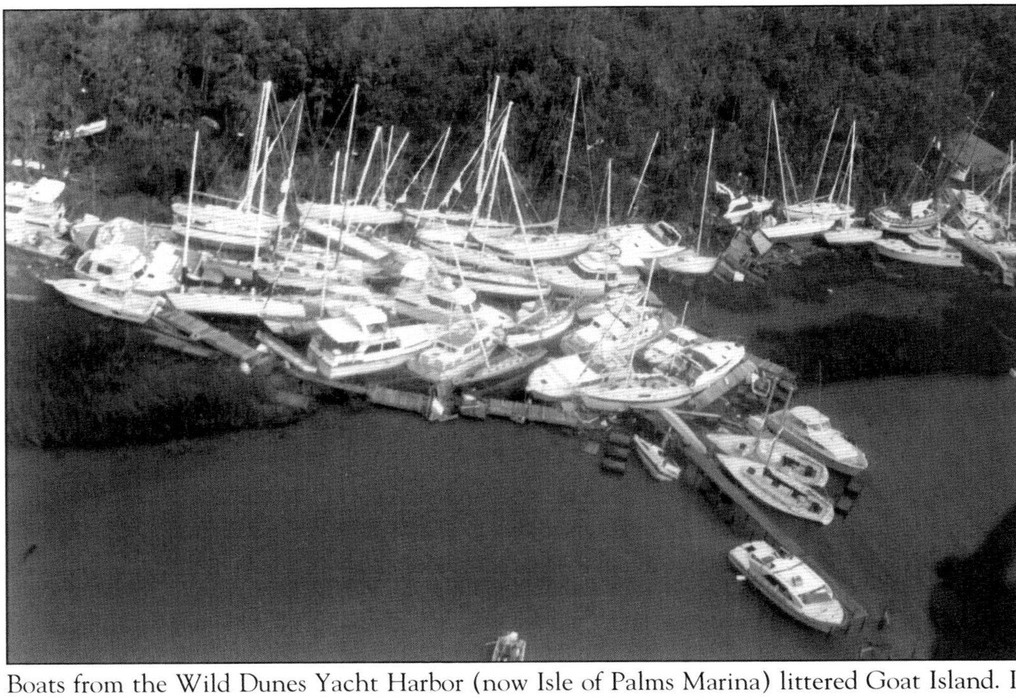

Boats from the Wild Dunes Yacht Harbor (now Isle of Palms Marina) littered Goat Island. It did not matter how well the boat was secured to its mooring, it was coming off!

Debris on Ocean Boulevard along Front Beach was scattered everywhere. The stench of rotten food filled the air, and live wires twisted all over the street. It was not a safe environment.

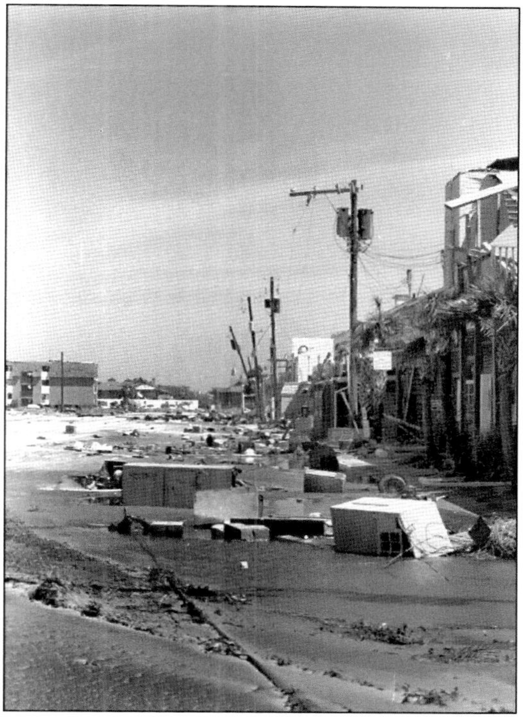

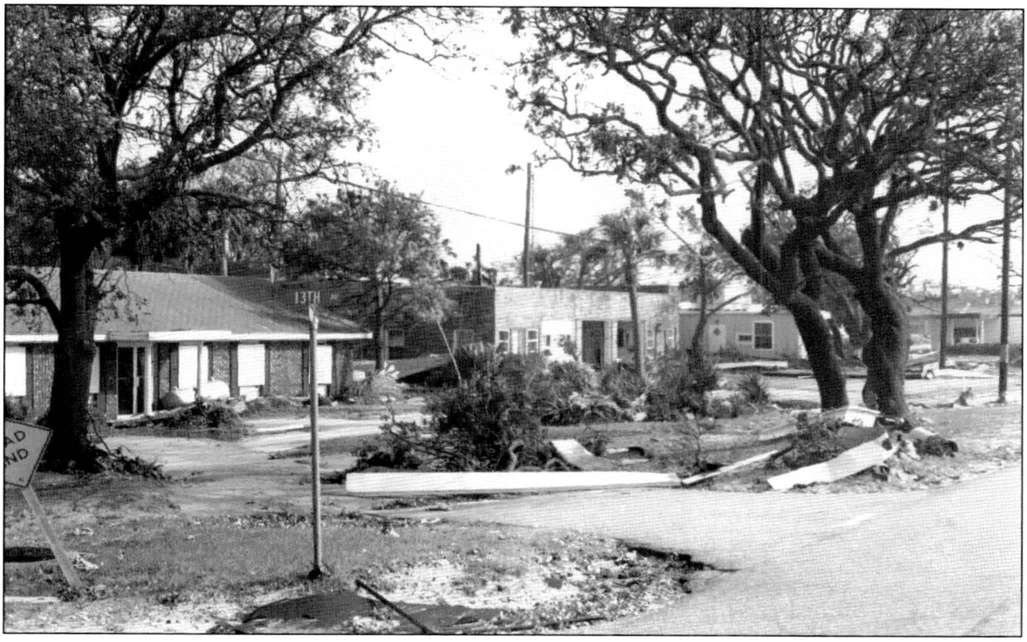

The mud-soaked city hall was unusable. The City of Isle of Palms functioned out of the Lutheran Church Retreat Center for months. In 1986, Mayor Carmen Bunch donated a generator to the center and got a key in case of an emergency. Without that foresight, Isle of Palms would have been homeless. The center also housed the National Guard, South Carolina State Law Enforcement Division (SLED), and Mayor Bunch herself.

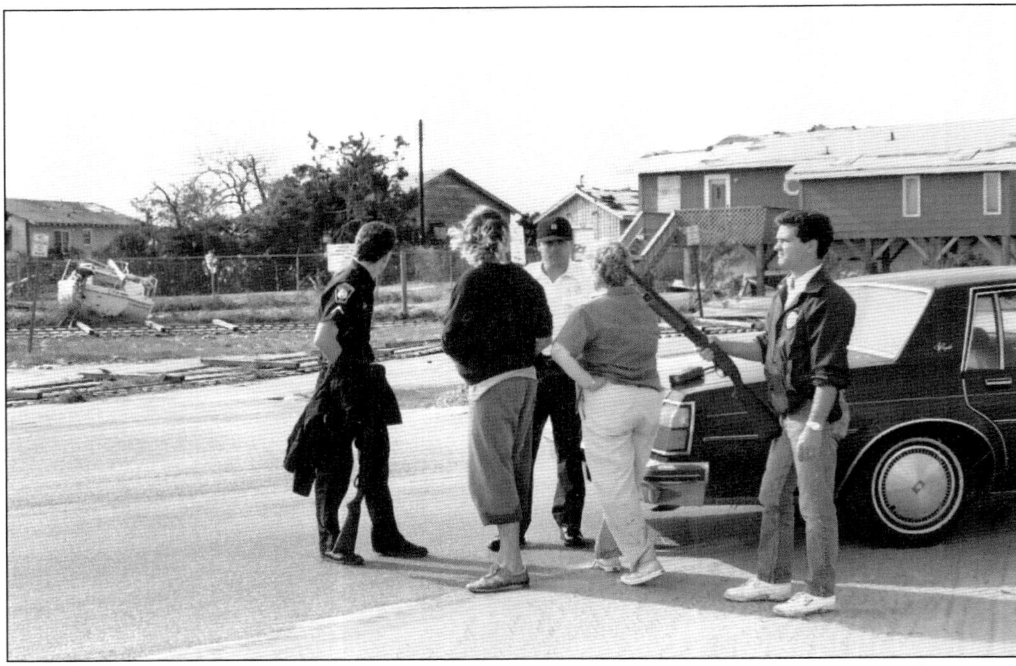

Everyone coming on the island was questioned by Isle of Palms police officers. Residents were checked for identification and asked their reason for being on the island. The officers, along with National Guardsmen, carried pump shotguns and M-16 rifles to scare away any looters who might have sneaked on the island.

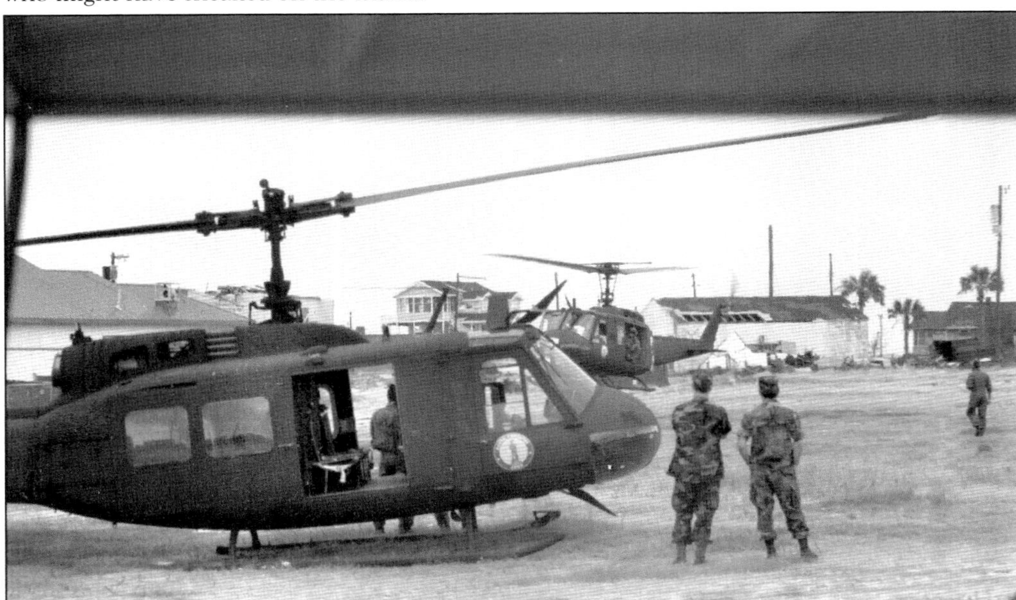

Military helicopters buzzed the island and landed troops behind the Pavilion Shops on Front Beach to search for looters. A curfew was established to monitor activity on the island. The Army, the Marines, the Army Corp of Engineers, and National Guardsmen were not only here to protect, but to also help Isle of Palms residents rebuild their lives and their property.

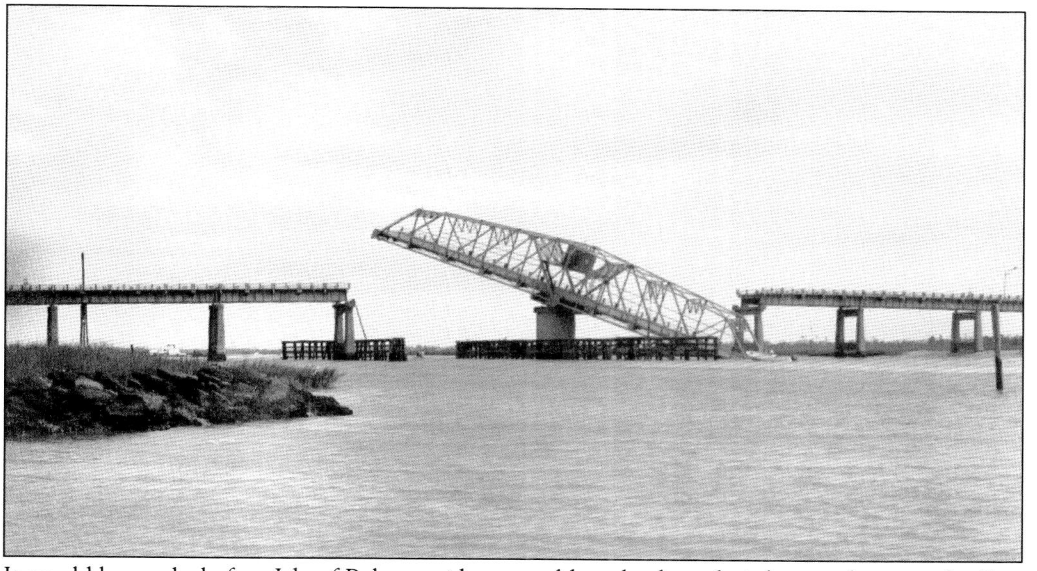

It would be weeks before Isle of Palms residents could get back to their homes, because the Ben Sawyer Bridge had been blown into the Intracoastal Waterway. The impassable bridge was the island's only link to the mainland. The Campsen family, who had founded Fort Sumter Tours in 1961 to carry visitors to Fort Sumter National Monument, volunteered the *General Beauregard* to transport residents to and from Isle of Palms. The vessel departed from Patriots Point and took them to Wild Dunes free of charge.

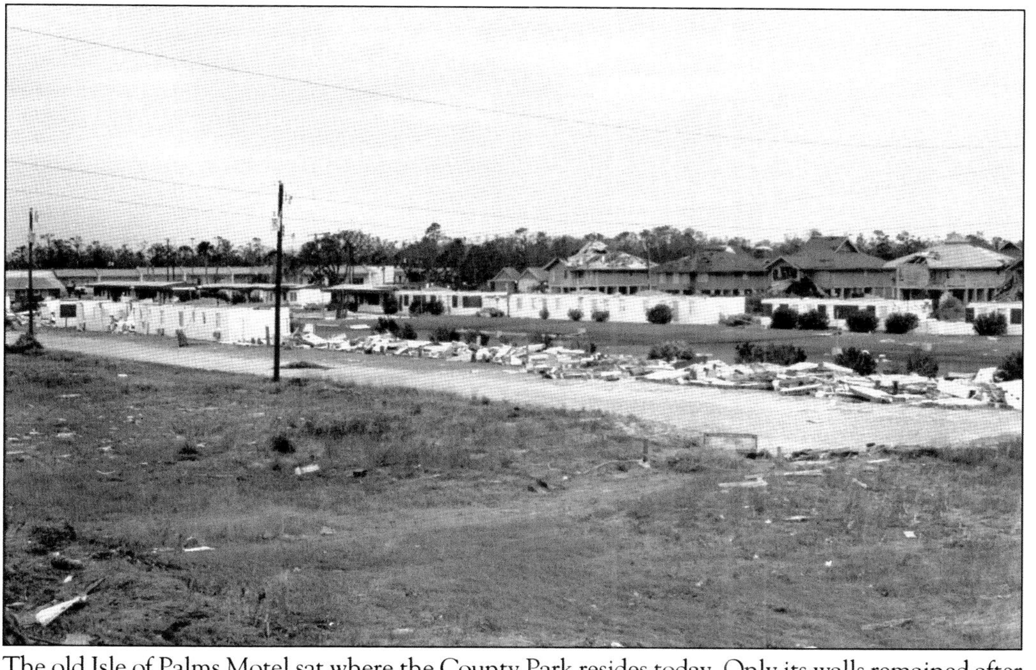

The old Isle of Palms Motel sat where the County Park resides today. Only its walls remained after Hugo ravaged the quaint lodging establishment. There was a ten-ton weight limit on the Ben Sawyer Bridge when it reopened to one-lane traffic, prohibiting large trucks from carrying debris off the island, so Isle of Palms used the city parking lot on Pavilion Drive for a debris site.

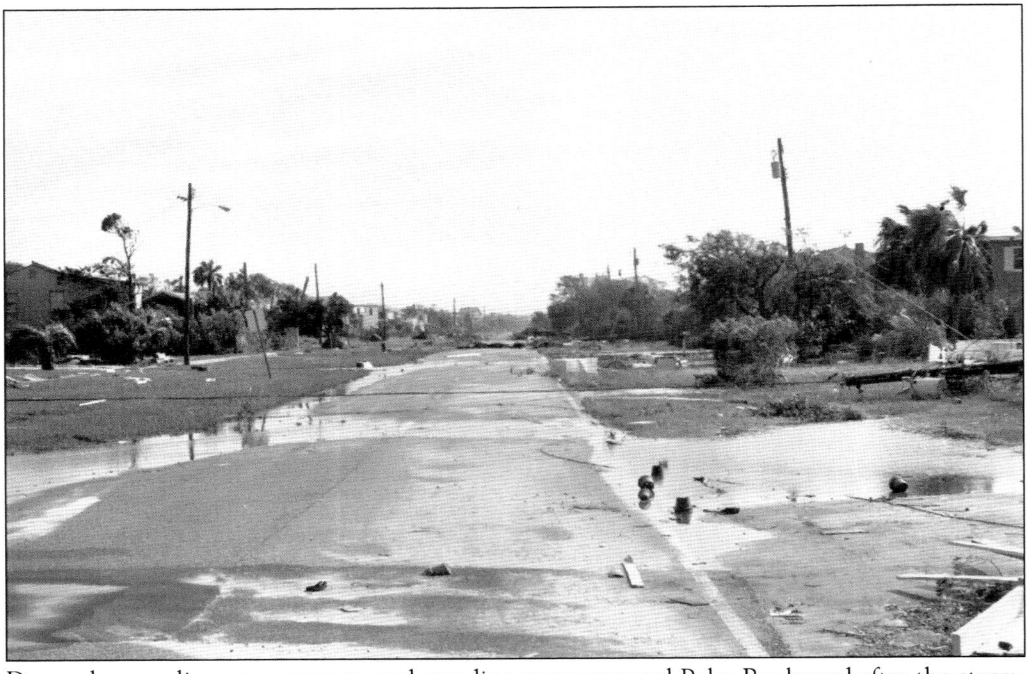

Downed power lines, raw sewage, and standing water covered Palm Boulevard after the storm. Puddles were deceiving. What looked like a couple of inches of water could have been a seven-foot-deep cavern in the middle of the street.

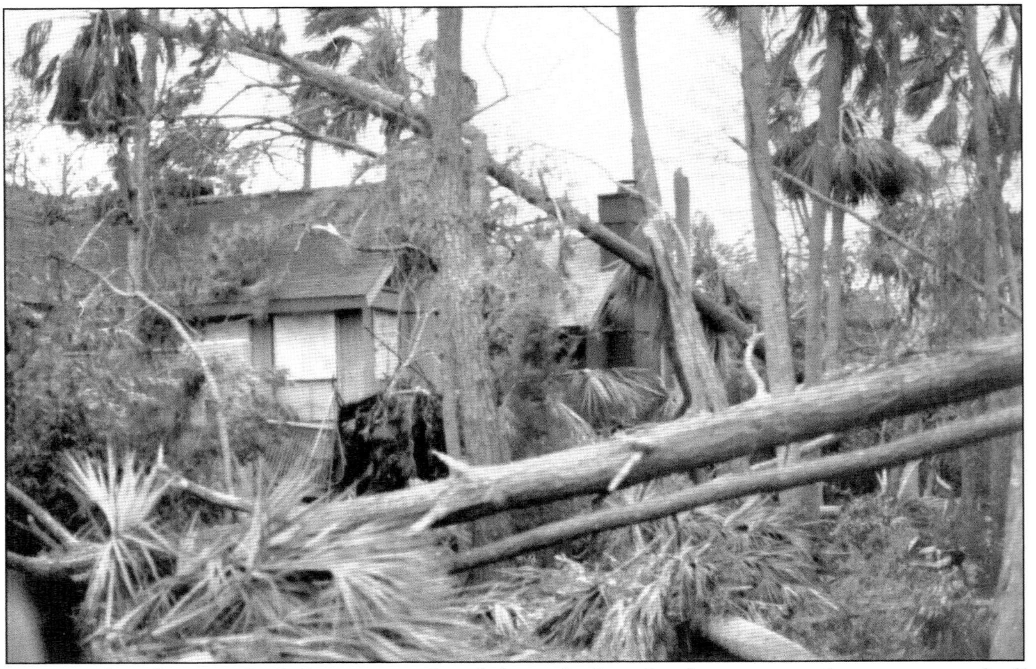

For months, the sound of chainsaws echoed through the island as tree trunks were moved off houses, power poles, and cars. The hum of generators continued through the night, allowing residents to enjoy a few of the creature comforts of home they once took for granted.

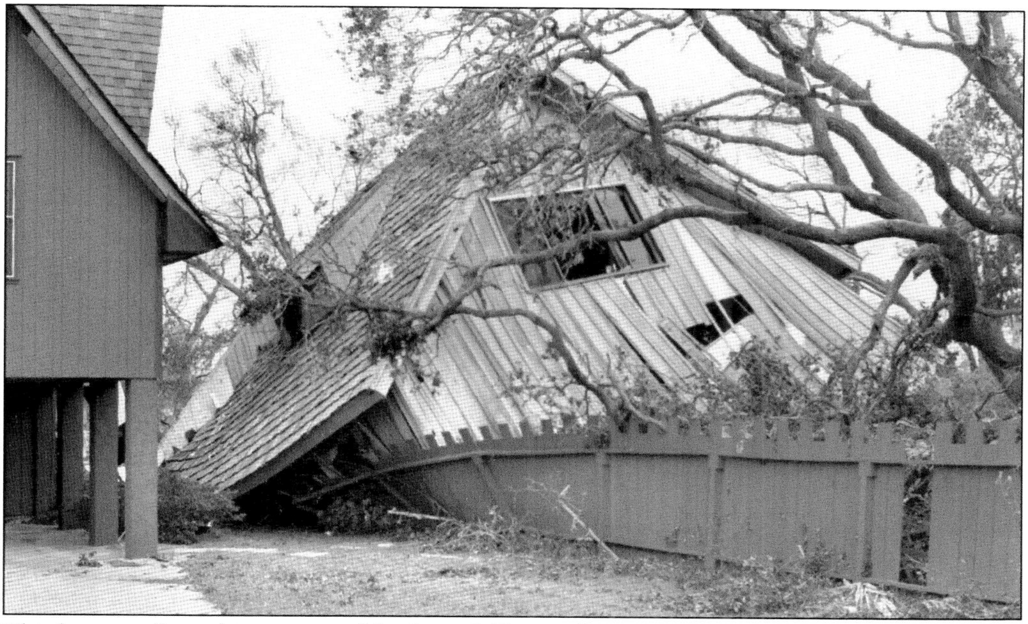

This house collapsed into its neighbor's yard. Fences that once separated families were mended after Hurricane Hugo. They say a picture can tell a thousand words, but no single picture can describe the outpouring of support that followed this disaster. Residents did not give a second thought to helping out their fellow man, even after a long day of salvaging their own belongings—if any—and putting what they could of their lives back together.

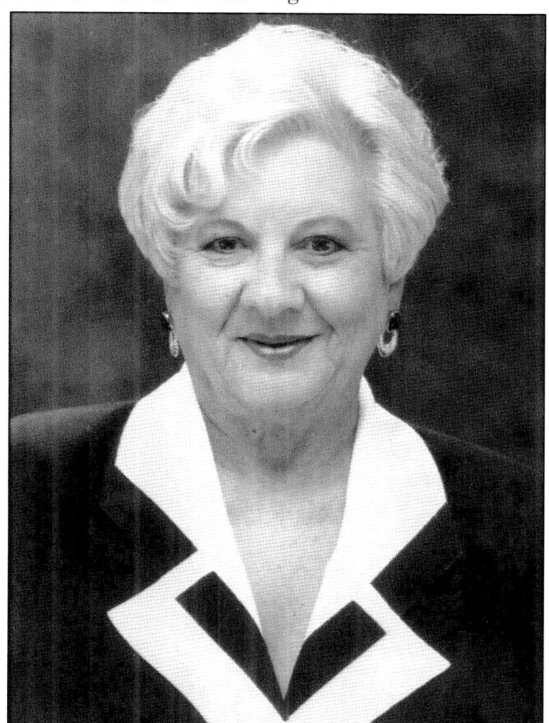

Mayor Carmen Bunch served from 1985 to 2001. The longest-serving mayor on Isle of Palms, Carmen was the only woman to ever hold the position. She put full-time hours towards a job she'd been preparing for over 40 years. From the time she came to the island in 1945, she campaigned for other candidates and served two terms on council. She was narrowly defeated the first time she ran for mayor but won the next four elections. Mayor Bunch put her constituents and her beloved Isle of Palms at the forefront of every decision.

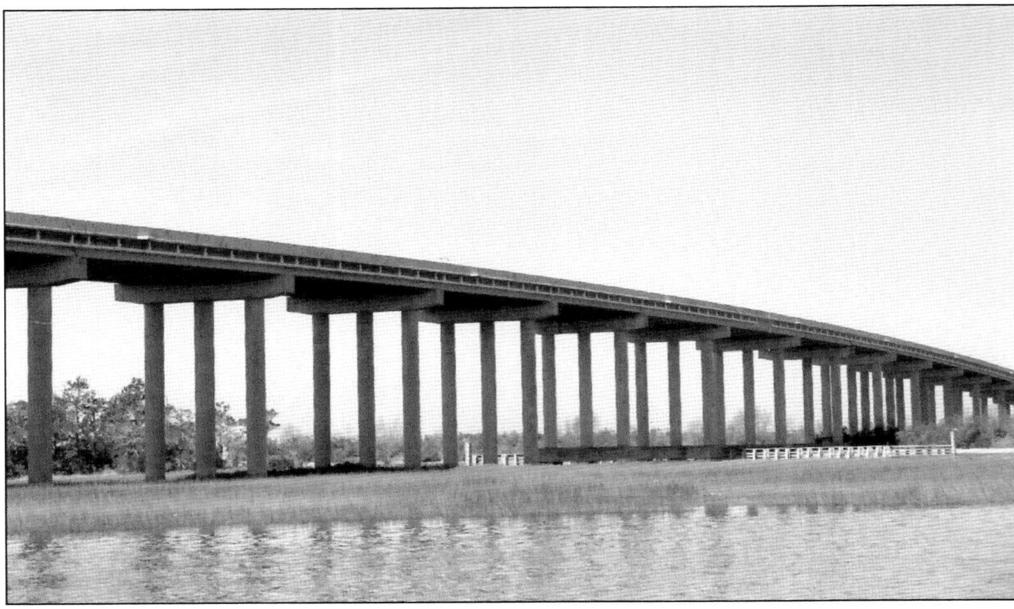

The Clyde Moultrie Dangerfield Bridge, otherwise known as the Isle of Palms Connector, opened to traffic on October 2, 1993, after almost 20 years of debate. About half of the island's residents saw a strong need for another way off the island, while the other half wanted to protect the small community's identity. Hurricane Hugo changed a lot of people's minds. On its dedication day, Mayor Carmen Bunch said, "This opens a new avenue to us all. We will never be kept from our homes again."

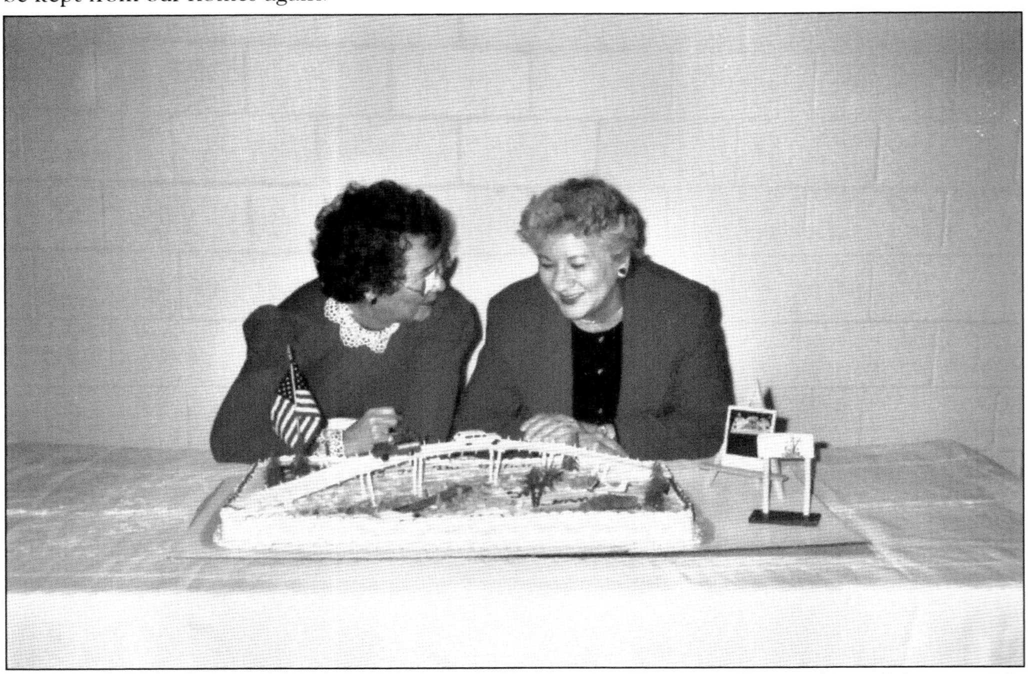

Mrs. Buttrum and Mayor Carmen Bunch admire a cake adorned with a replica of the new Isle of Palms Connector.

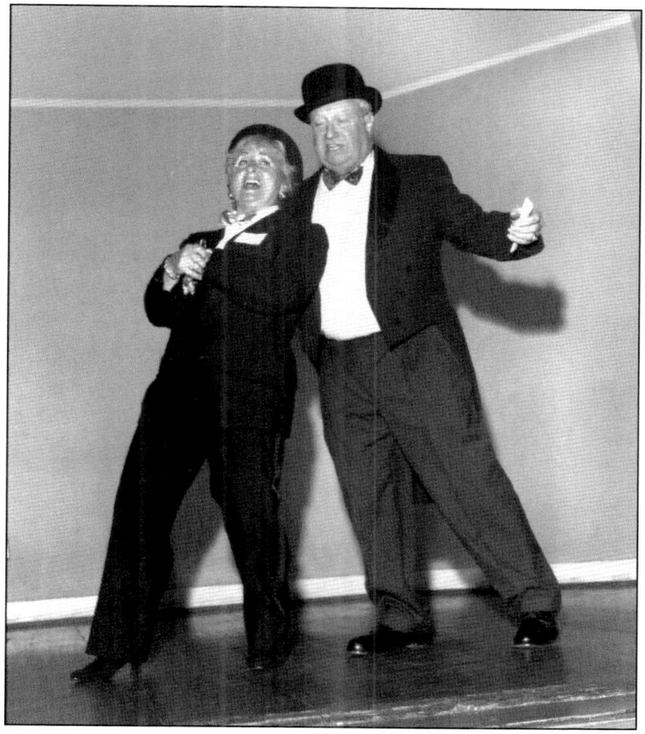

Phyllis Shaffer and Henry Berlin rehearse a number from *Step 'N Time*, a show co-founded by Phyllis to raise money for the American Cancer Society. Mrs. Shaffer is affiliated with the United Way, the YMCA, the March of Dimes, the American Cancer Society, and the Hollings Cancer Center. In the 1950s, she taught children how to swim while directing summer camps. She served on city council from 1978 to 1980. After Hurricane Hugo, she initiated the very successful Plant-A-Palm project. In 1993, the Charleston Exchange Club gave Mrs. Shaffer the Golden Book of Deeds Award.

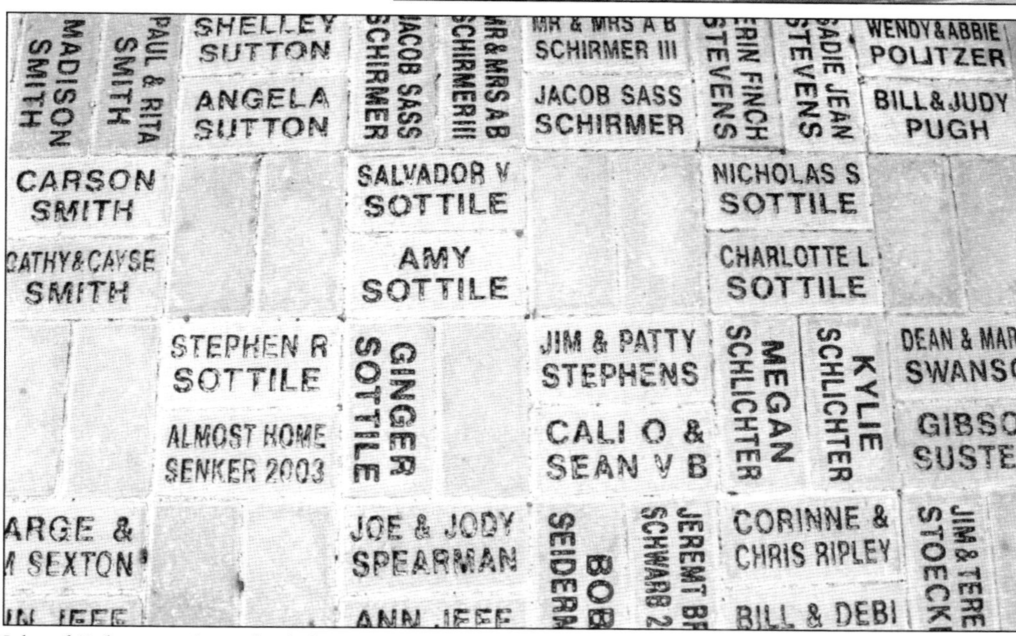

Isle of Palms residents had the opportunity in 2004 to purchase engraved bricks for $30 that were placed in the crosswalks of the newly designed Front Beach area. A total of 5,000 bricks were sold, thanks to Cathy Kennedy, the Isle of Palms staff member who proposed the idea. Along with the bricks, the city sold 26 benches and 110 palm trees labeled with granite plaques. Many people bought the benches and palm trees in memory of a loved one.

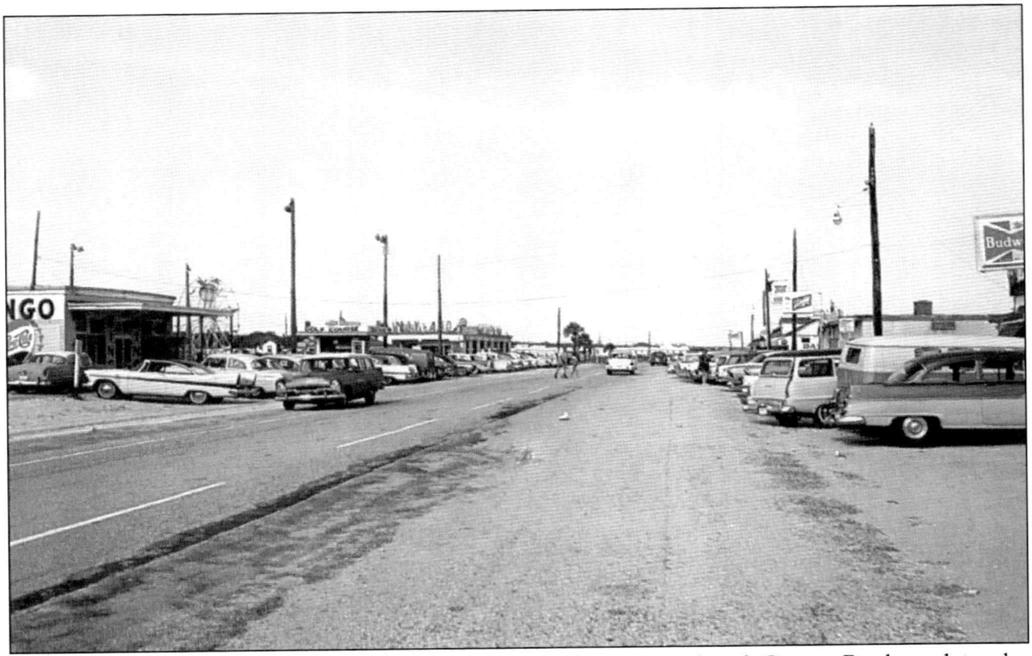

Power poles, one-story buildings, and meterless parking spots lined Ocean Boulevard in the 1960s.

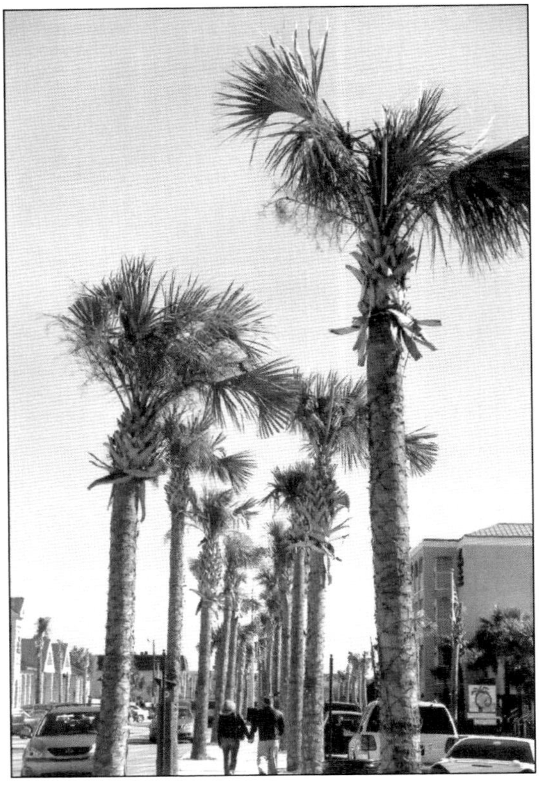

After the successful beautification project in 2004, blooming palmettos now line the middle of Ocean Boulevard between Tenth and Fourteenth Avenues. The streetscape renovation was cleverly dubbed "Aisle of Palms."